THE EXPORT PERFORMANCE OF THE UNITED STATES

Political, Strategic, and Economic Implications

Edited by

Center for Strategic and International Studies

PRAEGER

PRAEGER SPECIAL STUDIES • PRAEGER SCIENTIFIC

Published in 1981 by Praeger Publishers
CBS Educational and Professional Publishing
A Division of CBS, Inc.
521 Fifth Avenue, New York, NY 10175 USA

Library of Congress Catalog Card Number: 81-12021
ISBN: 0-03-059672-6

123456789 145 987654321
Printed in the United States of America

ACKNOWLEDGMENTS

A special word of thanks is due to a number of colleagues and friends who contributed to the U.S. Export Competitiveness Project and its studies: Penelope Hartland-Thunberg, Robert A. Kilmarx, Raymond F. Mikesell, and Robert A. Sammons for offering useful criticism of all or part of the studies contained in this two-volume text; Nancy Eddy and Jean Newsom for their editorial assistance; and Desiree Blackwell, Steve Cibull, Patricia Dodson, Sheila Payne, John Pauley, and Patricia Pefley for typing and proofing assistance.

Jennifer J. White
Project Editor
U.S. Export
  Competitiveness Project

Michael A. Samuels
Executive Director
U.S. Export
  Competitiveness Project

CONTENTS

v

INTRODUCTION

Many factors shape the strategic balance. The commercial competitive posture of a nation, that which strengthens its currency and provides impetus to its economic growth, is, however, often overlooked as an integral element of national power. In the 1980s, the United States will face increasing competition from all quarters. In this period, the strategic balance will be shaped by more than military might and strategic competence. It will also be influenced by the nation's economic strength and resilience.

For a nation to function as a great power, national economic growth and national profitability must be at the core of the power base. Yet in recent years we have witnessed relative national economic decline, frequent unwillingness and inability to compete, and a reactionary, defensive approach to world trade. At home, the existence of entire industries is being challenged by successful marketing from other countries; abroad, U.S. global market shares in key product areas have been eroded by competitors. U.S. productivity gains are close to nil, ranking the United States sixth among the world's top seven industrial nations. Oil imports continue to drain the U.S. economy of foreign exchange and contribute to the large balance of trade deficits witnessed throughout the decade.

Given these alarming trends, there are fundamental questions that must be addressed. What role do U.S. exports play in the U.S. national power equation? If they are indeed an important element, can the U.S. afford to ignore the declining competitiveness of U.S. products? What has caused the erosion of U.S. export performance? What approaches can government and industry take to revitalize the export drive? Are there lessons to be learned from our competitors? These are the basic questions that must be answered to launch an actively internationalistic, offensive approach to the challenges of the 1980s and beyond.

Three years ago, the Georgetown University Center for Strategic and International Studies set out to investigate these compelling questions. Through its U.S. Export Competitiveness Project, 20 studies were commissioned to examine the various components of U.S. export needs and policy directions. The study has proceeded from the hypothesis that one of the distortions in the U.S. national power base is that U.S. policy, in contrast to that of other major developed countries, has discouraged rather than encouraged exports. Faced with excessive export controls, financial and legal constraints, and active promotion by U.S. competitors, U.S. exporters have suffered serious loss of market shares. Consequently, not only has U.S. industry suffered but the prestige of the nation in the world economy has been severely challenged.

The seriousness of the U.S. export competitiveness problem must be understood not just by the normal observers of export and trade policy, the economists, and the businessmen, but more importantly by all Americans concerned with the overall economic and political strength of the United States domestically and internationally.

This two-volume work brings together the results of three years of research on the decline of U.S. export competitiveness. Volume One, The Export Performance of the United States, examines the political and strategic importance of exports and their role in the U.S. economy. Consideration is given to the effect of U.S. foreign direct investment on U.S. export performance and an examination is made of the U.S. regulatory, financial, and political environment for exports. The impact of recent multilateral agreements on U.S. exports is also evaluated.

Volume Two, World Trade Competition, examines the extent to which U.S. market shares have been lost vis-à-vis U.S. competitors and reviews the export experience of certain key U.S. trading partners. The outlook for trade competition in the 1980s is also addressed.

In both volumes, particular attention is given to trade competition with the industrialized world in the markets of the developing world. U.S. exports to the Third World, the fastest growing world market, represent a larger share of total U.S. exports than Europe and Japan combined. The objective here is to concentrate on U.S. export performance vis-à-vis other major exporting countries, given the developing world import market as a constant.

The study is also limited to manufactured exports since the U.S. competitive position in agricultural products has been fairly well maintained and, in the short run, agricultural exports are largely affected by worldwide crop variations. Moreover, international trade in nonmanufactures generally is subject to influences that cannot be explained by short-run changes in the measures of export competitiveness.

We hope that this two-volume work will serve to increase public understanding of the current export problem and will stimulate public concern for the direction of U.S. export policy. There are times when a nation must consciously change its course. Both empirical observation and economic facts say that time is now. The U.S. government and the nation must come of age, see the challenge and the opportunity, and take the offensive with a coordinated national export policy.

Jennifer J. White
Project Editor
U.S. Export Competitiveness
  Project

Michael A. Samuels
Executive Director
Third World Studies

1

THE POLITICAL AND STRATEGIC IMPORTANCE OF EXPORTS

Penelope Hartland-Thunberg

CONTENTS

I. INTRODUCTION

For two decades after World War II, U.S. foreign policy and world strategy were perceived at home and abroad as an integrated, internally consistent set of interrelated parts, all of which operated to preserve peace and strengthen democratic forces around the world. Foreign policy, military strategy, and economic policy were directed toward maintaining U.S. strength in order to contain nondemocratic forces and thus to preserve the hard-won peace. U.S.-initiated military alliances, diplomatic alignments, and international institutions were established as instruments to support these goals. Although there were constant disputes and discussions in the United States over the appropriateness of individual initiatives or doctrines as a means for achieving stated objectives, national policy and strategy were broadly satisfying to the United States and its allies because they were comprehendible, and because they seemed to work.

Since the mid-1960s, the opposite has been increasingly true. U.S. foreign policy and world strategy have become difficult to comprehend and have with increasing frequency been accused of being internally inconsistent, a hodgepodge of isolated initiatives seemingly operating at cross purposes to one another. Foreign policy no longer seems to work. Somewhere, apparently on the road to Vietnam, something went wrong. What happened?

It is the thesis of this paper that, for a variety of reasons, the mix of U.S. national goals and foreign policy instruments appropriate for the world scene of the immediate postwar years was maintained long after the conditions making that mix appropriate had changed; that the failure of the United States to redefine national goals after about a decade is responsible for the subsequent weakening of U.S. influence in the world; that until national goals are adjusted, U.S. world strategy will be perceived as confused, and -- the ultimate condemnation -- a failure. Specifically,

3

the foreign policy instrument whose role has been least understood and most misused is foreign <u>economic</u> policy. More specifically, within the economic component it is the central role of exports that is key to the reestablishment of a coherent, successful U.S. national policy and world strategy.

The instruments of foreign policy consist of the various elements of national power. The box of tools available to a nation-state for sustaining or increasing its relative power position in the world contains diplomacy, military force, economic (including financial) influence, and social and cultural prestige. When all elements of national power are being employed in tandem toward a set of national goals that are themselves coherent and not mutually exclusive, national policy appears consistent, unified, and integral. If national goals are internally inconsistent or if the implements of national policy are employed in such a way as to frustrate each other or the accomplishment of one or several national goals, the results are popular confusion and foreign or domestic policy failure.

In the early 1960s, the United States failed to adjust its national goals to take account of the new balance of economic power that was emerging in the world. The completion of postwar reconstruction and the rapidly growing competitive strength of other industrial countries should have signaled to the United States the importance of maintaining relative competitive strength and economic influence. This recognition of the changing importance of foreign economic policy was not forthcoming. Even today, two decades later it still seems to be lacking.

A basic truism of the world scene in the 1970s, is the increasing interdependence of nation-states. Such interdependence contains powerful implications for national policy because the domestic scene -- political, economic, social, and cultural developments at home -- is much more influenced by events abroad than used to be true. It also means for a country as large as the United States that domestic developments frequently have important repercussions elsewhere. Today, for example, tariffs are everywhere acknowledged to be a subject of concern to other countries, but it was not until the twentieth century that this interdependence was recognized. Previously, tariffs as the chief source of national revenue, were considered a purely domestic concern and determined unilaterally without discussion with trading partners. Today, fiscal and monetary policies are still treated in many quarters as purely domestic matters to be determined solely with reference to the requirements of the domestic economy. At the same time, however, economists point to fiscal and monetary policy divergencies among major countries as the main reason for balance of payments deficits and surpluses. They go on to urge that countries "synchronize" their policies in order to avoid importing inflation.

Every national leader would, of course, prefer to be able to determine domestic policy with reference only to requirements at home, but increasingly leaders are being forced to acknowledge that "interdependence" requires adjustment of the domestic to the world scene. The difference, in other words, between domestic policy and foreign policy has become increasingly blurred. National policy today is foreign policy and domestic policy has little meaning beyond a reference to the impact of national policy on domestic regions and localities.

The continued separation of national policy into domestic and foreign components is a form of cultural lag that will eventually disappear. In the meantime, however, this separation is partially responsible for the confusion and misunderstanding generated by U.S. foreign policy. For any country, it is meaningful to speak of foreign policy in relation to those national goals primarily directed toward relations with other nation-states only while recognizing that these goals are determined by and determining of domestic priorities. It is significant that the major piece of postwar legislation in which U.S. economic goals were defined, the Employment Act of 1946, nowhere mentions international economic relations. Lack of mention of international payments balance or any aspect of the balance of payments is indicative of an implicit assumption that domestic policy could be fashioned independently of any consideration of the rest of the world. In 1946 that was true; it no longer is.

The problem of differentiating between domestic and foreign policy is especially acute in the United

States because of its size and dominance on the world scene. U.S. national policy has more intensive and extensive repercussions on the rest of the world than that of any other country. Also, the worldwide scope of U.S. interests and responsibilities means that developments in every byway of the world are of significance to the United States; the same is not true of most other countries. At the same time in the field of economic policy the relative independence of the U.S. economy encourages the illusion that a meaningful distinction can be made by this country between its domestic and foreign economic policies. It was after all, only about a decade ago that U.S. exports amounted to less than 5 percent of GNP, in contrast to most other industrial countries where the importance of foreign trade was in the vicinity of 20 percent or more. Thus, the illusion of an objective distinction between foreign and domestic policy is more prevalent in the United States where unfortunately it can do more damage, and not only to Americans.

To understand the lag in recognizing the role of exports in the successful implementation of U.S. national policy and strategy, one must consider the degree to which successive administrations and secretaries of state took for granted American preeminence in the world economy and implicitly assumed that the dollar shortage of the immediate postwar years continued to be reality. A brief sketch of the basic postulates of U.S. foreign policy since World War II is therefore in order.

II. FOREIGN POLICY POSTULATES:
THE EARLY POSTWAR YEARS

Upon the conclusion of the war, the overriding concern of President Truman and his foreign policy advisors was the establishment of a secure and lasting peace. All instruments of foreign policy including the resources on the domestic economy were to be employed toward this end. It was an article of faith that peace depended on political stability within and between countries and that political stability depended on economic growth. To secure a lasting peace, therefore, a series of U.S. foreign policy initiatives was undertaken to create new international institutions that would provide the foundation for sustained economic growth and development around the world.

Economic growth elsewhere became a goal of U.S. national policy and U.S. international economic policy was the main tool used by successive administrations for achieving this end. The Marshall Plan, the General Agreement on Tariffs and Trade, the Bretton Woods Agreements, the "Point Four" program and its expansion into various programs of economic aid to developing countries were all economic initiatives of U.S. national policy to ensure a durable peace. These initiatives were enthusiastically supported by U.S. foreign policymakers and buttressed by the detailed administration of U.S. commercial and financial policy.

Conceived in the immediate aftermath of the war, the Marshall Plan committed U.S. productive power and financial resources to the restoration of European economies whose devastated facilities and infrastructures had to be rebuilt. Europe's financial resources had been exhausted in fighting the war, and the United States was the only source of goods and finance available on a sufficiently large scale to do the job quickly enough to minimize the change of political instability.

World leaders of the time had learned the lesson of World War I and the Weimar Republic -- that reparations imposed by the victor on the vanquished can boomerang to the point of nearly destroying both parties. In an act of humanitarianism and farsighted self-interest probably unprecedented in history, the

7

United States, rather than seeking reparations and warbooty, contributed vast quantities of its own resources to allies and vanquished alike. At the start, the American Congress was not totally convinced of the worthiness of the proposal. Indeed, the passage of the necessary legislation was viewed as risky until the Russian army marched into Czechoslovakia in the spring of 1948. That bold act of aggression turned the tide and the Marshall Plan was mandated. At about the same time, a similar program (GARIOA -- Government Aid and Rehabilitation in Occupied Areas) was initiated to aid reconstruction in Japan and West Germany. The prime motivation was the counteracting of the growing strength of Communist parties in Europe (especially in France and Italy), and Asia, widely perceived as politically destabilizing and hence a threat to peace.

A corollary of the basic postulate of foreign policy, that economic growth is necessary for political stability, was that an expanding volume of world trade was essential to economic growth. Again, world leaders demonstrated that they had learned lessons from history. During the Great Depression of the interwar years, major trading countries, seeking to buoy their own declining levels of employment at home by selling more abroad, erected ever-higher barriers to imports while attempting to stimulate exports through "beggar-thy-neighbor" policies of exchange rate depreciation, trade and currency controls, and bilateral balancing of trading accounts between partners. The results were a disastrous collapse of the volume of world trade. As all countries engaged in cut-throat competition and progressively tighter import barriers, declines in national employment levels were aggravated and unemployment soared.

In order to forestall the repetition of such self-defeating practices the General Agreement on Tariffs and Trade (GATT) established rules of conduct for international commerce based on the principle of nondiscrimination described as "most favored nation" treatment (MFN). It also provided a mechanism for an orderly and balanced expansion of trade through reciprocal tariff concessions in multilateral bargaining sessions. A series of such GATT "rounds" of tariff reductions characterized the 1950s and 1960s.

The Bretton Woods institutions -- The International Bank for Reconstruction and Development (World Bank) and the International Monetary Fund (IMF) -- were created to establish rules of conduct governing international financial activities. The controlling principles were fixed exchange rates and convertible currencies, with mechanisms provided for exchange rate changes only in the face of a "fundamental disequilibrium" in a country's balance of payments. International credit was made available to a limited degree to supplement a deficit country's international reserves during a cyclical shortfall.

Most important, recognizing that currency convertibility and a sustained expansion of world trade were possible only if international reserves were distributed among trading countries in rough proportion to their trade volumes, the U.S. undertook programs designed to correct the prevailing imbalance in the distribution of reserves. As a result of the political turmoil of the prewar years and the huge expansion of U.S. exports during the war, international reserves had become concentrated in this country. In 1950, fifty percent of international currency reserves were held by the United States.

In consequence, U.S. policies in the early postwar years consciously aimed for a U.S. balance of payments deficit in order to correct the imbalance in the ownership of world reserve assets. Payments for U.S. imports of goods and services typically fell short of receipts from exports, the difference being settled by drawing down U.S. reserve assets or most often by dollar deposits being accumulated as reserves by foreigners. Despite the nearly insatiable appetite of the rest of the world for American goods and the resulting worldwide dollar shortage, the United States achieved a series of balance of payments deficits through a variety of mechanisms. A series of military and economic aid programs first to Europe and Japan, then to the developing countries, provided U.S. goods on "concessional" terms -- i.e., at less than market prices.

III.   THE   LINGERING   "MARSHALL   PLAN   MENTALITY"

Through the 1950s exports of <u>other</u> countries were
encouraged by strict adherence by the United States to
the GATT principles of nondiscrimination and open
markets; U.S. tariff reductions were not counter-
balanced by the erection of nontariff barriers.   In
contrast, in Europe and Japan trade and financial
controls were maintained in order to speed reconstruction.   Exchange rates for the currencies of war-ravaged
economies were originally set at levels in terms of the
dollar which would stimulate their exports and U.S.
imports.[1] When in 1958 European currencies were made
convertible, exchange rates were fixed at levels that
continued to overvalue the dollar without U.S. protest.
Such a move was perceived as necessary to encourage
Europe's commitment to and involvement in expanding
world trade.   The depressing implications for U.S.
exports were ignored by U.S. policymakers who continued to assume -- a decade later -- that the postwar
dollar scarcity should and could determine U.S. policy.
The de-emphasis of U.S. exports was becoming
institutionalized.

In addition, European initiatives toward economic
integration starting early in the postwar period were
vigorously encouraged by U.S. diplomacy as an instrument that would lead to European political unity.   Here
again the postulate underlying U.S. policy was political stability through economic development.   Two major
wars had originated in Europe as an outgrowth of
political and economic instability there.   U.S. policy
sought to establish conditions that would prevent a
third.   It was recognized in U.S. policy discussions
from the beginning that the successful establishment of
a European Common Market would be detrimental to U.S.
exports to Europe.   In the climate of the time,
however, when markets for American goods were almost
limitless, this was viewed as a small price to pay for
peace.   The elimination of tariffs among members of the
Common Market, moreover, was not expected to be
entirely diversionary.   While in part, European sources
would replace American when intra-European tariffs were
written down to zero, the stimulus that such free trade
would provide to European income and production was
expected to boost their demand for noncommunity
dutiable imports beyond what it would otherwise have

10

been. The net effect on U.S. exports to Europe, it was opined at the time, would not be large and might well be plus rather than minus. Once again, the expendability of U.S. exports for political and economic purposes was institutionalized.

Like U.S. foreign economic policy, U.S. military policy was harnessed in the interest of preserving and securing peace, but so implemented as to encourage U.S. imports, discourage U.S. exports. A system of alliances starting with NATO and extending soon after around the world was fashioned with the twin goals of preventing internal subversion and external aggression. Shortly after the establishment of NATO, the communist invasion of Korea in mid-1950 underlined the vulnerability of developing countries to military aggression and resulted in a series of mutual security pacts between the United States and nonindustrial countries. Through these alliances U.S. military and strategic strength was extended to provide most of the rest of the world with the basic military protection necessary to encourage investors to commit resources to production in an environment that might otherwise have been too risky. The alliances themselves provided the mechanism for transferring the military hardware required for their security to these countries at little cost to them.

These U.S. military aid programs in addition provided a mechanism for generating the U.S. balance of payments deficit necessary for the redistribution of world international reserves. Through U.S. expenditures abroad during the 1950s for programs involving weapon production, a mutual weapons development program, purchases of foreign supplies and equipment and offshore procurement in NATO countries, U.S. military assistance was extended to an increasing number of countries, reaching a peak of 69 in 1963. In addition, U.S. government expenditures abroad included direct dollar payments for troop deployment and the maintenance of American overseas military establishments. U.S. expenditures abroad for military purposes rose from an average of $590 million annually 1946-50 to $3.1 billion during the second half of the 1950s.[2] The deliberate policies of U.S. procurement abroad were undertaken for the express purpose of stimulating the economies of Europe and Japan and thereby helping to establish there the economic strength necessary for

11

political stability. A more resounding de-emphasis of U.S. exports would be hard to cite.

Similarly, U.S. programs of economic aid to developing countries were an economic policy response to the basic goal of peace through political stability. Because the potential for instability in the developing regions was perceived to be high, programs fostering economic growth in these regions could contribute to peace there directly and in addition be so administered as to strengthen further Europe and Japan. In the early years of the program, economic aid took the form primarily of grants that were not tied to procurement in the United States. While in those years most U.S. economic aid dollars were spent directly or indirectly in the United States, the accumulation of reserves abroad and the decline in domestic reserve assets indicate that not all U.S. expenditures abroad generated American exports. More important, the emphasis was on administering the aid programs to further the goal of enhancing the exports and economic strength of America's competitors -- once again de-emphasizing U.S. exports.

All of these initiatives were undertaken by the United States for political reasons; foreign economic policy was used exclusively as an instrument of national political and security goals, not as an end in itself. The administration of U.S. foreign policy, foreign economic policy, and foreign military policy at home and abroad was entirely consistent with the basic goal of securing peace through worldwide economic growth. The conduct of U.S. foreign affairs was perceived as coherent and internally consistent. Its consistency and coherence, however, were made possible by the relegation of economic policy to the level of a tool by excluding international economic considerations from the list of national goals. Simplifying the list of goals, of ends to be sought in national policy and strategy in this fashion, enormously eased the complications of fashioning the foreign policy of the world's leading power. It also made foreign policy easy to comprehend. The benefits were real but there were equally real costs associated with this exclusion of economic policy from the list of national goals. The costs were the weakened competitive position of the U.S. economy. The emphasis of policy and its administration was on U.S. imports and on providing scarce

12

dollars to foreigners to enable them to acquire needed goods or services from wherever they were available, not necessarily from the United States. The de-emphasis of exports, later referred to in the 1971 report of the Commission on U.S. Foreign Economic Policy (the "Williams Commission") as the "Marshall Plan mentality", endured long after the immediate postwar years to which it was appropriate.

Currency convertibility and the European Economic Community became a reality in 1958. That these two interrelated objectives were attained that early in the postwar period (despite overly optimistic earlier estimates of the IMF) was directly traceable to U.S. policy initiatives and support. The Marshall Plan, for all practical purposes, was completed and ahead of schedule. The Japanese economy was remade in our image on the basis of competition. The German economy was re-equipped with a new and efficient industrial plant and was now able to participate as a leading force in the expansion of world trade. International reserves had been redistributed; the U.S. share of a larger world total was approaching 30 percent down from 50 percent a decade before. World production and trade had expanded, the former by 100 percent, the latter by 110 percent; tariffs had been reduced to some degree. The U.S. share of world output had declined from over 40 percent to less than 35 percent. The new international institutions were in place and equipped to cope with the challenge of open financial markets and liberal commercial policies. In fact, the reconstruction period had been successfully completed.

IV. THE ILLUSION OF THE "OPTIONAL EXTRA"

The fact that by the end of the 1950s U.S.-supported postwar reconstruction abroad had been successfully completed, should have stimulated a government review of basic foreign policy postulates and priorities to determine whether those of 10 to 15 years earlier were still appropriate to the world position of the United States in the 1960s. Such an examination of the basic foundations of U.S. foreign policy never occurred. With the advantage of hindsight, it is fairly easy to deduce why.

First, there were still some loose ends to be tied. Although isolated voices expressed discomfort over the continuing U.S. balance of payments deficits, the main concern of most experts versed in the mysteries of international finance was over the adequacy of international reserves and the dependence of the international financial mechanism on the U.S. deficit for the creation of new reserves. Except in the U.S. Treasury, considered notorious by many for its enduring "protect-the-revenue" philosophy, the deficit per se was not a cause for worry. The fact that U.S. exports represented a declining share of world exports was perceived as the concomitant of recovery in Europe and Japan and a measure of the success of American policy. Declining U.S. gold reserves and accumulating U.S. liquid liability to foreigners similarly represented the redistribution of reserve assets necessary to the maintenance of fixed exchange rates, currency convertibility, and an open world trading system.

There were, moreover, important foreign policy objectives to be pursued. The developing countries, restive over their colonial status and the increasing gap between the standards of living in their own countries and those in the rich industrial countries, organized themselves into the Group of 77 in the early 1960s and demanded to be heard. At the same time, the Soviet Union was on the offensive in Berlin and probing farther afield in a clear attempt to expand its influence and power position in the world. Its early successes in the Middle East were alarming to U.S. policymakers. The increasingly close relations between Cuba and the USSR in the early 1960s, the Cuban missile crisis, and Castro-sponsored insurgencies in this

14

hemisphere generated a spurt of policy interest in Latin America, a region of typically low foreign policy priority. As the decade of the sixties advanced, Indochina captured more and more of the administration's time and concern.

In addition, although the necessity for reserve redistribution always implied some finite time period for U.S. deficits, neither the timing appropriate for the disappearance of the deficits nor limits on their size was ever articulated by the United States. In the late 1940s, the problems of reconstruction were so enormous, the financial constraints so compelling, the risks of failure so intimidating, it did not seem necessary to spell out a phased program of transition from deficit to balance in the U.S. payments position. The Marshall Plan, moreover, had a programmed schedule and was originally understood as accounting for the bulk of the U.S. deficit. It was implicitly assumed that when that was completed the U.S. deficit would correct itself.

The failure to recognize the new realities was also partly due to the internal organization of the State Department. For two decades after World War II, international economics was considered a subject that could be relegated to technicians, left in the hands of experts, and about which the private citizen need not concern himself. Indeed during the 1950s and most of the 1960s, the arcane subject of foreign economic policy was one which even the average foreign service officer could safely ignore, over which the average secretary of state had little command, and which was left to a small group of department specialists. These economic experts, moreover, were regarded as second-class citizens in matters of salary and rank within the foreign service. The path to the top was via the political officer's post, not through the "E-Area". This denigration of international economic affairs within the hierarchy of the State Department was reflective of the prevailing view of foreign economic policy as a means not an end, a tool not a goal, and something therefore safely relegated to second-order diplomats.

Some shifts that to a small degree lessened the emphasis on imports in U.S. policy implementation did occur in the early 1960s. U.S. economic development programs in the Third World began to rely more on credits, less on grants, and aid was increasingly tied to U.S. procurement. This shift was a direct response to concern over the American balance of payments but also evidence of a mounting weariness with foreign aid efforts. Military aid programs were also adjusted in the same direction, as much for budgetary as for balance of payments reasons. Offshore procurement was drastically reduced after the mid-1950s, and other forms of dollar expenditures overseas for military purposes were also reduced. These measures were, however, increasingly offset by growing U.S. involvement in Southeast Asia as the 1960s advanced.

What was totally ignored through most of the 1960s was the bias in the structure of commercial and financial administrative decisions originally undertaken in haste to implement foreign policy postulates. There was the prevailing level of exchange rates, which increasingly overvalued the dollar. There was the relative lack of nontariff barriers as an offset to duty reductions in the United States and then the increasing implementation of them abroad. There was the support first of the European Common Market and then other similar customs unions all of which were prejudicial to American goods in world trade. In short, all of these decisions served to heighten the competitiveness of the rest of the world vis-à-vis the United States and to continue the de-emphasis of U.S. exports.

In addition, the fact that the U.S. dollar has served as the international financial reserve for the rest of the world meant that the United States could not easily adjust the foreign exchange value of its currency in response to changing competitive conditions as other countries could and did. A continual appreciation of the U.S. dollar in real terms until 1971 enabled Americans traveling abroad to feel rich; the dollar bought a lot. Foreigners, meanwhile, were increasingly concerned to observe American business taking over their industries through direct investment. In the face of such foreign concern over the competitiveness of American business located within their own boundaries, it was difficult for the United States to become apprehensive over the dwindling U.S. trade balance.

16

The new institutions and their implementation created a pattern of worldwide vested interests in their maintenance. Thus, for example, the sanctity of the existing Yen-dollar exchange rate which was originally fixed in 1949, went unchallenged for two decades of profound changes in the Japanese economy. Such exchange rate changes as occurred were primarily depreciations against the dollar undertaken for foreign competitive advantage. The strengthening abilities of other countries to compete effectively in world markets created a group of industries oriented toward exports. Export-led growth, correctly perceived by other governments to be the source of domestic prosperity, increasingly became the dominant consideration abroad in fashioning both domestic and foreign policies. In contrast, U.S. policy implementation continued the postwar pattern of favoring imports and obstructing exports under the illusion that the domestic economy was autonomous and independent of the rest of the world. High-growth domestic economic policies in the United States, mandated by the Employment Act of 1946 were dominant. As the 1960s progressed, they too sucked in imports and further discouraged exports.

Appreciation of the importance of exports, of course, was much more natural for the other major trading countries. With domestic markets much more limited in size and dependent to a far greater extent than the United States on imported supplies and materials, exports have always been given high priority. Exports have been widely considered by entire populations as necessary to their country's existence. Even in the fifth grade in Japan, for example, textbooks stress the importance of exports to national welfare.[3] In contrast, the vast American market could be exploited by domestic producers with ease at low risk. Aggressive marketing efforts were directed toward this huge free trade area where the same familiar language, laws, and institutions prevailed. Exports, moreover, in the later 1940s and 1950s sold themselves; they did not have to be marketed. Foreign buyers literally came knocking, by post, telephone, wire, to make inquiry about the availability of American goods. U.S. producers, selling only domestically and unacquainted with the procedures of exporting, frequently ignored these overtures -- and still do.[4]

17

As time passed, moreover, experienced U.S. exporters found it more and more difficult to compete in foreign markets as the dollar became an increasingly overvalued currency and as nontariff barriers abroad served to counter the impact of GATT-sponsored tariff reductions. Their solution was to establish operations abroad as a substitute for exports from this country, as the overvalued dollar made both imports and purchases of foreign plants increasingly attractive. In fact, the contribution of cheap imports to the U.S. record of price stability during the 1960s has only recently come to be recognized.

The rising tide of U.S. foreign direct investment during the 1960s was accompanied by a rapidly expanding American business presence. In Europe, the imminence of the Common Market added the desire for a position behind the new set of tariff barriers to the attraction of foreign investment created by the overvalued exchange rate. Top level executives from U.S. multinational companies as well as middle management and technical personnel took up residence abroad, creating a larger-than-life image of world dominance by the American economy. The ubiquitous presence of American personnel, accustomed to a relatively higher standard of living than many of their foreign counter-parts, was made obtrusive by their ability to live at least in the manner to which they were accustomed. In fact, it was probably the rising number of American business representatives living abroad rather than American ownership of productive facilities per se that prompted the foreign perception of an American threat to sovereignty, national identity, and competitive strength that culminated in the widely quoted Le Défi Américain, by J. J. Servan-Schriber.

During the 1960s what these fears of an American threat failed to recognize was the evolving shift in the American trade balance. The outflow of American capital took the form of U.S. exports of machinery and equipment that during the period of capital transfer buoyed U.S. exports. It also later stimulated U.S. exports of materials and supplies to U.S. branches abroad to the extent that by the end of the 1960s, intracorporate trade accounted for about half of American manufactured exports.[5] Without the capital outflow, however, U.S. exports would probably have been considerably smaller than they were, being increasingly discouraged by the overvalued exchange rate. Certainly, their mix would have been different by the 1970s.

In the present context what is important is that all of these developments -- foreign policy challenges in the diplomatic and military areas, the shifting nature of American trade relationships, growing foreign fears over the competitive strength of American multinational enterprise -- served to support a basic American disinterest in exports, and to divert attention from the persistent payments deficit. As Sir Andrew Shonfield, former director of the Royal Institute of International Affairs, has written, Americans have always viewed themselves "as a nation for whom external relations were a kind of optional extra."[6]

Perhaps of greatest importance in explaining the lack of official U.S. concern over exports and the payments deficits during these years was the enormous convenience for successive administrations to continue to play ostrich with the matter. In the early postwar years, presidents and secretaries of state basked in the unprecedented blessing of being able to fashion domestic and foreign policy initiatives without having to consider their cost or their balance of payments impact. Indeed, the blessing was twice-graced because not only could the cost of foreign policy initiatives be ignored, but a specific U.S. policy goal would even be furthered by the negative balance of payments impact of an import emphasis. Policymakers at the highest level, genuinely concerned with foreign policy and world strategy but ignorant of and diffident about matters of economics and international finance, assimilated this happy state of affairs with alacrity (although they probably did not properly appreciate it as a blessing, and a transitory one at that). It was, moreover, congenial to the American syndrome of viewing external relations as "an optional extra."

Thus furthered by national proclivites to downplay the significance of the foreign sector and by personal concerns over foreign policy issues narrowly defined, the comfort of being able to ignore deficits in the early postwar years quickly became habit in successive administrations. Abroad, national proclivities frequently underlined if not exaggerated the significance of exports and of reserve accumulation and thus served to further the acceptance of prevailing exchange rates, and administrative and institutional structures without question. As Wilbur Monroe has commented, "changes in existing parities for major currencies came to be viewed as something to be avoided at all costs" (during the 1950s and first half of the 1960s).[7] That most of the world ignored the changing role of the United States in the world economy was recognized by only a very small minority. With hindsight, however, it is clear that U.S. administrations continued implicitly to assume that U.S. payments deficits remained in the best interest of the United States and the rest of the world alike and that the government could therefore continue to pursue national policy initiatives regardless of their cost and without impact on the domestic economy or national priorities.

The U.S. balance of payments deficit which had averaged $1.5 billion during the 1950s rose to over $3 billion for most of the 1960s, and then mushroomed to $22 billion in 1971. U.S. exports, which amounted to one-quarter of the world total in 1948, had declined to 17 percent by 1958 and to 14 percent by 1970. Between 1950 and 1970, world production expanded 4½ times, U.S. production by less than 3½ times; world trade expanded five-fold over the same period, U.S. trade by less than 4½ times. U.S. gold reserves, which in 1948 had been more than three times the level of dollar claims of foreigners against the United States, by 1971 had declined to 10-15 percent of those claims.

When the coup de grâce hit, it was unexpected, created panic, poorly-suppressed, at home and abroad, and resulted in abrupt deflation of foreign perceptions of American economic might. The fears of the 1960s of a shortage of international reserves had subsided as the supply of dollars owned by foreigners mounted with the U.S. deficit. Aggravated by the financing of the war in Vietnam, the supply of dollars abroad became excessive about the turn of the decade, and in August 1971 the United States was forced to suspend dollar convertibility. After an 18-month period of groping, in early 1973 the international community -- or at least the most important trading nations -- agreed to a system of floating exchange rates. Since then, U.S. balance of trade and balance of payments have fluctuated wildly, aggravated by a quantum jump in the price of oil, responding to a once-again desynchronized

20

international business cycle and divergent rates of inflation among trading partners. Dollar exchange rates, floating but with varying degrees of official interference, have with some lag fluctuated accordingly.

V.   THE ROLE OF THE GOVERNMENT

Over the past 15 years the U.S. government has announced five "new" export expansion policies. The frequency of these announcements by itself suggests something less than total commitment by the government to these initiatives. It suggests in addition that the "Marshall Plan mentality" and the sense of "the optional extra" are still prevalent. As Frank Weil, Assistant Secretary of Commerce for Trade and Industry, commented before the Joint Economic Committee on 29 September, 1978, "Each year, within a year or so from the commencement of a strong export program, the financial winds change and the balance of payments problem grows less. Thus each time . . . the desire for an export solution to these problems diminishes. . . . There is a risk that if our current account deficit shrinks, as we all hope it will, that the will behind the effort will be sapped away by other priorities."

The "other priorities" continue to be at least as much those of the government as those of private industry. The fact remains that since the balance of payments crisis of 1971, U.S. policy toward exports has been ambivalent and inconsistent. Despite official importuning of private industry to export more, despite discrete instances of export encouragement (e.g., creation of DISCs) U.S. government policy has continued to view exports and foreign economic policy in general as an implement of international politics and strategy, a tool rather than an enduring goal of high priority.* In November 1978, in the face of increasingly chaotic financial markets around the world and a collapsing value of the dollar exchange rate, another new program was announced, specifically aimed at supporting the dollar and recognizing once again that in the long-run

---

*It is true that since the 1973 OPEC oil embargo, the United States has treated the Middle East as an area of top foreign policy interest because of its importance as a source of oil to the United States and its allies. Because of the strategic importance of oil, however, security of oil supply is as much a military as an economic goal.

the strength of the dollar would depend on a robust export performance. Whether other priorities will dissipate this latest effort remains to be seen.

Old habits die hard. Despite a genuine, if spasmodic, effort since 1971 to encourage exports, the occupants of the White House and their top aides have continued to encroach on U.S. export performance through creeping incrementalism. Successive laws, regulations, and initiatives, not one of which has great export significance in isolation, have added increments of export restraint that cumulatively have served to counter the new policies aimed at export expansion. Each one of these increments was undertaken either for valid, noneconomic foreign policy purposes or to further some purely domestic goal. The list is familiar -- the abrogation of soybean contracts; restrictions on exports of U.S. wood products; constraints on North Slope crude oil exports; ban on exports to the South African army or police; anti-Arab boycott regulations; restrictions on Export-Import Bank credit; corrupt practices prohibitions; strategic export controls; denial of exports or export financing for purposes of controlling nuclear proliferation, arms availability, human rights violations, or environmental restrictions -- to cite only those increments which come most readily to mind. In most cases the volume of frustrated exports has not been large (although this statement certainly does not apply to Export-Import Bank financing) but it undoubtedly has had a cumulative impact.

In addition, these post-1971 increments have been added to previously existing laws and regulations that continue to operate to restrict exports (e.g., antitrust act implementation; earlier Export-Import Bank financing restrictions; price requirements for military sales; various export controls; discriminatory tax provisions). Of at least equal importance, this gradual incrementalism has created confusion at home and abroad about American seriousness of purpose in coping with its economic problems. Potential U.S. exporters have been discouraged by the existing burden of export regulations and the fact that unforeseen new restrictions are constantly being added. In their perception, it is much easier and cheaper to sell only at home where the rules of the game do not change so quickly. Actual exporters have been forced to

23

withdraw. Abroad, where the importance of exports has traditionally been recognized, the difference between official U.S. words and action is taken as evidence either of incompetence or duplicity. In many foreign quarters the belief is still strong that the dollar's decline in 1978 was the result of a conscious U.S. attempt "to talk the dollar down" for competitive advantage. Addressing their own preoccupations with the international competitiveness of their own economies, they ascribe such motivation to others.

Unfortunately, U.S. preoccupations have continued to remain with politics and strategy and not within the importance of exports. Concern with competitiveness and exports comes only spasmodically and in extremis. Since 1973, despite the series of export promotion programs, real U.S. exports (correcting for inflation) have remained practically constant while those of the other industrial countries have grown by 4 percent annually, and that growth excludes their exports to the United States.[8]

VI.   REPERCUSSIONS ON FOREIGN POLICY EFFECTIVENESS

The economic instrument in the national policy tool-kit is not the only one which has been weakened. For a number of reasons the diplomatic and military instruments have also been weakened.

The continuing momentum of old habits affects officials throughout the foreign service, not only those at the top. For about two decades after World War II, American diplomats, as representatives of the country that provided to the rest of the world either military security or needed finance and goods or both, never had to hone the art of diplomacy to the extent that their foreign counterparts did. Readily available exports on concessional terms were the major instrument of foreign policy. The rest of the world was, by and large, in the position of the supplicant seeking the favor of the protector or the provider. The supplicant has little bargaining advantage and knows it. Frequently, without overt pressure from the powerful, he seeks the favor of the rich by accommodating himself to the latter -- following his lead. U.S. initiatives, in consequence, were in many cases followed by its allies and clients without the need for exercising those diplomatic skills of persuasion that are so necessary to the foreign service officers of nearly every other country. Those of U.S. diplomats, it seems likely, were at least to some degree allowed to atrophy.

Diplomacy may be an art Americans have partially forgotten. The French, in contrast, are masters. They have shaped, for example, the European Community into the kind of organization they view as most useful for these own national priorities, one that enhances their own stature and furthers the achievement of their own goals. The British, too, are diplomatic artists. Experienced U.S. foreign service officers speak with nostalgia of support they received from their British counterparts in international forums in the days before resource constraints forced the British into an essentially passive foreign policy posture. In fact, the changed British circumstances provide the example par excellence of the importance of a strong international economic position in giving force to diplomatic initiatives. The strength of the British export performance before World War I reinforced British foreign policy. Since then, they have of necessity increasingly relied on the art of diplomacy in implementing a passive foreign policy.

The failure since 1973 of U.S. exports to keep pace with imports, despite a series of official export promotion programs and the subsequent depreciation of the dollar on international money markets, has been accompanied by a pronounced diminution of American influence in the world arena. Currency value has traditionally been a symbol of national prestige around the world -- perhaps more so abroad than in the United States. The symbolism of the depreciated dollar, moreover, probably has been exaggerated in foreign perceptions by the fact that the value of the dollar had for so long remained constant at Bretton Woods parities. The depreciated dollar is viewed as reflecting a failure of the U.S. economy and the decline in perceived U.S. economic strength has been accompanied by declining levels of foreign diplomatic acquiescence to U.S. initiatives. American prestige in the rest of the world at the end of the 1970s is probably lower than it has ever been in this century. Whether justified or not, the denigration of U.S. power is being evidenced in a rising chorus of criticism of U.S. actions and policies by our closest allies, and in a new assertiveness on the part of foreigners in regard to U.S. domestic as well as foreign policies. It is, in short, not only U.S. economic influence that has waned; U.S. influence in political and military matters has declined as well.

Referring to the comportment of two heads of government at the July 1978 summit meeting, Hobart Rowen commented in the Washington Post at the time, "But what lifted the eyebrows of summit participants was Schmidt's willingness to be as critical to Carter's face on U.S. energy policy as he had in some of his private talks. When echoed by Japan's Prime Minister Takeo Fukuda, it was as if the two wealthy nations, each with a sizable surplus and a low inflation rate, had determined that they would not be pushed around."

Nothing succeeds like success, or fails like failure. The diminished political significance of the United States, stemming from its weakened international economic position, has economic repercussions as well.

A case in point lies in the report that an important prod to the November 1978 decision to raise U.S. interest rates in defense of the dollar was the insistence by West Germany on such a move as a price for its cooperation. (Washington Post, 28 January 1979).

Budget and balance of payments considerations began around 1960 to cause changes in the pattern of U.S. military expenditures abroad. First, offshore procurement was strictly limited and the initial offset agreements were negotiated involving partial compensation for U.S. overseas expenditures. Since that time, the United States has exerted more and more pressure on Europe and Japan to increase the amount of such offsetting purchases. Military aid programs, meanwhile, have been increasingly limited in scope and except for the period of the war in Vietnam, the U.S. military presence abroad has been greatly contracted, a result of foreign as well as U.S. initiative. This balance of payments induced contraction in the American presence in the developing countries has contributed to the new assertiveness of their leaders. Energized recently both by the U.S. military defeat in Vietnam and its economic defeat at the hands of OPEC, most if not all developing countries are encouraged to push their demands on the United States and their probings of the American position. At the least, they hope for improved terms of trade, at the most, for a position of power and influence on the world scene.

The consequence of the economizing on U.S. military expenditures abroad has been a reduction of U.S. naval power worldwide and an increasing concentration of U.S. military strength on the Soviet threat in Europe. It has resulted in increasing alarm among U.S. political and military planners that in so doing, the United States is no longer able to protect vital national interests elsewhere. Concentration on the Soviet threat in Europe is a natural response to growing Soviet military and strategic capabilities. The practial result is that, in local crises, as former Secretary Kissinger has said: "Soviet capacity for intervention must become more politically significant than in the past. And will be perceived as being more significant. The conduct of American policy in crises will inevitably become more cautious. This is an event of geopolitical significance."[9]

The emasculation of U.S. influence in the world is not solely the result of a weakened economic performance. The rapid increase over the past decade in Soviet military, naval, and strategic capabilities was, of course, independent of the U.S. economic decline. The U.S. economic decline, however, coming as it did at the time the USSR was achieving strategic parity and extending its ability to intervene around the world, caused American global influence to diminish in something approaching a geometric progression.

The decline in relative U.S. economic superiority is, in fact, quite analogous in its impact to the decline in relative U.S. strategic superiority. The absolute superiority of the U.S. economy over that of any other country is unquestioned. Arguably, the United States still maintains a significant margin of strategic superiority over the USSR. In popular perceptions of relative national power, however, the absolute margins of difference are given little weight; what is important is the direction of change. A simultaneous decline in both U.S. economic and strategic superiorities combined with an out-of-practice foreign service has decimated U.S. global influence. From the American point of view, the economic decline could not have occurred at a worse time.

An emasculated American negotiating position combined with the advent of a Soviet capacity for intervention around the world causes allies and neutrals alike to undertake overtures to the USSR, directly or indirectly, by adopting a policy stance less distant from that of Moscow, more distant from that of Washington. Recent examples of such policy adjustments are multiple and include Turkey, Saudi Arabia, and West Germany.

The foreign policy position of any country cannot be taken for granted as fixed. It is constantly evolving in response to changing perceptions of relative power positions among states, especially among neighbors and world powers. If any one of the instruments in the national policy tool-kit of a major power is generally perceived to be seriously impaired, the effectiveness of the entire kit is weakened as one country and then another reacts. When the two most potent tools are weakened simultaneously, the emasculation of power gains a momentum of its own, unless something happens to halt the process.

In today's world, the economic implement in the tool-kit of national policy encompasses more than just exports and imports -- more than solely a country's international transactions. Because imports are a function of a country's level of business activity and prices, the exports of other countries will be influenced by shifts in the domestic economy. Similarly, one country's exports and therefore the level of its business activity are subject to policy decisions abroad. No single country can completely control its own economy or the level of activity elsewhere; some are more vulnerable to influences from abroad than others. All are vulnerable, however, to some degree, including the United States. The potency of the economic instrument in the U.S. tool-kit is still formidable, but it is less awesome than it used to be because of the increasing vulnerability of the U.S. economy to external events. This vulnerability is directly traceable to the decline in U.S. exports relative to imports.

It used to be said in the early 1950s that when the U.S. economy sneezed, Europe got pneumonia, with the implication that Europe's pneumonia would not affect the United States. For all practical purposes that was then true. It ceased being true some time ago. Europe and Japan can and have prospered when the United States was operating at less than full capacity. Rising prosperity in the United Sates no longer necessarily means full employment abroad and therefore it is no longer true that U.S. exports will keep pace with U.S. imports. The United States, therefore, can no longer be oblivious to the balance of payments implications of domestic economic policies that are not in accord with those of other countries. It no longer is a locomotive dragging engineless cars behind it.

Looking back, one can state with assurance that about two decades ago, the United States should have undertaken a reevaluation of its foreign policy goals and the instruments then available to it for pursuing those goals. In the immediate postwar period, the United States could safely assume that it had unlimited resources for implementing foreign policy for that period when a U.S. balance of payments deficit was sought for the purpose of redistributing international reserves. During these years, the United States could implement policies that would affect imports and exports but treat them as if they were unrelated and independent, as if the country's capacity for absorbing imports was unrelated to the level of exports. The accomplishment of the reserve-sharing program implied, eventually, a new era when the means available for policy implementation would be limited, when imports and exports could no longer be assumed to be unrelated.

Instead, the Marshall Plan mentality continued to prevail. Political goals remained at top priority and their balance of payments impact was ignored. The implicit assumption was that the United States so dominated the world economy it could chart its course at home and abroad by behaving as though it existed in economic isolation -- as though the relation between exports and imports were unimportant.

Diminution of U.S. relative economic power in the world was of course implicit in the successful accomplishment of its immediate postwar goals. A decline in U.S. exports as a share of world exports was expected and acceptable, but not a decline of the degree and to the extent that actually has transpired. The Marshall Plan mentality prevailed for too long.

VII.   WHAT THEN CAN BE DONE?

What then can be done? Is the weakened U.S. international economic position permanently impaired? Can the United States recover its former relative position of power in the world? Of course it can, but not overnight and not without recognizing the nature of the problem.

The relative power position of the United States in the immediate post-World War II years is not recoverable, and recovery to that degree is not a proper goal of U.S. policy. U.S. power was then for all practical purposes unlimited. American leaders quite correctly recognized that such a position of infinite power was not consistent with the basic goals of U.S. national policy -- an economically healthy, politically stable, democratic world.

The relative power position of the United States at the start of the 1960s, however, with U.S. exports at 15 percent of the world total while considerably diluted from that of 1947, was sustainable, given appropriate policy priorities. What continues to be required is recognition that national goals cannot be determined without consideration of national resource availabilities, especially in the international sphere. In the world arena, resource availabilities are determined by the volume of a country's exports of goods and services. Recovery of U.S. stature in the world scene is dependent on a vibrant export performance.

A boom in U.S. exports cannot be accomplished by the private sector alone because export weakness has stemmed at least as much from public policy as it has from private initiative. A reversal of public policy requires far more than another export drive.   It requires an end to the practice of creeping incrementalism and a reversal of the habit of obstructing exports by legislative and administrative mandate.   In addition, it requires a reversal of the Marshall Plan mentality: the thirty-odd year practice of treating foreign economic policy solely as a means and not as an end in itself, as an instrument rather than a goal of policy.   And of greatest importance, it requires a vibrant, flexible, innovative domestic economy producing goods the world wants.

It is instructive to note that not until 1978 was the country's balance of payments mentioned in a list of U.S. national goals. In that year, the Humphrey-Hawkins Act stated an "improved trade balance" as one of the goals of national policy. As Governor Henry Wallich observed in New York on 4 January 1979, the Employment Act of 1946 does not include balance of payments equilibrium among U.S. economic objectives; in contrast, the West German equivalent of this legislation does list external equilibrium as a goal.

Because U.S. export performance has deteriorated to such a degree relative to U.S. imports and world exports, recovery will require sacrifices for this country. Recovery could be achieved by balancing downward, by a reduction of U.S. imports to the level of exports. In fact, such a downward adjustment of imports was initiated by the 1 November 1978 measures to defend the dollar. If, in addition, a sharp reduction in U.S. exports were followed by a rising share of U.S. exports in world trade, this would probably be the regrettable consequence of a collapse of world trade initiated by the U.S. protectionist stance and a worldwide recession or depression. Such a downward adjustment would imply a retreat by the United States from international specialization, a diminution of the productivity of U.S. labor and capital, and a lower real U.S. standard of living.

The alternative is balancing upward -- raising U.S. exports to the level of imports -- and is vastly to be preferred. Its achievement will be far easier for the U.S. private sector than for the national government. Both the legislative and the executive branches have been spoiled by the habit of obstructing exports, a habit ingrained by three decades of practice. Members of both political parties, at both ends of Pennsylvania Avenue, must learn to resist the temptation to pursue national goals by introducing initiatives that further obstruct U.S. exports. To change the habit of creeping incrementalism will require self-discipline in the public sector; such self-discipline will, however, only serve to halt the deterioration in U.S. export performance.

To reverse the trend will require draconian measures. Every current domestic and foreign policy initiative should be examined in terms of its balance of payments impact in order to evaluate the effect of current policy on exports. In addition, every new initiative proposed to the White House should be accompanied by an impact statement. Any negative or positive impact should be viewed by the White House, not in isolation, but as an increment to a cumulative total and the direction of the cumulative total must be changed from negative to positive. For a period of time any initiative that has a negative impact on the U.S. balance of payments must be postponed until it can be implemented with another that has a positive impact at least as large. Public policy must be made to work with, not against, the efforts of the private sector to expand exports.

The change in public practice that is required is enormous and should pervade all levels of government service, resulting in a basic change of attitude concerning the nation's priorities. The Marshall Plan mentality of favoring imports over exports must be totally demolished.

Such a change in attitude would be facilitated by the creation of a new government Department of Trade that would gather together under one Cabinet-level secretary the trade responsibilities now scattered throughout the government. The assignment of trade policy as the sole responsibility of a Cabinet-level secretary is essential if the national policy interests dependent on expanding exports are to be argued effectively within the administration. Senator Ribicoff has stated the case well: "The Secretary of State is concerned with geopolitics. What we must now realize is that eco-politics is possibly even more important."

The secretary of state is not the only presidential advisor recommending measures detrimental to exports, however; the secretary of labor argues forcefully for the protection of his constituency as do the secretaries of agriculture, treasury, and commerce -- for all of whom domestic market considerations are at least as influential as are those of trade. Exchange rate policy, for example, has a major impact on government revenues and expenditures indirectly through its impact on prices and directly through its influence on debt management, tax receipts, and currency reserves. At the same time, exchange rate policy is of vital importance to the trade balance through its differing impacts on imports and exports as the entire postwar history of Japan and the United States vividly illustrates. A secretary of trade would be in a position to argue that a realistic exchange rate for the dollar is one that does more than just equate prices here and elsewhere. A realistic rate equates trade flows because it equates not only prices but effective demand at those prices. If, because of tradition, government controls, or for any reason, the effective demand of Japan for imports at 200 yen to the dollar causes Japanese exports greatly to exceed imports, that level of the dollar in relation to the yen is too high. The secretary of the treasury, concerned with the impact of dollar depreciation on domestic inflation might or might not be sympathetic to the trade argument. What is important is that the trade case not be prejudiced by the inferior status of its proponent.

The change in attitude must start at the top. Nothing is more revealing of the reasons for the enduring assumption that economic subjects are not properly included in a discussion of U.S. foreign policy goals than President Carter's address on 20 February 1979 at the Georgia Institute of Technology. The address was billed in advance by the White House as "a major foreign policy statement." The only mention of any economic subject matter came in the preamble when the president said, "We have the world's strongest military forces. . ." Then two paragraphs later, having continued on strategic matters, "We help sustain a world trading and monetary system that has brought greater prosperity to more of the world's people than ever before in history" (all true but not relevant). And finally, after three short paragraphs containing generalizations about national goals, "in short, we provide the bedrock of global security and economic advance in a world of unprecedented change and conflict. In such a world, America has four fundamental security responsibilities:. . ." After listing the four (see below) he went on to discuss Iran, the Mideast peace treaty, Indochina, the SALT II treaty, the importance of his defense budget, and relations with the Soviet Union.

34

What emerged was the clear implication that the U.S. economy and U.S. government expenditures are the means to be employed in efforts to provide for four fundamental security responsibilities: to provide for our nation's strength and safety; to stand by our allies and friends; to support national independence and integrity; and to work diligently for peace. No place was there any hint that the nation's strength and safety are dependent on economic performance. No place was there any suggestion that national independence and integrity are a function of economic strength and vitality. No place was there recognition that our allies and our friends will remain allies and friends only so long as they perceive our friendship to be in their national interest. No place was there any acknowledgement that U.S. pursuit of world peace can be effective only if the U.S. economy is generally perceived as strong enough to be able to resist political, economic, and military aggression against the United States or its allies. The United States will not remain a potent force on the world scene if "foreign policy" continues to be so narrowly conceived at the highest policy level.

FOOTNOTES

[1]Volcker, Paul A., "The Political Economy of the Dollar" Federal Reserve Bank of New York, <u>Quarterly Review</u>, Winter, 1978-1979.

[2]International Economic Policy Association: <u>The U.S. Balance of Payments: An Appraisal of U.S. Economic Strategy</u>, Washington, 1966.

[3]Hadley, Eleanor M., "Japan's Export Competitiveness in Third World Markets," <u>Significant Issues Series</u>, (Washington, D.C.: Georgetown University Center for Strategic and International Studies), (forthcoming).

[4]Tesor, George, "Dynamics of Export Consulting," paper presented at the National Meeting of the Academy of International Business, New York, November 12-14, 1976. (mimeo)

[5]Bradshaw, M. "U.S. Exports to Foreign Affiliates of U.S. Firms," <u>Survey of Current Business</u>, May 1969.

[6]<u>International Economic Relations of the Western World</u>, <u>1959-71</u>, <u>Volume I</u>, <u>Politics and Trade</u>, (London: Royal Institute of International Affairs 1976), p. 59.

[7]Monroe, Wilbur, <u>The New Internationalism</u>, (Massachusetts: Lexington Books 1976), p. 53.

[8]Katz, Julius L., Assistant Secretary of State, in testimony before the Joint Economic Committee of the Congress, 29 September 1978.

[9]Kissinger, Henry, <u>Economist</u>, 3 February 1979, p. 18.

SELECTED BIBLIOGRAPHY

American Enterprise Institute. International Payments Problems: A Symposium. Washington, D.C., 1966.

Bradshaw, Marie T., "U.S. Exports to Foreign Affiliates of U.S. Firms," Survey of Current Business. May, 1969.

Congressional Research Service. "Regulations of Direct Foreign Investment in Australia, Canada, France, Japan, Mexico." Foreign Investment Act of 1975. Hearings before the Subcommittee on Banking, Housing and Urban Affairs. United States Senate. 94th Congress. 1st session. 1975. p. s425.

Council of Economic Advisers. Annual Report. January, 1964.

Hadley, Eleanor M. Antitrust in Japan. Princeton University Press. 1969.

International Economic Policy Association. The United States Balance of Payments: An Appraisal of U.S. Economic Strategy. Washington, D.C., 1966.

Monroe, Wilbur. The New Internationalism. Massachusetts: Lexington Books, 1976.

Morgan, A. D. and D. Martin. "Tariff Reduction and U.K. Imports of Manufactures: 1955-71." National Institute Economic Review. no. 72. May 1975.

Moynihan, D. P. "United States in Opposition." First World and Third World. ed., Karl Brunner. University of Rochester, Center for Research in Government Policy and Business, 1978.

North Atlantic Treaty Organization. NATO Handbook. Brussels. March 1977.

Organization for Economic Cooperation and Development. Resources for the Developing World: The Flow of Financial Resources to Less Developed Countries. 1962-1968.

Perle, Richard. "Echoes of the 1930s." Strategic Review. Winter 1979.

Shonfield, Sir Andrew. International Economic Relations. Center for Strategic and International Studies. Washington Papers. vol. IV., no. 42. Sage Publications: Beverly Hills. 1976.

Shonfield, Andrew, ed. International Economic Relations of the Western World 1959-1971: Volume I, Politics and Trade. Royal Institute of International Affairs. New York. 1976.

Shonfield, Andrew. Europe: Journey to an Unknown Destination. Baltimore: Penguin Books, 1973.

Tesar, George. "Dynamics of Export Consulting." paper presented at the National Meeting of the Academy of International Business. 12-14 November 1976. New York.

Vernon, Raymond. Sovereignty at Bay. Cambridge: Harvard Business School Basic Books. 1971.

Vernon, Raymond. "Economic Consequences of U.S. Foreign Direct Investment." U.S. National Economic Policy in an Interdependent World. (Williams Report). Washington, D.C.: Government Printing Office. 1971.

Volcker, Paul A. "The Political Economy of the Dollar." Quarterly Review. Federal Reserve Bank of New York. Winter. 1978-1979.

2

THE ECONOMIC IMPORTANCE OF EXPORTS TO THE UNITED STATES

Jack Carlson
Hugh Graham

CONTENTS

I.   INTRODUCTION

Since World War II, international trade has increased at a much faster rate than world output. For example, between 1953 and 1979, the volume of world trade grew at an average annual rate of over 7.3 percent compared with a real world output growth rate of under 5 percent per year. After a modest slowdown over the next few years, this trend of rapid growth in world trade is likely to continue during the 1980s, resulting in a significant increase in the degree of international economic interdependence. It has already been a major factor behind the increasing degree of political cooperation and exchange that has evolved over the past few years, such as the annual economic summit meetings of major trading countries. The growth of international trade, particularly in imports of Western industrialized countries, has provided a rapidly expanding market for the products of developing nations, both primary commodities and manufactured products. Together with the spread of capital, technology and entrepreneurial skills through direct foreign investment, increased international trade, perhaps more than any other factor, has contributed to increased standards of living in both developed and developing countries.

The growth in importance of foreign markets has been most rapid in the developed countries. Since the mid-1950s, the share of Western industrial countries' output exported to other countries has risen from less than 10 percent to almost 17 percent. This increased dependence on foreign trade has been especially notable in Europe and Japan (see Table 5).

While the United States remains an active participant in world trade and has enjoyed the benefits of the rapid postwar expansion of trade, the growth rate of U.S. exports has lagged significantly behind that of most other major trading countries. Since 1953, U.S. exports have grown on average at under 6 percent per year, or nearly 1.2 percentage points

41

below the average annual increase in world trade. Despite this comparatively slow growth, U.S. exports have grown considerably faster than U.S. domestic production during the postwar period. Since 1953, U.S. domestic production grew at an average annual rate of about 3.4 percent, nearly 2.5 percentage points slower than the growth rate of exports.

The poor performance of U.S. exports compared to that of many other major Western industrialized countries is even more evident in trade in manufactured goods. World trade in manufactured goods has grown at a remarkable 7.8 percent per year since the mid-1950s while U.S. exports of manufactured goods have increased at only 5.1 percent per year.

As a result of this slow expansion of U.S. manufactured exports, the preeminence of the United States in world trade has been steadily declining. The U.S. share of world exports of manufactures declined from 25 percent in 1955 to about 13.6 percent in 1977 before improving slightly to 15.5 percent in 1979. While the growth rate of U.S. manufactured exports is forecast to accelerate over the next 10 years, it is likely that the United States will experience a continuing decline in its market share of world exports in the next decade.

In large part, the decline in the U.S. share of manufactured goods trade is attributable to the rapid postwar recovery of Western Europe and Japan and the relatively slow growth of industrial production in the United States. As these areas grew in economic importance to levels rivaling the United States, a large number of firms in Europe and Japan became increasingly competitive with U.S. firms.

Recently, the rapid growth of manufacturing exports from several developing countries such as Brazil, South Korea, and Taiwan has also made inroads into U.S. domestic and export markets. The competitiveness of these countries in world markets can be expected to grow even further over the next decade, placing increased pressure on U.S. exporters in retaining their existing market shares.

The increased instability of the international economic system in the 1970s, as evidenced by the collapse of the fixed exchange rate system of Bretton Woods and the increasing power of the OPEC oil cartel, has placed additional pressure on governments to insulate their domestic economies from international repercussions, at least on the import side, and has encouraged a marked increase in protectionist sentiments in both industrialized and developing countries. Slower overall growth in developed countries, resulting, in part, from the tenfold increase of crude oil prices during the decade of the 1970s, has made many domestic industries increasingly vulnerable to changes in foreign competition. At the same time, many nations have been tempted to look (largely in vain) to external sources for relief, hoping for increased exports to stimulate domestic economic growth. In other cases, and often in the same countries, protectionist sentiments have been encouraged by seemingly persistent balance of payments problems. In the major Western industrial countries, including the United States, textiles and clothing, steel and other metal products, footwear, electronic goods, and rubber products have all been the subject of trade actions in recent years designed to protect local industry from foreign competition.

The success of the OPEC oil cartel in raising export revenues for oil exporters also encouraged other developing countries to seek similar strategies for other commodities and to demand the implementation of the "new international economic order" under which developing countries would receive a larger share of the gains from trade. Primarily, these objectives would be accomplished through increased cartelization of world trade, particularly in commodity markets. This strengthening mood of protectionism threatens to arrest the underlying trend toward freer trade that the world has enjoyed since the Second World War and to slow the rate of growth of world trade.

In light of these developments, the decision in April 1979 by most of the Western industrial nations and some developing countries to conclude the Tokyo Round of the multilateral trade negotiations represents an important step toward diminishing the thrust of the protectionist argument. Under the proposed agreement, industrial nations will cut the remaining tariff levels by an average 33 percent over the next eight years and, for the first time, a significant multilateral effort

43

has been made to reduce the major nontariff barriers to free trade, such as discriminatory government procurement policies and customs evaluation practices.

While the Tokyo Round of trade negotiations will reduce barriers facing U.S. exporters and increase the rate of growth of U.S. manufactured goods exports in the long run, the short run outlook for U.S. exports is somewhat mixed. The very large depreciation of the U.S. dollar against the currencies of major trading partners in 1978 resulted in modest progress toward decreasing the U.S. trade deficit as U.S. exports became more competitive in world markets and export volume expanded by over 10 percent. The large increases in oil prices in 1979, however, resulted in a deterioration in the combined current account for developed countries from a surplus of $8 billion in 1978 to a deficit of $30 billion in 1979, with a further deterioration to a $50 billion deficit anticipated for 1980. This massive change in the terms of trade in favor of oil exporters will almost certainly slow economic activity in most Western industrial countries during the early 1980s. As a result, the growth rates of world trade and output are expected to moderate somewhat over the next three years. It is forecast that the volume of world manufacturing trade will grow at about 4 percent per year during the early 1980s, while the volume of primary commodity exports (including energy) will increase at less than 3 percent per year (see Table 1). These growth rates are significantly lower than those achieved during most of the postwar period. In the longer term, the growth of world trade should return to more normal levels, about 6 percent to 7 percent per year. Provided the U.S. exporters can retain at least their present share of world markets and maintain international competitiveness, the long run prospects for a substantial contribution to U.S. economic growth from the foreign trade sector are therefore bright, perhaps adding each year a one-half percentage point to U.S. GNP growth, and providing 500,000 new jobs.

Recent Trends in U.S. Trade Performance

The recent major depreciation of the dollar against the currencies of many of our major trading

TABLE 1

THE GROWTH OF WORLD TRADE[1]
(Average Annual Percent Change in Volume)

	Actual 1960-1979	Forecast 1979-1983	Forecast 1983-1990
DEVELOPED COUNTRIES	7.1	4.0*	5.7
United States	6.3	3.0*	5.3
Canada	7.0	3.1	5.0
Japan	8.3	6.0	5.8
United Kingdom	4.4	2.1	3.5
France	8.2	2.9	5.5
West Germany	7.0	3.3	6.0
Italy	4.5	1.1	3.8
DEVELOPING COUNTRIES	5.5	1.4	4.9
CENTRALLY PLANNED COUNTRIES	12.5	4.0	5.5
WORLD	6.5	3.7*	5.5
Manufactured Goods	8.1	4.7	6.5
Food and Raw Materials	4.3	1.4	3.0
Services	5.0	2.7	4.5

[1]National data are exports of goods and services (national income account basis) in local currency at 1970 prices. Regional and commodity data are converted from national data at 1970 exchange rates.

*authors' estimates.

Source: Wharton Econometric Forecasting Associates for actual data and, unless otherwise specified, 1979-1983 forecasting; 1983-1990 forecasting by authors.

45

partners has focused public attention on the large deficits in the U.S. merchandise trade balance in 1977, 1978 and 1979 (see Figure 1). These large deficits, however, were the latest reflection of an increasingly uneven and generally lackluster trade performance by the United States since 1970.

Through the 1950s and 1960s, the United States generally enjoyed a moderate surplus in its balance of merchandise trade (see Table 2). By 1971, however, the overall merchandise trade balance had slipped into a slight deficit. This situation persisted into 1972, in part due to a moderate increase in the value of fuel imports in those years, and the pronounced deterioration in the U.S. surplus in net exports of manufactured goods. After enjoying a surplus in trade in manufactured goods of over $4 billion throughout the 1960s, by 1972 the United States was in deficit in its trade balance in manufactures.

The deterioration in the overall U.S. trade position in the late 1960s and early 1970s, coupled with large-scale capital outflows, resulted in enormous pressure on the dollar in international financial markets, culminating in the August 1971 suspension of convertibility into gold for foreign currencies, the imposition of a 10 percent surcharge on imports by the United States and the general devaluation of the dollar under the Smithsonian Agreement in December 1971.

Despite the 1971 devaluation of the dollar, which was intended to make U.S. goods more competitive in world markets, the U.S. trade position worsened in 1972. The trade deficit in manufactured goods reached $2.4 billion in 1972, chiefly due to the surge in manufactured imports. The overall merchandise trade balance in all goods was even larger at $6.4 billion.

This slow response of the U.S. trade position to the corrective measures taken in 1971 continued to cause alarm in international currency markets during 1972, resulting in massive speculation against the dollar during the first half of 1973. A second devaluation of the dollar in February 1973, followed by the adoption of a generalized system of floating rates by the major industrial countries, resulted in further depreciation of the dollar against several other currencies, including the West German mark.

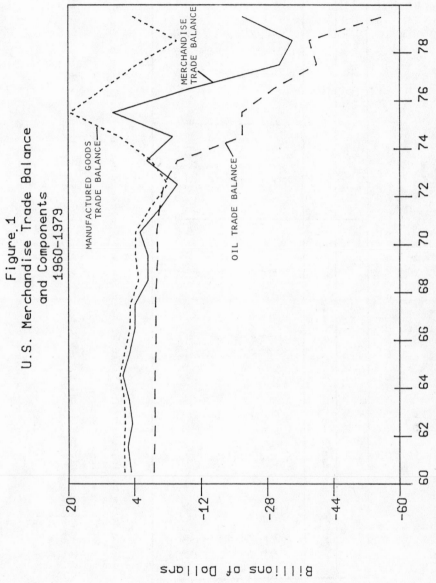

Figure 1
U.S. Merchandise Trade Balance
and Components
1960-1979

MANUFACTURED GOODS
TRADE BALANCE

MERCHANDISE
TRADE BALANCE

OIL TRADE BALANCE

Billions of Dollars

Source: Wharton Econometric Forecasting Associates and Forecast Center, U.S. Chamber of Commerce.

TABLE 2

U.S. TRADE BALANCE
($U.S. billions)

	MERCHANDISE TRADE[1]				SERVICES[2]	BALANCE OF TRADE IN GOODS AND SERVICES[3]
	TOTAL	Manufactured Goods	Agricultural Goods	Fuels		
1960	4.6	6.2	1.1	-0.7	3.2	5.1
1965	5.3	7.0	2.1	-1.3	5.8	8.3
1970	2.7	4.6	1.4	-1.5	7.0	5.6
1971	-2.0	1.2	1.9	-2.2	8.9	2.3
1972	-6.4	-2.4	2.9	-3.2	10.4	-1.9
1973	1.3	-0.3	9.2	-6.5	15.8	11.0
1974	-2.3	7.3	11.6	-22.0	20.3	9.3
1975	11.0	19.9	12.4	-22.0	19.1	23.0
1976	-5.9	12.4	12.2	-32.4	22.6	9.6
1977	-26.5	3.6	10.8	-43.1	24.5	-9.4
1978	-28.5	-5.9	14.9	-41.3	31.0	-8.8
1979	-23.6	3.8	17.4	-55.6	34.6	-1.1

[1]Census basis.
[2]Balance of payments basis, excluding official services but including net interest from private U.S. assets abroad.
[3]Including official services payments.

Source: Bureau of Economic Analysis, Survey of Current Business, various issues, and the U.S. Chamber of Commerce, Forecast Center.

48

By late 1973, however, the U.S. trade balance had begun to improve. Two years of very strong growth in exports of manufactured goods in 1973 and 1974, together with a massive surge in the value of agricultural exports in 1973, resulted in a return to a small surplus in the overall merchandise trade balance in 1973 and only a slight deficit in 1974. This improvement in the overall trade picture occured in spite of the huge increase in the price of imported oil during late 1973 and 1974.

The pronounced economic slowdown in the United States in 1974 and 1975 and the delayed effects of the 1973 currency realignments further improved the U.S. trade position during 1975 and 1976. In fact, in 1975 the United States experienced an almost embarrassingly large trade surplus of over $11 billion, due mainly to a sizeable surplus for manufactured goods.

As the United States recovered from the depressed conditions of 1974 and 1975, this short-lived trade surplus evaporated as rapidly as it had appeared. Oil imports surged and the trade deficit for fuels grew from $22 billion in 1975 to $56 billion in 1979. This was only part of the story, however. Imports of manufactured goods also grew at an astounding rate, increasing by 106 percent in value and over 56 percent in volume between 1975 and 1979. Unfortunately, exports of manufactures failed to increase at the same rate as imports. Although the value of exports of manufactured goods rose from $71 billion in 1975 to $119.6 billion in 1979, much of this increase was due to inflation; higher prices generally and higher export prices in particular tended to drive up the value of U.S. exports even when the volume of exports was growing fairly slowly. In volume terms (adjusted for inflation) U.S. exports of manufactured goods increased only 28 percent between 1975 and 1979, less than the growth in U.S. manufactured imports over the period. More importantly, this increase in U.S. exports of manufactures was also significantly less than the 32 percent growth in trade in manufactured goods for the world as a whole.

Together with the large increase in the fuel imports bill over the period, this poor trade performance resulted in a $24 billion trade deficit in 1979, compared with an $11 billion surplus in 1975.

About half of the $35 billion deterioration in the trade balance between 1975 and 1979 was attributable to the increased cost and volume of fuel imports and the rest to the slow growth of U.S. manufactured goods exports and the surge of U.S. imports of manufactures. Part of the slow growth of U.S. manufactured exports since 1975 was in turn attributable to the relatively slow growth in our major trading partners, especially in Western Europe and Japan (see Figure 2).

It is doubtful, however, that the below average growth in its major trading partners reduced U.S. exports of manufactured goods by more than $2-3 billion per year (or 2 to 3 percent) below the level that would have occurred if growth had been at the historic average in Europe and Japan. This is only about a quarter as large as the loss of U.S. exports of manufactured goods due to the decline in its share of world markets over the period. For example, had the United States been able to maintain even its 1975 share of world exports of manufactured goods during the 1976 to 1979 period, exports of manufactures would have been about $8 billion per year higher than they actually were over these four years. Rather, this poor U.S. export performance reflects a continuation of a fundamental long-term decline in the relative position of the United States as an exporter of manufactured goods. Between 1956 and 1979, the U.S. share of world trade in manufactures declined from 25 percent to 15.5 percent, although most of this decline occurred before 1972. Even during periods when the value of U.S. exports increased particularly rapidly, as for example in 1974-1975 and 1979, the share of U.S. exports in world exports of manufactures did not increase markedly above trend levels (see Table 3). In contrast, Japan, France, West Germany, and Italy all significantly increased their share of world trade in manufactures during the postwar period.

While the recent merchandise trade deficits justifiably have raised considerable concern over the trend of declining U.S. export shares and the burgeoning oil import bill, the very concept of merchandise trade deficits needs to be treated with considerable caution. The merchandise trade balance is but one of many subtotals in the overall classification of U.S. financial relations with the rest of the world and often merchandise trade deficits are wholly or

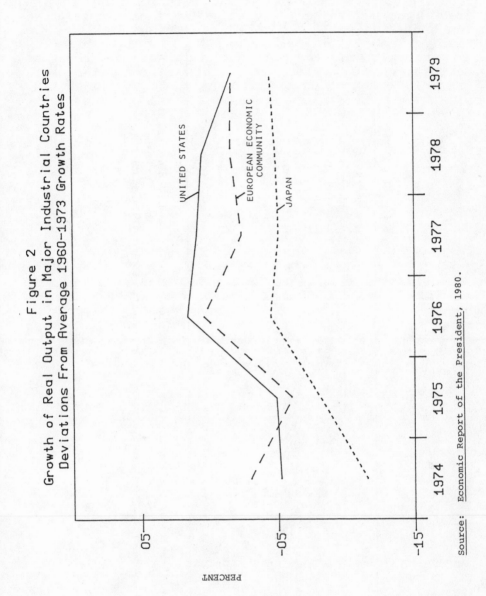

Figure 2

Growth of Real Output in Major Industrial Countries
Deviations From Average 1960-1973 Growth Rates

UNITED STATES

EUROPEAN ECONOMIC
COMMUNITY

JAPAN

PERCENT

05

-05

-15

1974   1975   1976   1977   1978   1979

Source: Economic Report of the President, 1980.

51

TABLE 3

WORLD TRADE IN MANUFACTURED GOODS
(Percent Share by Country and Region)

	1956	1960	1965	1970	1975	1977	1978	1979[1]
United States..........	25.0	19.6	17.0	14.7	15.6	13.7	14.1	15.6
Canada................	4.1	3.5	3.8	4.8	4.1	4.4	4.4	4.5
Japan.................	3.4	4.3	7.0	8.7	10.1	11.0	10.2	11.0
European Economic Community...........	26.1	32.0	33.8	35.7	34.7	35.8	36.4	44.4
United Kingdom........	15.0	12.7	10.2	8.1	7.2	6.9	6.8	6.4
France................	5.2	6.6	6.3	6.6	7.0	7.0	7.2	7.2
West Germany..........	12.0	14.6	14.3	14.8	13.8	14.4	14.4	13.8
Italy.................	2.0	3.3	4.8	5.2	5.3	5.6	5.9	6.5
Developed Countries[2].	82.6	81.5	81.8	82.7	82.1	81.8	82.4	83.4
Developing Countries.	6.9	6.6	6.1	6.7	7.3	8.1	8.0	7.6
Centrally Planned Countries...........	10.5	11.9	12.1	10.6	10.6	10.0	9.6	9.0

[1] Estimated
[2] Includes all members of the Organization for Economic Cooperation and Development plus South Africa.

Source: U.S. Chamber of Commerce, Forecast Center, Wharton Econometric Associates.

partially offset by surpluses in other components of the U.S. balance of payments (see Figure 3). For example, the United States has traditionally run a sizeable surplus in its net receipts of foreign investment income and other services (see Table 2). This surplus of U.S. trade in services offset all but $3.2 billion of the merchandise trade deficit in 1979 and has meant that over the 1970s, the United States enjoyed a modest $4.0 billion average annual surplus on its balance of trade of goods and services combined. And, while the United States certainly has a strong interest in reducing its massive merchandise trade deficits, it must be recognized that other countries might then argue that this should be accompanied by some reduction in the size of the U.S. surplus on net foreign investment receipts and other service inflows.

Trade in Services in the Balance of Payments

The very considerable surplus enjoyed by the United States in its trade balance in services tends to receive far less attention than the more commonly recognized merchandise trade balance (i.e. trade in goods). Service exports under the balance of payments definitions consist predominantly of receipts on U.S. investment abroad and other receipts of interest on foreign assets, tourist expenditure in the United States, and sales of transportation services (see Table 4).

Since 1960, U.S. service exports have grown exceptionally rapidly, averaging over 13 percent per annum in value terms and 7 percent in volume. Significantly, investment receipts have been the fastest growing component of services exports, increasing an average 14.6 percent a year over the last 20 years. While service exports have grown rapidly over the last two decades, imports of services have increased even faster in volume terms, averaging over 8 percent per year growth since 1960. This expansion of service imports is primarily the result of the explosive increase in payments on foreign owned assets in the United States, which grew at over 13 percent per year in volume over the period.

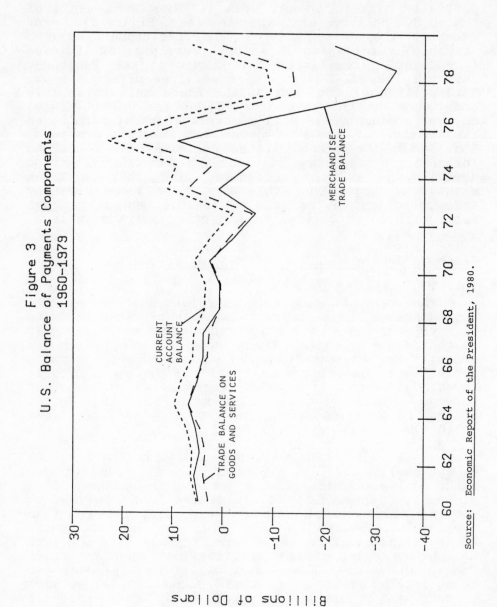

Figure 3

U.S. Balance of Payments Components
1960-1979

Billions of Dollars

Source: Economic Report of the President, 1980.

54

TABLE 4

U.S. TRADE IN SERVICES
1960 - 1979

($U.S. billions)

Year	EXPORTS					IMPORTS					Balance
	Total	Receipts on U.S. Investment Abroad	Travel	Passenger Fares	Transportation	Total	Payment on Foreign Assets	Travel	Passenger Fares	Transportation	
1960	8.9	4.6	0.9	0.2	1.6	5.9	1.2	1.7	0.5	1.4	3.0
1965	13.8	7.4	1.4	0.3	2.2	8.3	2.1	2.4	0.7	2.0	5.5
1970	21.7	11.8	2.3	0.5	3.1	15.3	5.5	4.0	1.2	2.8	6.4
1975	44.6	25.4	4.8	1.0	5.8	29.8	12.6	6.4	2.3	5.5	14.8
1976	51.4	29.2	5.8	1.2	6.7	33.0	13.3	6.9	2.6	6.6	18.4
1977	55.6	32.1	6.2	1.4	7.0	36.3	14.6	7.5	2.8	7.3	19.3
1978	68.5	41.5	7.1	1.6	7.8	45.7	21.6	8.4	3.1	8.2	22.8
1979[1]	92.8	61.6	8.6	1.7	9.5	60.3	32.1	9.9	3.9	9.4	32.5

[1] Estimated.

Source: Survey of Current Business, various issues. Estimates by Jack Carlson and Hugh Graham, Forecast Center, U.S. Chamber of Commerce.

55

Despite the faster growth of U.S. service imports than exports, the services surplus has increased continuously over the last 20 years, mainly due to the large surplus experienced at the end of the 1950s and the slightly faster increase of service export prices. As a result, the trade surplus for services reached a record $34.5 billion in 1979.

Although growth in many overseas countries may slow slightly in the next decade compared with the past 20 years, U.S. direct investment receipts are expected to increase strongly, possibly averaging more than 10 percent growth per year between 1979 and 1990. Similarly, improving living standards in Europe and Japan and the recent depreciation of the dollar against many other currencies can be expected to provide a substantial boost to tourist receipts over the first half of the next decade. Overall, service exports are expected to grow at around 5 percent per year in volume terms and 11-12 percent in value over the next decade, or about the same rate as service imports. While the nominal surplus for services can therefore be expected to increase strongly over the period to 1990, in real (price adjusted) terms, it is anticipated that little change in the current surplus will occur.

The Importance of Exports in U.S. Output

Despite the relatively slow U.S. export growth and declining share of the United States in world trade, U.S. exports of goods and services have grown faster than domestic output as a whole. As a result of this rapid growth of exports, the share of exports (and imports) of goods and services in gross national product has risen dramatically (see Table 5). In 1960, exports of goods and services accounted for only about 4.7 percent of U.S. domestic production. By 1979, this figure had risen to 8 percent and can be expected to increase to over 10 percent by 1990.

Exports, however, remain less important as a source of demand for domestic goods and services in the United States than for other Western industrialized countries. The ratio of exports to total output for the United States, at 8 percent, is significantly below the average of 16.8 percent for all developed countries

TABLE 5

IMPORTANCE OF FOREIGN TRADE IN
TOTAL NATIONAL OUTPUT[1]

	1956	1960	1965	1970	1975	1977	1978	1979
Developed Countries[2]	9.6	10.3	11.1	13.6	15.8	16.7	16.8	17.6
United States	5.0	4.7	4.8	5.7	7.0	6.7	7.0	8.3
Canada	16.7	16.2	17.6	23.3	20.7	22.6	23.7	24.0
Japan	6.8	7.7	9.5	10.5	14.7	17.2	16.2	17.0
United Kingdom	19.4	19.4	19.7	23.5	26.6	29.3	29.0	29.1
France	9.7	12.3	12.6	16.3	20.5	22.4	23.2	24.3
Germany	15.1	15.7	16.6	21.1	25.4	27.1	27.2	27.8
Italy	7.6	11.5	16.1	19.3	23.5	26.6	28.8	30.5
Developing Countries	15.9	15.4	16.3	16.6	15.2	16.0	15.6	16.0
Centrally Planned Countries	4.4	4.7	4.9	4.4	4.0	3.9	3.8	3.7
WORLD	10.3	10.2	10.5	11.8	12.8	13.4	13.6	14.1

[1]Exports of goods and services on a national income accounts basis as a percent of gross domestic product, both valued at 1970 prices and exchange rates.
[2]All members of the Organization for Economic Cooperation and Development plus South Africa.

Source: U.S. Chamber of Commerce, Forecast Center.

and has been growing at a slower rate over the last 20 years. For example, between 1956 and 1979, the share of exports in the Japanese gross domestic product rose from 6.8 percent to 17.0 percent. Over the, same period, the share of exports in the European Economic Community gross domestic product increased from 15.5 percent to 29.3 percent and similar increases have occurred in other Western industrial countries.

Though enjoying fairly rapid growth in exports, neither the developing countries as a whole nor the centrally planned economies showed significant increases in the share of exports in total output over the last 20 years. In these areas, the rapid growth rate for exports was matched by an equally rapid growth rate in total output -- between 1956 and 1979, output in the developing countries grew at an average annual rate of 5.3 percent, about the same rate as these countries' exports. As a result, the share of exports in total output for the region as a whole stayed roughly constant over the period at around 15 percent, although still significantly higher than in the United States. In the centrally planned economies, output grew faster than exports between 1956 and 1979, resulting in a slight fall in the share of exports in national output from 4.4 percent to 3.8 percent over the period.

In terms of foreign trade then, the United States remains relatively inward-looking and oriented toward production for the domestic market, in part the result of the size and diversity of resources and markets in the United States.

II. THE COMPOSITION OF U.S. EXPORTS

Exports consist of all those goods and services produced by a nation's residents and sold overseas, including sales to private citizens in foreign countries, sales to foreign companies and foreign governments, and even sales to overseas branches of American corporations.

As with other components of demand, exports include services as well as goods sold overseas, since the production of services requires the use of a nation's resources in the same way as the production of more tangible goods. For example, service exports include freight and insurance charges received from overseas by U.S. shipping companies for the transport of goods (not necessarily only U.S. goods). When foreign tourists fly on American-owned airlines, the United States also has exported transportation services.[1]

Almost two-thirds of U.S. exports of goods and services are in the form of merchandise goods (excluding military sales). The rest consists of receipts for services of various kinds. About 45 percent of total exports are manufactured products and about 13 percent are agricultural commodities. Crude minerals and fuels account for another 9 percent of total exports.

This pattern of exports differs markedly from the relative importance of these sectors in U.S. output. Agricultural commodities account for only 3 percent of private output in the United States, much less than the 13 percent share of agricultural products in exports of goods and services. Similarly, the manufacturing sector accounts for only 27 percent of private U.S. production, but for 45 percent of total exports. This high propensity of the agricultural and manufacturing sectors to export compared to the commercial and service sectors is hardly surprising. For the most part, the output of the service sectors is not transportable or transferable over large distances since it requires close proximity and contact between buyer and seller. For example, it is very difficult for the sellers of laundry services to export their product, but it is a lot easier for the makers of

TABLE 6

U.S. MERCHANDISE EXPORTS
BY COMMODITY CLASS
1978-1979

	Value $ U.S. Billion		Percent of Total[1]	
	1978	1979	1978	1979
TOTAL DOMESTIC EXPORTS	141.1	176.6	100	100
Food and Live Animals	18.3	21.8	13.0	12.3
Meat	1.0	1.1	0.7	0.6
Grains	11.6	14.1	8.2	8.0
Beverages and Tobacco	2.3	2.2	1.6	1.2
Crude Minerals[2]	15.5	20.3	11.0	11.5
Minerals Fuels and Lubricants	3.9	5.5	2.8	3.1
Organic Oils and Fats	1.5	1.8	1.1	1.0
Manufactured Goods	94.5	115.6	67.0	65.5
Chemicals	12.6	17.1	8.9	9.7
Nonelectrical Machinery	32.2	24.8	16.4	14.0
Electrical Machinery	13.8	17.8	9.8	10.0
Transportation Equipment	22.2	25.7	15.7	14.6
Other Manufactures	22.7	30.2	16.1	17.1
Other Goods	9.0	9.3	6.3	5.3

[1] Sums may not add to totals because of rounding.
[2] Excluding fuels.

Source: U.S. Department of Commerce. Highlights of U.S. Export and Import Trade, December 1979.

TABLE 7

U.S. FOREIGN TRADE: AGRICULTURAL PRODUCTS[1]

($U.S. billions)

	Exports	Imports	Balance
1958	3.9	3.9	0
1960	4.9	3.8	1.1
1965	6.2	4.1	2.1
1970	7.2	5.8	1.4
1971	7.7	5.8	1.9
1972	9.4	6.5	2.9
1973	17.7	8.4	9.2
1974	22.0	10.4	11.6
1975	21.9	9.5	12.4
1976	23.0	11.0	12.0
1977	23.6	13.5	10.1
1978	29.4	14.8	14.6
1979[2]...........	32.0	16.2	15.8

[1]Exports and imports are free alongside ship transaction values, except prior to 1974 where imports are customs values.
[2]Fiscal year ended September 1979.

Source: International Economic Report of the President, 1976, and U. S. Department of Agriculture, Foreign Agricultural Trade of the United States, February 1979.

washing machines to do so. When American firms wish to sell services overseas, it is often necessary for them to establish a branch or subsidiary in the foreign country concerned. This is especially important in certain service sectors such as banking and insurance. These difficulties in exporting the output of the service sector account for the relatively low propensity to export services.

U.S. Agricultural Exports

In contrast to the interwar period and the decade of the 1950s, when the United States was a net importer of agricultural commodities, the nation again become a net exporter of agricultural goods in the early 1960s. Throughout the 1960s, however, the U.S. net trade surplus for agricultural commodities remained fairly small, averaging less than $1.6 billion per year. Despite the persistent but modest agricultural trade surplus during the 1960s, the growth rate of agricultural exports remained fairly low, averaging only about 4 percent per year in value over the decade.

After 1973, however, U.S. exports increased very rapidly. Aided by massive purchases of U.S. wheat by the Soviet Union and a more than 50 percent increase in food export prices, agricultural exports rose from $9.4 billion in 1972 to $17.7 billion in 1973, an increase of nearly 80 percent. While the volume of agricultural trade fell markedly in 1974 from the very high levels of the previous year, higher farm prices were sufficient to ensure a further increase in the value of agricultural trade in 1974. Since 1974, both export volumes and prices for agricultural exports have generally risen rapidly, pushing the value of agricultural exports in 1979 to a record $34.5 billion. Although agricultural imports also rose strongly between 1973 and 1979, the increase was significantly less than the growth of imports. By 1979, the United States had a very sizeable surplus in its agricultural trade of $17.4 billion. Despite the recent imposition of a partial embargo on grain sales to the Soviet Union, the United States is expected to maintain a growing trade surplus in agricultural commodities over the next few years.

The composition of U.S. agricultural exports has also undergone major changes since the second world war. In the early postwar years, cotton and tobacco dominated agricultural exports, accounting for nearly half the total. By 1979, these two items had declined in importance to only 10 percent of agricultural exports. The share of grain in agricultural exports, on the other hand, had risen from 29 percent in 1950 to 39 percent in 1978, while the share of oilseeds increased from 6 percent to 28 percent.

Although the United States has suffered a slight decline in its total share of world agricultural exports since 1960, this has not been as pronounced as for manufactured goods and there has been some improvement in market shares since 1970, mainly due to the upsurge in grain exports after 1972.

The United States remains preeminant in world grain trade, accounting for between 50 and 55 percent of world exports in recent years. Because of its unique ability to expand domestic production rapidly to meet the upsurge in grain imports by the Soviet Union and Eastern European countries, the United States captured nearly 80 percent of these recent increases in world grain trade.

Despite a declining share of world trade in soybeans, cotton, and tobacco, the United States also remains the world's largest exporter of these agricultural commodities. The spectacular growth of soybean exports from Brazil and other developing countries has reduced the U.S. share of world soybean trade from 92 percent in 1965 to around 65 percent today. Nevertheless, the volume of soybean exports has grown strongly, averaging over 8 percent per year in recent years. Similarly, cotton exports have again attained record levels, even though subject to intense competition from exports from the Soviet Union, Turkey, and the Ivory Coast.

The continuation of these recent trends toward rapidly rising U.S. exports of agricultural products depends on a variety of factors. In the short run, prospects for a significant expansion of trade with the Soviet Union have been clouded by recent military and political events in the Middle East and the imposition of a political embargo on U.S. grain exports to the

Soviet Union. Nevertheless, record agricultural output in the United States in the 1980 marketing year, together with an anticipated decline in agricultural output in many other major producing areas in the world should sustain last year's record export levels during this year. In the long term, world demand for grains, oilseeds, and meat is expected to continue to grow fairly strongly over the next decade due to the forecasted rising per capita incomes in centrally planned economies and middle income developing countries. The limited ability of many of these countries to expand production fast enough to meet the rising demand should ensure that this increase in demand is translated into a sizeable increase in world export trade, although climactic factors may result in substantial variations in demand from year to year.

With world demand for agricultural imports expected to grow strongly over the next decade, the growth of U.S. agricultural exports over the next decade is in large part dependent on the ability of the United States to sustain the recent growth in domestic agricultural output. While the scope for major increases in land area and to a lesser extent labor and capital devoted to agriculture are fairly limited, continued growth in productivity in agriculture should boost agricultural output substantially in the United States over the next decade.[2]

Currently, agricultural exports account for about a quarter of farm receipts in the United States, although this proportion varies widely across products and states. For example, Illinois is dependent on exports for 45 percent and Indiana for 40 percent of state farm income, while agricultural industries in the New England and Middle Atlantic regions are only minimally dependent on export markets. In all, eighteen states rely on agricultural exports for more than 25 percent of total farm income (see Table 9). As would be expected, those states that are leading producers of wheat, feed grains, soybeans, and other major agricultural exports are also those states relying most heavily on export markets (see Table 8).

While no exact estimates of the number of jobs directly dependent on agricultural exports are available, about 3 million workers and farmers are engaged in agricultural activities in the nation as a

TABLE 8

U.S. AGRICULTURAL EXPORTS VALUE BY COMMODITY

($ U.S. billions)

	1965	1970	1975	1976	1977	1978[1]	1979
Animals and Animal Products	0.8	0.9	1.7	2.4	2.7	3.0	3.6
Percent of total	12.9	12.3	7.7	10.4	11.3	10.1	11.3
Cotton	0.5	0.4	1.0	1.0	1.5	1.7	1.9
Percent of total	8.1	5.5	4.5	4.6	6.5	5.9	5.9
Grains and Preparations	2.6	2.6	11.6	10.9	8.7	11.5	12.6
Percent of total	42.9	35.6	53.1	47.3	36.7	39.2	39.4
Oil Seeds and Products	1.2	1.9	4.5	5.4	6.6	8.4	8.6
Percent of total	19.3	26.0	20.3	22.1	28.0	28.4	26.9
Tobacco, Unmanufactured	0.4	0.5	0.9	0.9	1.1	1.4	1.3
Percent of total	6.5	6.8	4.0	4.1	4.6	4.6	4.1
Other	0.7	1.0	2.2	2.7	3.0	3.4	4.0
Percent of total	11.2	13.7	10.0	11.7	12.7	11.5	12.5
TOTAL	6.2	7.3	21.9	23.0	23.6	29.4	32.0

[1]Fiscal year October 1978 - September 1979.

Source: U.S. Department of Agriculture, Foreign Agricultural Trade of the United States, various issues.

65

TABLE 9

LEADING STATES FOR AGRICULTURAL EXPORT SHARES
By Leading Export Commodities
1978

($U.S. millions)

Commodity	United States	Leading 5 States by Rank				
All commodities........	27,298.0	Illinois 2,769.5	Iowa 2,115.1	Texas 2,074.4	California 1,926.7	Minnesota 1,484.8
Soybeans and products	6,410.9	Illinois 1,223.8	Iowa 914.6	Missouri 541.5	Indiana 252.2	Minnesota 487.0
Feedgrains and products	5,983.1	Illinois 1,103.8	Iowa 813.9	Nebraska 721.5	Indiana 597.5	Minnesota 474.1
Wheat and products...	4,138.7	Kansas 741.1	N.Dakota 420.2	Oklahoma 377.1	Montana 253.3	Texas 252.5
Cotton inc. linters..	1,706.9	Texas 652.4	California 331.0	Mississippi 195.3	Arizona 134.6	Arkansas 122.8
Tobacco	1,131.8	N.Carolina 564.4	Kentucky 140.2	S.Carolina 107.1	Georgia 104.2	Virginia 97.0
Fruits and preparations	976.5	California 543.2	Florida 200.0	Washington 45.1	Texas 37.2	Arizona 32.7

Source: U.S. Department of Agriculture, Foreign Agricultural Trade of the United States, March/April 1979.

66

whole. Although it is not strictly legitimate to infer that exports employ a quarter of those engaged in agricultural activities, it is likely that 0.5 million workers in the agricultural sector are dependent on exports. The direct employment effects of agricultural exports in the leading producing states is obviously also quite high. Illinois, the leading exporting state, has over 97,000 wage and salaried farm workers and 117,000 farmers. With agricultural exports in the state so dominant in farm income, the implied number of jobs directly dependent on exports is obviously quite large, approaching one half.

In addition, the indirect employment effects from these exports in those industries supplying inputs and services (including transportation and "post production" services) to agriculture are obviously greater. For example, every $1 billion worth of agricultural exports requires, directly and indirectly, the input of about $0.4 billion worth of both manufactured goods and services such as farm tractors and chemical fertilizers and thereby increases employment in these sectors. It has been estimated that, in addition to the roughly 0.5 million people employed in the agricultural sector, another 0.65 million nonfarm jobs are associated with trade and service industries (about 0.3 million jobs) and food processing and other manufacturing activities (0.25 million jobs).

Exports of Manufactured Products

According to the latest available census of manufactures in the United States, exports account for about 7 percent of all shipments of manufactured goods in this country and about 11.3 percent of all manufacturing employment (see Table 11). The importance of exports as a source of demand for U.S. manufactured products, however, is partially underestimated by these figures, since the total value of shipments (but not exports) from census data unavoidably includes substantial double counting of goods shipped from one industry to another and within each industry itself. For example, the value of steel is recorded once in the form of the output of the steel plant and again implicitly in the value of shipments of products made from steel. This double counting artificially

TABLE 10

AGRICULTURAL EXPORTS, FARM INCOME AND EMPLOYMENT
BY STATES, 1978
($U.S. millions)

States	Agricultural Exports	Farm Income	Agricultural Exports as % of Farm Income	Agricultural Exports as % of State Personal Income	Farm Workers (1,000)[1]	Number of Farms (1,000)
Alabama	299.5	1,895	16%	1.3	--	76
Alaska	0	12	0	negl.	--	--
Arizona	277.2	1,471	19	1.6	82	7
Arkansas	1,027.4	2,678	38	7.6	179	68
California	1,926.7	10,369	19	1.0	--	.75
Colorado	339.8	2,635	13	1.6	43	29
Connecticut	20.0	230	9	0.1	--	4
Delaware	46.6	320	15	0.1	--	4
Florida	378.8	3,238	12	0.6	112	38
Georgia	432.9	2,543	17	1.3	66	69
Hawaii	19.1	380	5	0.3	--	4
Idaho	231.5	1,434	16	3.9	29	27
Illinois	2,769.5	6,123	45	2.8	97	117
Indiana	1,407.8	3,478	40	3.4	88	95
Iowa	2,115.1	8,228	26	9.3	155	128
Kansas	1,360.2	4,446	31	7.2	96	76
Kentucky	485.9	2.040	24	2.1	110	117
Louisiana	524.8	1,420	37	2.0	--	43
Maine	15.4	410	4	0.2	--	8
Maryland	122.1	771	16	0.4	--	17
Massachusetts	12.7	242	5	negl.	--	5
Michigan	493.5	2,127	23	0.6	63	72
Minnesota	1,484.8	4,852	31	4.7	105	114
Mississippi	636.7	1,999	32	4.6	41	78
Missouri	1,068.9	3,576	30	3.0	118	133
Montana	325.2	1,232	26	5.9	40	23
Nebraska	1,331.6	4,732	28	11.5	78	68
Nevada	11.1	168	7	0.2	--	2
New Hampshire	1.8	87	2	negl.	--	3
New Jersey	42.3	372	11	negl.	--	8
New Mexico	102.6	964	11	1.3	22	13
New York	118.0	1,919	6	negl.	72	57
N. Carolina	915.8	3,236	28	2.5	93	115
N. Dakota	702.0	1,866	38	14.3	52	42
Ohio	1,055.9	3,003	35	1.3	77	108
Oklahoma	627.5	2,379	26	3.1	52	85
Oregon	181.9	1,268	14	1.0	--	34
Pennsylvania	151.5	2,152	7	0.2	67	72
Rhode Island	0.3	30	1	negl.	--	1
S. Carolina	288.4	979	29	1.6	--	45
S. Dakota	379.7	2,085	18	8.1	61	43
Tennessee	386.5	1,625	24	1.3	59	110
Texas	2,074.4	7,548	27	2.1	178	197
Utah	58.6	457	13	0.7	26	13
Vermont	3.5	309	1	0.1	12	7
Virginia	229.0	1,231	19	0.8	--	61
Washington	367.3	2,124	17	1.2	58	36
W. Virginia	12.1	187	6	0.1	--	26
Wisconsin	381.1	3,644	11	1.1	132	99
Wyoming	45.0	527	9	1.2	--	8
U.S. TOTAL	27,290.0	111,041	24.5	1.6	3,297[2]	2,680

negl. Negligible
-- Indicates reliable figures not available

[1]Excludes self-employed farmers and non-paid family workers
[2]Includes self-employed farmers and non-paid family workers

Source: U.S. Department of Labor, and U.S. Department of Agriculture.

68

TABLE 11

EXPORTS AND EXPORT-RELATED EMPLOYMENT BY INDUSTRY: 1976

	Value of Shipments			Manufacturing Employment			
	Total ($U.S. billions)	For Export ($U.S. billions)	Exports as % of Total	Total (thousands)	Direct Export Related (thousands)	Supporting[1] Exports (thousands)	Export Employment % of Total
All industries, Total[2]	1,185.7	83.1	7.0	18,753	1,173	952	11.3
Lumber and Wood Products	31.2	1.2	3.8	628	14	35	7.8
Furniture and Fixtures	14.2	0.1	0.7	425	2	4	1.3
Stone, Clay, and Glass	30.6	0.8	2.5	599	14	28	7.0
Primary Metals	93.0	2.8	3.0	1,110	36	155	17.2
Fabricated Metals	77.5	2.9	3.7	1,470	52	93	9.9
Nonelectric Machinery	105.5	14.1	13.3	1,960	215	112	16.7
Electrical Equipment	73.9	5.4	7.2	1,580	115	98	13.4
Transportation Equipment	141.0	13.0	9.2	1,670	160	49	12.5
Instruments	25.0	3.1	13.5	518	61	16	14.9
Food and Related Products	180.9	3.7	2.1	1,530	23	20	2.8
Tobacco	8.8	0.8	9.0	64	7	3	15.2
Textiles	36.4	0.7	1.8	875	13	39	5.9
Apparel	34.8	0.2	0.7	1,270	4	14	1.4
Paper and Allied Products	48.2	1.9	3.9	614	17	37	8.8
Printing and Publishing	42.8	0.4	0.9	1,080	7	13	1.8
Chemicals and Products	104.1	6.4	6.1	851	48	55	12.1
Petroleum and Coal Products	82.3	1.0	1.2	144	2	3	3.5
Leather and Leather Goods	7.2	0.1	1.2	247	1	1	1.0
Rubber and Plastics	31.8	0.9	2.9	624	16	42	9.2
Miscellaneous Manufactures	16.3	0.7	4.3	410	14	6	4.8

[1]Manufacturing employment at establishments producing components, parts, and supplies, etc. for use by plants producing for export.
[2]Includes employees of central administrative offices and auxiliaries serving operating manufacturing establishments which are not classified by industry.

Source: U.S. Department of Commerce, Annual Survey of Manufacturing: 1976.

69

increases the value of shipments and so decreases the relative importance of exports that are not subject to double counting. After eliminating for the effects of double counting, exports of manufactures as a share of the net output of the manufacturing sector are higher (at 18.3 percent) than the share of exports in shipments.[3] By any measure, however, exports constitute a sizeable and increasingly important source of demand for U.S. manufactured goods.

A disproportionately large share of exporting of manufactured goods is done by a few large innovative firms. Of the approximately 39,000 U.S. firms that export manufactured goods, the largest 200 exporters account for over 40 percent of all manufactured exports, and the largest 10 firms account for about 15 percent of U.S. manufactured exports.

The United States has often been seen to have a comparative advantage in exports of industrial goods involving high amounts of skilled labor, advanced technology, and sophisticated capital equipment, and/or entrepreneurial skill in their production. In high wage countries such as the United States (or West Germany), industries involving standardized production techniques or that utilize a high proportion of only moderately skilled labor are unlikely to be able to penetrate foreign markets to any substantial degree.

This view of the determination of U.S. comparative advantage is at least partially confirmed by the industrial makeup of U.S. exports of manufactures. The nonelectrical and electrical machinery, transportation equipment, and scientific and professional instruments sectors -- all industries involving intensive use of research and development -- show above average dependence on export markets. The tobacco and chemicals industries also show moderate export dependence. As would be expected, however, the textile and apparel industries are not heavily export-oriented (see Table 11).

Overall, nearly 1.2 million jobs in manufacturing in the United States are directly related to exports and another one million jobs are involved in producing components and parts for use by plants producing for exports. A further 1.3 million employees in nonmanufacturing industries supply materials and services to

70

the manufacturing sector for export production. In all, nearly 3.5 million jobs are associated with exports of manufactured goods.

About 400,000 of these export related jobs in manufacturing are in the nonelectrical machinery sector and about 300,000 export related jobs are in the electrical machinery sector. Another 250,000 export related jobs are in the transportation equipment industry.

The importance of exports in total manufacturing shipments varies significantly across states (see Table 12). In most of the larger industrial states, including California, Illinois, Michigan, Ohio, and Pennsylvania, export-related jobs (including the supply of parts and components) are about 12 percent of total manufacturing employment. Even in New York, where the proportion of export-related manufacturing employment is lower than the national average, over 150,000 jobs, or 10.5 percent of total manufacturing employment, is export related. While several states such as Delaware, Montana, Nevada and New Mexico, export only a very small proportion of their manufacturing output, these states have only small manufacturing sectors.

In some states, the indirect employment effects of manufactured exports are crucial in providing manufacturing employment in the area. For example, the largest single employer in the manufacturing sector in Washington state is The Boeing Company, which exports about 56 percent of its output. Moreover, many additional jobs in manufacturing in the state of Washington depend on supplying Boeing with parts used in aerospace construction and so depend, indirectly, on the exports of The Boeing Company.

Exports also provide a source of stability in manufacturing sales and employment, helping to smooth out fluctuations in domestic demand. Again The Boeing Company provides an excellent example from the aircraft industry, wherein, for a period of 18 months in the early 1970s, no orders were received for commercial aircraft from domestic companies. During this period nearly all the jobs in the Boeing Commercial Aircraft Company, the commercial jet division of The Boeing Company, were dependent on exports. As the share of exports in total production of U.S. manufactures

TABLE 12

EXPORTS AND EXPORT-RELATED EMPLOYMENT BY STATES: 1976

	Value of Shipments			Manufacturing Employment			
	Total ($U.S. billions)	For Export ($U.S. billions)	Export as Percent of total	TOTAL (thousands)	Direct Export Related (thousands)	Supporting[1] Exports (thousands)	Total export Employment as Percent of total
U.S. TOTAL	1,185.7	83.1	7.0	18,753	1,173	952	11.3
Alabama	18.0	0.8	4.6	330	12	18	8.9
Alaska	1.0	0.2	23.4	7	1	1	14.3
Arizona	6.2	0.6	10.3	99	11	6	17.1
Arkansas	10.6	0.7	6.1	188	7	8	7.7
California	102.0	8.1	7.9	1,600	124	73	12.3
Colorado	9.5	0.6	6.5	142	9	6	10.6
Connecticut	18.2	2.0	10.7	405	36	21	14.1
Delaware	5.0	0.2	3.7	66	1	2	5.2
Florida	18.1	1.4	7.5	331	20	13	9.9
Georgia	28.4	1.4	4.8	468	21	20	8.7
Hawaii	1.9	0.2	9.9	24	2	0	8.3
Idaho	3.4	0.2	4.9	52	2	2	8.3
Illinois	82.3	6.6	8.1	1,250	86	70	12.5
Indiana	45.2	2.8	6.2	677	40	41	12.0
Iowa	20.8	1.5	7.2	231	19	8	11.9
Kansas	14.7	0.6	4.3	167	10	7	10.2
Kentucky	20.3	1.1	5.6	277	12	13	9.1
Louisiana	25.2	1.4	5.5	189	9	9	9.3
Maine	4.4	0.3	5.7	99	4	4	7.8
Maryland	14.8	0.6	4.3	242	10	12	8.9
Massachusetts	26.9	2.5	9.3	590	48	29	13.0
Michigan	80.3	6.9	8.6	1,040	73	74	14.1
Minnesota	20.4	1.6	7.6	321	23	15	11.7
Mississippi	10.9	0.7	6.4	209	9	6	7.2
Missouri	27.5	1.6	5.9	424	22	18	9.5
Montana	2.5	0.0	1.7	21	2	1	5.7
Nebraska	8.8	0.3	3.5	87	3	3	7.0

72

TABLE 12 (continued)

EXPORTS AND EXPORT-RELATED EMPLOYMENT BY STATES: 1976

	Value of Shipments			Manufacturing Employment			
	Total ($U.S. billions)	For Export ($U.S. billions)	Export as Percent of total	TOTAL (thousands)	Direct Export Related (thousands)	Supporting[1] Exports (thousands)	Total export Employment as Percent of total
Nevada	0.7	0.0	3.7	13	0	1	4.6
New Hampshire	3.5	0.3	8.3	87	6	4	11.5
New Jersey	45.7	2.7	5.8	735	34	41	10.2
New Mexico	1.5	0.1	4.5	30	0	1	3.3
New York	76.1	5.3	7.0	1,450	84	70	10.6
North Carolina	35.8	2.2	6.1	738	32	30	8.3
North Dakota	1.2	0.1	6.8	14	1	0	9.3
Ohio	83.6	5.8	6.9	1,280	86	79	12.9
Oklahoma	10.1	0.6	5.7	150	8	6	9.1
Oregon	12.2	0.8	6.7	187	13	9	11.9
Pennsylvania	71.9	4.7	6.5	1,310	82	78	12.2
Rhode Island	4.5	0.3	5.9	115	5	5	9.0
South Carolina	16.6	0.9	5.6	371	16	19	9.4
South Dakota	1.6	0.1	4.2	21	1	1	7.6
Tennessee	24.8	1.3	5.1	478	18	20	7.9
Texas	77.1	5.2	6.7	824	59	38	11.8
Utah	4.6	0.2	4.8	71	7	4	14.9
Vermont	2.1	0.2	9.7	41	3	2	12.4
Virginia	20.5	1.5	7.5	375	21	14	9.4
Washington	18.8	3.2	17.1	244	30	12	17.1
West Virginia	7.9	0.4	5.6	120	4	10	11.3
Wisconsin	35.4	2.2	6.2	519	32	28	11.5
Wyoming	0.8	0.0	1.2	7	0	0	0.0

[1]Manufacturing employment at establishments producing components, parts, supplies, etc. for use by plants producing for export.

Source: U.S. Department of Commerce, Annual Survey of Manufacturing: 1976.

73

increases, the stabilizing role of export markets could become even more important. A more detailed breakdown of those industries having the largest number of export-related jobs in manufacturing within each state is given in Table 13.

Trade in Services

Trade in the services sector in the U.S. has traditionally been a neglected area in most analyses of trade patterns. A major factor inhibiting a detailed discussion of the contribution of the service sector to U.S. international trade has been the lack of readily available, comprehensive data on the service sector and even a lack of consensus of the definition of the service sector itself.

Exports and imports of services is one area where the definitions adopted by statisticians in deriving estimates of the nation's gross national product differ significantly from what most nonstatisticians would imagine the term to mean. The scope of the service sector itself is very broad and includes a wide variety of heterogenous activities. Under many U.S. definitions, the service sector includes those industries providing health, legal, engineering, and other professional services, personal, business, repair, and amusement services, educational institutions, and hotels. Often the financial sector, wholesale and retail trade sector, insurance and real estate, and even transportation and utilities industries are also included in the definition. Indeed, the service sector is more reasonably defined by what it is not rather than what it is -- the service sector broadly consists of those private sectors not engaging in primary production or manufacturing activities. The contribution of these sectors to gross national product is shown in Table 14 below.

TABLE 13

EXPORT-RELATED EMPLOYMENT IN MANUFACTURING
By State and Major Export Industry: 1976

	Employment in export (thousands)	Employment in export as Percent of total		Employment in export (thousands)	Employment in export as Percent of total
Alabama			**Montana**		
Textiles	1.9	4.2	Food and Related Products	0.2	5.9
Fabricated Metals	2.0	8.1	Lumber and Wood Products	0.2	2.8
Alaska			**Nebraska**		
Food and Related Products	0.4	11.8	Nonelectrical Machinery	1.0	9.7
Lumber and Wood Products	0.6	37.5	Electrical Equipment	0.7	8.1
Arizona			**Nevada**		
Nonelectrical Machinery	2.6	22.6	Chemicals and Products	0.1	10.0
Electrical Equipment	6.3	29.7	Fabricated Metals	0.1	14.3
Arkansas			**New Hampshire**		
Food and Related Products	1.1	4.1	Nonelectrical Machinery	2.4	20.0
Electrical Equipment	1.4	7.6	Electrical Equipment	1.6	13.0
California			**New Jersey**		
Electrical Equipment	31.9	16.3	Chemicals and Products	8.2	8.7
Transportation Equipment	29.3	12.0	Nonelectrical Machinery	7.5	12.7
Colorado			**New Mexico**		
Nonelectrical Machinery	2.6	21.0	Chemicals and Products	0.2	16.7
Instruments	3.9	25.8	Nonelectrical Machinery	0.2	10.5
Connecticut			**New York**		
Nonelectrical Machinery	6.0	10.9	Nonelectrical Machinery	19.8	15.3
Transportation Equipment	16.2	21.0	Electrical Equipment	20.3	13.7
Delaware			**North Carolina**		
Rubber and Plastics	0.4	12.5	Textiles	8.9	3.5
Nonelectrical Machinery	0.2	11.1	Nonelectrical Machinery	5.2	15.9

75

TABLE 13 (Continued)

EXPORT-RELATED EMPLOYMENT IN MANUFACTURING
By State and Major Export Industry: 1976

	Employment in export (thousands)	Employment in export as Percent of total		Employment in export (thousands)	Employment in export as Percent of total
Florida			**North Dakota**		
Electrical Equipment	5.1	13.8	Nonelectrical Machinery	1.0	27.0
Transportation Equipment	3.6	11.9	Miscellaneous Manufactures	0.3	60.0
Georgia			**Ohio**		
Textiles	4.2	3.9	Nonelectrical Machinery	25.0	13.7
Transportation Equipment	7.9	24.5	Transportation Equipment	20.0	12.9
Hawaii			**Oklahoma**		
Food and Related Products	2.6	22.8	Nonelectrical Machinery	4.5	17.1
Apparel	0.1	1.6	Electrical Equipment	1.0	9.4
Idaho			**Oregon**		
Food and Related Products	0.5	3.4	Lumber and Wood Products	3.8	5.5
Nonelectrical Machinery	0.6	18.2	Instruments	4.8	27.5
Illinois			**Pennsylvania**		
Nonelectrical Machinery	39.3	19.5	Nonelectrical Machinery	23.5	18.7
Electrical Equipment	12.9	9.0	Electrical Equipment	15.7	15.6
Indiana			**Rhode Island**		
Electrical Equipment	10.1	9.6	Nonelectrical Machinery	1.3	16.7
Transportation Equipment	12.1	12.7	Miscellaneous Manufactures	2.3	8.1
Iowa			**South Carolina**		
Nonelectrical Machinery	10.2	17.9	Textiles	3.5	2.4
Electrical Equipment	4.3	17.6	Nonelectrical Machinery	2.9	12.0
Kansas			**South Dakota**		
Nonelectrical Machinery	1.9	7.4	Food and Related Products	0.2	2.4
Transportation Equipment	5.6	14.9	Rubber and Plastics	0.3	59.5

TABLE 13 (Continued)

EXPORT-RELATED EMPLOYMENT IN MANUFACTURING
By State and Major Export Industry: 1976

	Employment in export (thousands)	Employment in export as Percent of total		Employment in export (thousands)	Employment in export as Percent of total
Kentucky			**Tennessee**		
Nonelectrical Machinery	3.9	9.5	Chemicals and Products	3.2	6.4
Electrical Equipment	1.9	6.5	Nonelectrical Machinery	3.1	10.8
Louisiana			**Texas**		
Chemicals and Prouducts	2.5	8.7	Nonelectrical Machinery	21.8	20.4
Nonelectrical Machinery	1.9	20.0	Transportation Equipment	8.8	14.7
Maine			**Utah**		
Food and Related Products	0.5	4.3	Nonelectrical Machinery	2.5	24.3
Paper and Allied Products	1.1	6.8	Electrical Equipment	0.4	10.8
Maryland			**Vermont**		
Nonelectrical Machinery	2.1	11.3	Fabricated Metals	1.2	36.4
Electrical Equipment	3.8	13.1	Nonelectrical Machinery	0.7	12.5
Massachusetts			**Virginia**		
Nonelectrical Machinery	13.3	17.3	Chemicals and Products	3.5	11.1
Electrical Equipment	12.9	16.3	Electrical Equipment	4.4	16.1
Michigan			**Washington**		
Nonelectrical Machinery	13.2	9.9	Lumber and Wood Products	6.8	15.2
Transportation Equipment	32.0	10.6	Transportation Equipment	16.6	29.7
Minnesota			**West Virginia**		
Nonelectrical Machinery	11.5	19.6	Chemicals and Products	1.9	10.1
Electrical Equipment	3.2	13.6	Primary Metals	0.6	2.5
Mississippi			**Wisconsin**		
Paper and Allied Products	1.6	27.6	Nonelectrical Machinery	16.0	15.4
Electrical Equipment	1.6	9.8	Electrical Equipment	5.2	12.0

TABLE 13 (Continued)

EXPORT-RELATED EMPLOYMENT IN MANUFACTURING
By State and Major Export Industry: 1976

	Employment in export (thousands)	Employment in export as Percent of total		Employment in export (thousands)	Employment in export as Percent of total
Missouri			Wyoming		
Electrical Equipment	4.5	13.5	Food and Related Products	0.1 [1]	5.0
Transportation Equipment	8.2	12.8	Stone, Clay and Glass Products		

[1] Export employment in the stone, clay and glass industry in Wyoming was less than 500 persons in 1976. Exports of stone, clay and glass, however, represent 3.6 percent of the state's total.

Source: U.S. Department of Commerce, Annual Survey of Manufacturing: 1976.

78

TABLE 14

SHARE OF THE SERVICES SECTOR IN GNP

Sector	Proportion of U.S. GNP[1] (percent)	
	1947	1979[2]
Transportation	5.8	3.9
Communications	1.3	2.6
Utilities	1.6	2.6
Wholesale and Retail Trade	18.9	16.6
Finance, Insurance and Real Estate	10.0	13.8
Miscellaneous Services	8.7	17.9
Total Private Service Sector	46.3	57.4

[1]Sums may not add to totals because of rounding.
[2]Partly estimated.

Source: Bureau of Economic Analysis and U.S. Chamber
          of Commerce, Forecast Center.

It would be natural to think of services exports as representing the sales to nonresidents of the output of these sectors in the same way that exports of manufactured goods represent the output of the manufacturing sector. Unfortunately, that is not the definition used in the national accounts or balance of payments definitions. Under the balance of payments and national accounts definitions, exports of services include such items as military sales contracts, income from foreign investment overseas (including direct investment), and receipts from royalties and licenses, none of which represents the output of the service sector. In fact, the exports of the output of the service sector represent only about 30 percent of the "services" component of the balance of payments accounts. This figure is even smaller if service purchases in the United States by foreign residents that are included under the balance of payments definition of service exports -- such as tourism -- are included.

Under the balance of payments definition, service exports represent about 5.4 percent of the value of output of the service sector. Under the more restrictive definition of the sales to nonresidents by the service sector, less than 2 percent of service sector output is exported. This compares to a correspondingly defined figure of 18.6 percent for manufacturing. The largest components of exports of service sector output include tourism, passenger fares, transportation receipts, management fees, and business services (see Table 15).

Often increases in exports of services are accompanied by increases in exports of manufactures as well. For example, U.S. engineering and construction firms are more likely to specify U.S. parts and equipment when undertaking contracts overseas. Associated exports of U.S. equipment represent approximately 25 percent of the value of overseas construction contracts.

Despite the very small percentage of the service sector's output that is exported, certain service industries are highly dependent on foreign markets. For example, between a third and a half of the construction industry's new contracts in 1975 were foreign contracts, although that was an unusually high proportion due to the very depressed conditions in the construction industry in the United States in that year.

These figures tend to understate the overseas sales of services of U.S. companies in at least one regard. In 1976 an estimated $50 billion in services were sold overseas by foreign affiliates of U.S. companies. The largest service sectors selling through overseas affiliates were banking, wholesale and retail trade, advertising, insurance, transportation, and communications. These sales are not directly recorded as U.S. exports since the sales are made by foreign corporations (albeit subsidiaries of U.S. parent companies). The profits from these sales, however, are reflected in U.S. service exports under the national accounting definitions as receipts from direct investment abroad.

80

TABLE 15

ESTIMATED FOREIGN SALES OF U.S. SERVICES INDUSTRIES,
1974[1]
($U.S. billions)

EXPORT SALES

Passenger Fares	1.1
Air Freight	.4
Ocean Freight	1.5
Other Transportation	.1
Film Rental	.3
Reinsurance	.6
Contractors' Fees[2]	.5
Communication	.5
Management Fees & Services to Affiliates	1.3
Business Services to Nonaffiliates	.7
Purchases in the U.S. by Nonresidents	8.7
of which:	
Tourism in U.S.	4.0
U.S. Port & Airport Charges	3.5
Other	1.2
Total	15.7

OVERSEAS AFFILIATES SALES

Banking	12.0	(e)
Insurance & Other Finance	2.1	
Wholesale/Retail Trade (Value-Added)	6.4	(e)
Advertising	3.4	
Franchising	1.5	(e)
Transportation, Communication, Utilities	2.7	(e)
Other[3]	14.9	
Total	43.0	

TOTAL FOREIGN SALES — $58.7

---

[1] Data in this table are derived principally from balance of payments and industry sources, but the data in this table measure flows of services rather than financial receipts. Some data, particularly for insurance, are weak.

[2] Overseas construction contracts led to an estimated $2.5 billion in follow-on merchandise exports from the United States in 1974.

[3] Probably largely composed of sales in hotel/motel, equipment leasing, and construction/engineering industries.

(e) Denotes estimates.

Source: U.S. Department of Commerce, "U.S. Service Industries in World Markets," Washington, D.C. 1976.

Unfortunately, it is very difficult to determine whether or not the U.S. share of total world trade in services has been declining in recent years. For the most part, no reliable estimates of world trade in these sectors are available. In at least one area -- contract construction -- the United States appears to have suffered a decline in export shares at least as large as in manufacturing. The National Constructors Association has estimated that between 1976 and 1978, the United States slipped from first to fourth place in overseas construction. Although the United States has about 40 percent of world contract construction capacity, only 10 percent of the $86 billion in Middle East construction awards between 1975 and 1978 went to U.S. firms. Over 50 percent of these contracts were awarded to European firms and 27 percent to firms in the Far East. This trend is also typical in areas other than the Middle East.

III. THE GEOGRAPHIC DISTRIBUTION
OF U.S. EXPORTS

Historically, most international trade has been between advanced manufacturing nations rather than between less developed nations and developed nations. Since World War II this tendency has increased further, particularly for manufactured goods. The volume of exports between industrial countries increased by 285 percent from 1960 to 1979, whereas the volume of exports from developing countries to developed countries grew by 166 percent over the same period. By 1979, about 72 percent of exports of goods from all industrial countries were to other industrial countries and only about 23 percent were to developing economies (including oil exporting countries). Approximately 4 percent of exports of all developed countries were to centrally planned economies in 1978.

Although the United States conforms to this overall pattern, a higher proportion of U.S. exports are made to developing countries than in most other industrial countries. In 1979, about 58 percent of U.S. merchandise exports were to other Western industrial countries, while 38.3 percent of exports were to developing countries (see Table 16). Only 3.1 percent of U.S. exports were to centrally planned economies.

The geographic pattern of U.S. exports is fairly similar for both manufactured goods and agricultural commodities, except that centrally planned economies account for a larger share of U.S. agricultural exports (9 percent) than in U.S. exports of manufactures (3.1 percent), while the reverse is true for developing nations. Although 39 percent of U.S. agricultural exports go to developing countries, this region accounts for nearly 45 percent of U.S. exports of manufactures. About 52 percent of U.S. agricultural exports and 54 percent of exports of manufactures are to other Western industrial countries.

The share of centrally planned economies in U.S. exports of manufactures is notably smaller than for many other exporters of manufactured goods. For example, about 7 percent of exports of manufactured goods by both West Germany and Japan go to centrally

TABLE 16

U.S. EXPORTS BY COMMODITY AND GEOGRAPHIC AREA[1]
1978
(percent)

	DEVELOPED COUNTRIES			CENTRALLY PLANNED ECONOMIES	DEVELOPING COUNTRIES
	Total	EC[2]	Japan		
Agricultural Products	52.1	25.6	15.1	9.1	38.8
Industrial Materials	63.2	25.8	11.6	1.4	35.4
All Manufactured Goods	53.9	20.2	6.6	1.2	44.9
Chemicals	56.0	25.6	7.5	1.4	42.6
Electrical Machinery excl. consumer type	41.9	20.3	4.2	0.6	57.5
Nonelectric Machinery excl. consumer type	57.9	25.2	4.8	2.2	39.9
Scientific Machinery	77.1	41.8	7.7	0.9	22.0
Computers	83.3	48.6	7.9	1.0	15.7
Automotive Equipment	25.3	14.0	1.2	0.5	74.2
Transportation Equipment excl. automotive	55.3	30.4	7.3	0.1	43.6
Consumer Durables excl. automotive	61.8	21.6	7.8	0.1	37.9
Consumer Nondurables	59.3	25.3	9.0	0.5	40.2
ALL EXPORTS[3]	58.6	22.3	9.0	3.1	38.3
Memo Items:					
Total Exports of EC by Destination	76.6	51.3	1.0	3.8	19.6
Total Exports of Japan by Destination	47.4	8.5	-	11.6	52.5
Total Exports of Canada by Destination	84.8	9.0	5.6	2.9	12.3

[1]U.S. exports to each area as a percent of total U.S. exports.
[2]European Economic Community (9 countries) consisting of Belgium, Denmark, France, Ireland, Italy, Luxembourg, the Netherlands, the United Kingdom, and West Germany.
[3]Includes other exports not shown separately.

Source: U.S. Department of Commerce, Highlights of Export and Import Trade, December 1978, and International Monetary Fund, Direction of Trade Yearbook, 1979.

planned economies. This relatively small share of U.S. manufactured exports is also reflected in the total imports by the centrally planned economies. In 1977, West Germany exported over $2.5 billion worth of nonagricultural products to the Soviet Union. Japan exported about $2.6 billion worth to the Soviet Union in the same year. U.S. nonagricultural exports to the Soviet Union, however, were worth only $0.6 billion. A similar situation currently exists in U.S. trade with the People's Republic of China.

Political factors have substantially contributed to this relatively poor performance of U.S. manufacturing exports to centrally planned economies. Among the communist nations, the United States has granted full most favored nation status (that is, has normalized trade relations) with Poland and recently, the People's Republic of China, while provisionally normalizing relations with Romania and Hungary. Other major competing industrial exporters have moved much further in this direction than the United States. Although the recent recognition of the People's Republic of China by the United States may add some impetus toward speeding up normalization of trade relations with some of the remaining centrally planned economies, the souring of political relations between the United States and the Soviet Union, may hamper long-term growth in U.S.-Soviet trade. In the short run, U.S. exports to the Soviet Union are likely to be reduced by more than $2.2 billion this year as a result of the U.S. embargo on incremental grain shipments and high technology exports.

IV. EXPORTS AND IMPORTS
IN THE U.S. ECONOMY

The high degree of interdependence among
industries in a modern economy ensures that exports
make a far greater overall contribution to economic
well-being than is even suggested by a consideration of
their direct employment effects. Workers employed in
export industries consume the products of nontraded
sectors and export industries also purchase inputs of
materials, energy, and investment goods from other
industries that are not necessarily exporters. These
indirect employment effects of exports may well be as
large as the more direct measures.

Some idea of the magnitude of the total impact of
exports and trade in general on the national economy
can be gained by examining the effect of increases in
export demand on the determination of the overall level
of economic activity in the economy.

The level of production and employment in the U.S.
economy as a whole and within each particular industry
depends on the relationship between the uses to which
goods are put (the demand for goods and services) and
the supply of those goods and services. In general,
the economy is continually adjusted toward a position
where the demand for all goods and services (including
export demand) equals the supply of all goods and
services (including imports) (see Table 17).

Exactly how this adjustment is achieved depends in
large part on the degree to which the productive
resources of the nation -- labor, capital, and entrepreneurial skills -- are being fully utilized. For
example, if the economy were currently operating with
moderate amounts of unused capital and labor -- some
factories were shut down or the machines in them were
running at less than full capacity and an above-normal
number of workers were unemployed -- any increase in
the volume of exports would tend to increase the level
of production in the economy as a whole. Firms would
increase hiring and employ more workers and operate
machines and factories at closer to full capacity. The
supply of goods and services, some of which were from
domestic production and some from imports, would
increase to match the higher level of export demand,

TABLE 17

U.S. GROSS NATIONAL PRODUCT AND COMPONENTS[1]
(1960-1990)

	1960	1965	1970	1975	1977	1978	1979[2]	1979 Percent of Total	Average Annual Growth Rate 1960-79 (Actual)	Average Annual Growth Rate 1979-90 (Forecast)
TOTAL DEMAND FOR GOODS AND SERVICES	767.1	966.9	1140.9	1269.8	1421.4	1484.3	1533.2	100.0	3.7	2.8
Consumption	453.0	558.1	668.9	774.6	861.7	900.8	924.5	60.3	3.8	2.7
Fixed Private Domestic Investment	101.0	138.8	150.4	152.4	186.9	200.2	204.6	13.3	3.8	3.2
-Business Fixed Investment	66.0	95.6	110.0	113.6	129.8	140.1	148.2	9.6	4.3	3.6
-Housing	35.0	43.2	40.4	38.8	57.7	60.1	56.5	3.7	2.5	2.0
Change in Business Inventories	4.4	11.3	4.3	-9.8	13.1	14.1	10.2	0.7	n.a.	n.a.
Government Purchases of Goods and Services	172.9	209.6	250.2	262.6	269.2	275.0	274.1	17.8	2.4	1.9
Exports	35.8	49.1	67.1	90.0	98.4	108.9	119.8	7.8	6.6	4.5
SUPPLY OF GOODS AND SERVICES	767.1	966.9	1140.9	1269.8	1421.4	1484.3	1533.2	100.0	3.7	2.8
Domestic Production (Gross Natl Product)	736.8	925.9	1075.3	1202.3	1340.5	1399.2	1431.1	93.3	3.5	2.8
Imports	30.3	41.0	65.7	67.5	88.2	97.9	102.0	6.7	6.6	3.2

[1]All figures are in constant (1972) billions of dollars.
[2]Figures for 1979 are preliminary estimates.
n.a. - not applicable.

Source: Actual: Survey of Current Business, various issues. Forecast: Jack Carlson and Hugh Graham using Wharton Econometric Forecasting Associates' Annual Econometric Model of the United States.

presumably without triggering a marked acceleration in inflation. A higher level of domestic output would also encourage some firms to expand the production capacity of their factories, resulting in higher level of investment. This would further stimulate domestic production and employment.

On the other hand, if this increase in export demand were to occur when the economy was close to full employment of its resources -- such as during 1973 or 1978 -- with factories working at closer to full capacity and relatively few workers unemployed, then a much smaller increase in the domestic output would occur since it would be more difficult to obtain the additional resources necessary to produce those extra goods. In this case, the economy would adjust to the increase in demand by overheating -- the rate of inflation would increase and some shortages would develop. With increases in domestic output limited by a shortage of capacity, imports would increase to meet the excess demand. Only very small changes in the overall level of employment would occur in this case.

Normally, of course, the economy operates with some degree of unused capacity in its stock of plant and equipment and a small amount of unemployment, allowing for moderate increases in employment and real output whenever export (or domestic) demand increases. Shortages, however, often develop in certain industries, with attendant inflationary effects, well before factories in all industries are running at full capacity or the work force as a whole is fully employed.

For example, at the beginning of 1979 firms engaged in manufacturing were operating at approximately 86 percent of capacity, slightly above the 83.4 average for the postwar period but below the 88 percent peak experienced at the height of the 1973 economic boom.[4] Similarly, the labor market did not exhibit exceptional tightness; the unemployment rate remained slightly above the postwar average, although shortages for several categories of skilled labor were evident.

Given these initial conditions, the $15 billion growth in exports in 1979 (at constant prices of 1978) can be expected to have a substantial impact on the

U.S. economy over the next few years. Based on the past performance of the economy, a $15 billion increase in manufactured exports can be expected to increase U.S. consumption by over $20 billion per year and employment by one million (see Table 18).

As a result of this export growth, U.S. output (GNP) should increase by about $37 billion per year at 1979 prices. This represents an expansion in volume of domestic production of about 1.6 percent. The growth in GNP will probably be about twice as large as the initial boost in export demand because the initial export expansion induces further increases in consumption.[5]

The increase in exports also boosts private investment as firms seek to expand their production capacity to meet the new demand for their products. A $19 billion increase in exports could increase private investment by about $4 billion per year (an increase of about 1.6 percent).

Overall, employment might increase by about 1 million jobs. This is significantly more than the approximately 400,000 additional people who would be directly employed in producing the extra export goods. It is also significant that quite sizeable increases in employment occur in both the nontraded goods and even import competing sectors of the economy (see Table 19) as a result of the overall expansion of the economy. This ensures that the benefits of increased overseas trade are enjoyed in areas that are not necessarily heavily dependent on exports. For example, almost 500,000 jobs will be created in the service sector of the economy as a result of the export expansion, and even those sectors subject to intense competition from foreign imports, such as the apparel and leather industries, will benefit substantially.

Although the increase in export demand may cause some increase in the rate of inflation, this effect should be very moderate -- the anticipated $15 billion increase in exports might increase the rate of inflation by about 0.2 percentage points per year over the next few years. The inflationary effect of the forecasted increase in U.S. exports in 1979 is certainly small when compared to inflationary pressures coming from other sources. For example, the increases

TABLE 18

ECONOMIC IMPACT OF A $15 BILLION INCREASE
IN U.S. MANUFACTURING EXPORTS ON THE U.S. ECONOMY
(Average Increase 1979-1982, Annual Rates)

	Billions of Dollars	Percent Change
Gross National Product	37.7	1.6
Consumption	21.5	1.4
Fixed Investment	4.2	1.6
Merchandise Trade Balance	9.5	—
Federal Government Receipts	9.7	1.9
State and Local Government Receipts	2.7	0.8
Industrial Production	—	2.0
Inflation (GNP Deflator)	—	0.2

— not meaningful

Source: Modeling by Jack Carlson and Hugh Graham using Wharton Econometric Forecasting Associates' Annual Model of the U.S. Economy.

90

TABLE 19

INCREASES IN EMPLOYMENT
FROM A $15 BILLION INCREASE IN U.S. MANUFACTURES EXPORTS[1]
(Average 1979-1982, Annual Rates)

	Thousands	Percent Change
TOTAL[2]	973.5	1.0
Agriculture	26.5	0.8
Mining	6.7	0.7
Manufacturing[2]	346.8	1.6
Lumber	6.2	0.8
Furniture	5.7	1.1
Stone, Clay, & Glass Products	11.9	1.6
Primary Metals	28.4	2.3
Fabricated Metal Products	34.6	2.0
Nonelectrical Machinery	89.8	3.6
Electrical Machinery	42.1	2.0
Motor Vehicles	20.3	1.3
Nonauto Transportation	26.7	2.6
Instruments	12.4	1.8
Food and Beverages	2.9	0.1
Tobacco	0.2	0.3
Textiles	7.4	0.8
Apparel	8.2	0.6
Printing and Publishing	8.1	0.7
Chemicals	12.9	1.2
Petroleum	0.5	0.3
Rubber	11.6	1.5
Leather	2.2	0.9
Other Manufactures	10.0	2.1
Transportation, Utilities	103.4	2.1
Communications, Commercial and Other	491.0	0.9

[1]Excluding autos to Canada.
[2]Details may not add to total due to rounding and conceptual differences between household and establishment data.

Source: Modeling by Jack Carlson and Hugh Graham using Wharton Econometric Forecasting Association's Annual Model of the U.S. Economy.

91

in OPEC oil prices increased the rate of inflation by about 3 percentage points by the end of 1979. The cost impact of many government policies such as increases in the federal minimum wage and social security taxes added another 1 to 2 percentage points to the inflation rate in 1979.

Governments would benefit from the higher level of economic activity due to the export increases. A $15 billion increase in manufactured exports would boost federal receipts by about $9.5 billion per year (in 1979 prices), or by nearly 2 percent. State and local government receipts would also grow, though not as strongly as federal receipts due to the greater reliance on progressive individual income taxes in the federal sector. State and local government receipts might be about $2.7 billion per year (in 1979 prices), or 0.8 percent, due to the $15 billion growth in exports of manufactures.

The Determinants of U.S. Exports and Imports

Despite the fact that in certain cases increases in exports can lead to large increases in the level of employment and real income for the country, it is not solely or even primarily for this reason that trade is beneficial to the United States. Nor are imports always harmful even though an increase in imports might lead to a decrease in employment in the short run in some cases.

International trade benefits a nation because it allows countries to specialize in the production of those goods in which they are relatively more efficient and to take advantage of the more efficient production techniques of other countries by importing those products where the country is not as productive. International trade also enables countries that are not well endowed with sufficient domestic quantities of essential raw materials for industrial and agricultural production to obtain these supplies from overseas.

Export goods and services from the United States represent foreign demand for U.S. production and as such, depend very closely on the overall level of economic activity overseas. U.S. exports compete, however, in those foreign markets with supplies of goods and services from many other exporting countries and domestically produced goods and services in the foreign market themselves.

The extent to which U.S. goods remain competitive in terms of both price and such nonprice factors as quality of goods, speed of delivery, after-sales service and so on, will determine the share of U.S. products in foreign markets. Similarly, the extent to which the demand for goods and services from U.S. consumers is satisfied by domestically produced goods versus imports depends on the competitiveness of imports compared to domestic goods. The volume of U.S. imports will also depend on the overall level of economic activity in the United States. Higher levels of domestic production will require larger imports of raw materials and investment goods, and higher levels of real expandable income in the United States boosts imports of consumer goods.

In general, the price at which goods and services sell in the international marketplace reflects in the cost of the resources -- labor, capital, entrepre-neurial skills, and natural resources -- used in the production of those goods and the productivity of these inputs, providing that these goods are produced and sold in competitive markets. Sometimes major discrep-ancies occur between production cost and the market price at which the goods are sold. The most compelling example of an internationally traded good where this occurs is crude oil. The production cost for much of the oil produced in the Middle East is less than $1 per barrel, but because of the OPEC oil cartel, such oil is sold above $25 during 1980. In other cases, government production subsidies may lower the price of traded goods below the cost of resources used in their production.

Subject to these qualifications, however, the price of most manufactured goods and agricultural commodities traded in international markets in general reflect production costs. A country will, therefore, be most competitive in those products it can produce at a relatively lower cost than other countries, and least competitive for those goods that have a relatively higher cost than in other countries.

This is the true source of the gain from international trade. Nations export those goods in which they are relatively most efficient in producing (those requiring least resources) and import those commodities in which they are relatively least efficient at producing. By concentrating its production activities in those areas in which it is relatively most efficient, the United States increases the amount of goods and services available for it to consume from its available resources.

The most obvious example of differences in production efficiency between nations occurs with trade in products that have a significant national resource component. For example, because of their enormous reserves of oil, both Saudi Arabia and Kuwait can export large volumes of energy and chemical feedstock at lower cost than such energy can be produced in most of Western Europe, Japan, and the United States, despite the massive increases in oil prices that have occurred since 1973. Similarly, the huge coal reserves of the United States and the iron ore, bauxite, and uranium reserves of Australia confer substantial export advantages on these countries for these products.

On the other hand, Western Europe, Japan, and other Western industrialized nations have a considerable advantage in the production of sophisticated manufactured goods in comparison with Saudi Arabia and Kuwait. It is therefore, beneficial to both the oil producing areas and industrialized countries to engage in trade; the industrialized nations gain access to essential raw materials needed for industrial production and the oil producing countries are able to import manufactured goods and foodstuffs at considerably lower cost than if these products were produced in their own countries. Indeed, without the opportunity to engage in international trade, Saudi Arabia and Kuwait would both be very poor countries and living standards in the Western industrial countries would be considerably below present levels.

Of course, the gains from international trade are not confined to trade between areas with substantial endowments of natural resources and industrial countries. Substantial variations in relative cost of production in different branches of manufacturing occur even among advanced industrial countries and many newly industrializing countries. These differences in relative production cost and efficiency in production provide substantial scope for international trade in manufactures.

What is perhaps most surprising is that the gains from trade do not depend on a nation being absolutely more efficient than other countries in producing some goods and absolutely less efficient at producing other goods. Rather, gains from trade arise when a country is relatively more efficient in the production of some goods than others; a principle known as "the law of comparative advantage."

This elusive and somewhat counterintuitive concept is perhaps best explained by a simple hypothetical example. An executive may be able to type twice as fast as his secretary and yet be three times as efficient at managing a firm than his secretary. The appropriate "division of labor" that would make the most efficient use of the firm's limited resources would be for the executive to devote his time to management tasks and for the typing to be done by his secretary. The same is true for economies as a whole. The United States may be able to produce either more machine tools or more textiles for any given quantity of labor and capital devoted to either of these activities than, say, South Korea. If, however, the United States was three times as efficient in producing machine tools but only twice as efficient in textile production as South Korea, then the United States and South Korea can both gain from trade if the United States exports machine tools (the goods in which it is relatively more efficient) to South Korea and imports textiles from South Korea.

Of course, the normal operation of the price mechanism unfettered by distortions due to government intervention would move resources into production and the export of those goods in which the nation has a comparative advantage and out of those traded goods in which it does not. This applies especially when the comparative advantage of a nation changes over time -- some (but not all) industries become uncompetitive either in domestic or foreign markets and domestic production in these industries declines. Other industries will normally be expanding sufficiently to absorb those domestic factors of production -- labor and capital -- released from the declining industries. Often, however, significant adjustment problems arise in transferring those resources into industries in which the nation's comparative advantage and competitiveness are increasing -- resulting in short run unemployment for some of the factors of production in the declining industries. For example, in the short run, it may be difficult for a New England textile worker displaced by imports to get alternative employment, or to convert a textile mill into other productive uses. Although it would be ultimately futile and economically wasteful to resist the transfer of resources out of industries declining in competitiveness, it may be desirable in such cases to provide some form of compensation or assistance to the employees of the declining industry to aid the adjustment process, but not to retard it. Of course, designing an equitable and efficient method of adjustment assistance for particular industries adversely affected by growing import competition is seldom an easy task in practice. It is often difficult to determine the extent to which an industry's decline is attributable to import competition and how much to changing patterns of demand in general.

Although the principle of comparative advantage will determine the pattern of trade -- which products are likely to be exported and which imported -- general competitiveness of a nation's exports also depends on the prevailing exchange rates (that is the cost of foreign currencies in terms of domestic currency) and domestic money wages and prices compared to those in other countries producing and exporting similar products. Nevertheless, in the long run, exchange rates and even domestic money wages and prices will adjust to ensure that those goods in which the country possesses a comparative advantage remain competitive in international markets.

What still needs to be explained is what determines the relative efficiency with which nations produce goods. What makes the United States three times as efficient as South Korea in producing machine tools but only twice as efficient in textiles production?

In general, nations tend to be most efficient in those products that require the largest proportion of resources -- labor, capital, land, entrepreneurial skills, and technology -- that they possess in relatively the largest amounts. For example, countries with very large quantities of labor and little capital and scientific skills will tend to be relatively most efficient in the production of goods that intensively utilize large amounts of unskilled or semiskilled labor, such as textiles, apparel, footwear, simple consumer electronics, and so on. Although the United States possesses large quantities of all types of labor and capital, its most abundant factors of production are its supplies of highly-skilled labor, technological and entrepreneurial skills, and to some extent its large area of fertile agricultural land in temperate climates.

In turn, the large stock of technological skills represents the effects of the high levels of research and development expenditure undertaken in the United States both by firms and by the government. Especially during the early 1960s, the proportion of GNP devoted to research and development (R&D) was much greater in the United States than in most other Western industrial countries (see Table 20).

TABLE 20

R&D SPENDING PATTERNS OF SELECTED COUNTRIES:
SELECTED YEARS
(percent of gross national product)

	1964	1967	1970	1975	1976	1977
United States	3.0	2.9	2.6	2.3	2.3	2.1
France	1.8	2.1	1.9	1.8	1.7	1.7
West Germany	1.6	2.0	2.2	2.4	2.3	2.3
Japan	1.5	1.6	1.9	2.0	2.0	1.9
United Kingdom	2.6	2.7	2.5	2.1	NA	NA
USSR	2.4	2.6	2.8	3.2	3.1	3.1

Source: National Science Foundation, National Patterns of R&D Resources, October 1978.

Most of this advantage lay in the area of government-funded research. The U.S. proportion of industry-funded expenditure on research and development in GNP was not significantly greater than that for other Western countries (see Table 20). The proportion of GNP devoted to research and development in the United States, however, has been steadily declining. In 1964, 3.0 percent of U.S. GNP was devoted to research and development -- by 1978, this share had fallen to 2.1 percent. Most of this decline is due to the slow rate of growth of federal R&D programs since 1964. With increased spending on energy and defense R&D programs, however the share of R&D in national output is expected to remain around its current level during the 1980s. The share of GNP devoted to research and development in other Western countries has, in contrast, been steadily rising since the early 1960s. Nevertheless, the sheer size of the U.S. economy has been sufficient to ensure that the United States continues to invest the largest absolute amount of funds in research and development, although even this lead may be decreasing.

Together with the large stock of highly skilled labor, the technological lead of the United States has meant that it possesses a comparative advantage in the production of technology intensive products. The production cost advantages conferred by a technological lead, however, do not remain static or constant over time. Although the United States traditionally led the way in the introduction of labor-saving technology, automated machinery and complex electrical goods, and chemical products, over time new products become more standardized as do their production techniques, and more conventional factors that determine production cost advantages, including lower labor costs, start becoming more important. In this way, U.S. technology-based industries face growing competition, not just from other countries that possess large stocks of skilled labor and devote large shares of output to expanding the existing stock of knowledge and applying this new knowledge, but also from countries that become increasingly able to standardize new technologies quickly and commence competitive production at lower costs.

Although the U.S. comparative advantage may not remain static in terms of individual products, the continual expansion of new technologically-intensive products is mainly located in a few industries -- for example, chemicals, electrical and nonelectrical machinery, and transportation equipment (see Table 21). Traditionally, the United States has had a significant and growing trade surplus in these industries (see Table 22).

The heavy dependence of the U.S. comparative advantage and international competitiveness on a high level of ongoing research and development activity, and the alleged recent decline in the U.S. technological lead over other advanced industrial countries has led many corporate leaders to call for increased government incentives to stimulate the innovative process, especially in the private sector. It has been alleged that the governments of other major industrial countries do more to foster domestic research and development than does the United States and that similar measures need to be adopted by the federal government to maintain U.S. comparative advantage and competitiveness in high technology products.[6]

There is considerable merit in these arguments for the need for additional stimulus for research and development. By its very nature, it is often difficult for a private firm to capture the full returns to the technology that it develops since competing firms are often able to incorporate the developing firm's innovation without appropriate compensation being paid. This can lead to underinvestment in research and development. Government support for increased basic and applied research and some development activities in these circumstances might be necessary to ensure that sufficient resources are devoted to innovative activity. In practice, however, it is very difficult to determine the amount of assistance necessary or even the desirable level of investment in research and development.

Not only does the large stock of skilled labor and technology encourage U.S. exports of products utilizing these resources intensively, but these same resources confer on the United States a comparative advantage in direct foreign investment overseas in firms producing these products. To some extent, a firm's decision to capitalize on technological advantages through exporting from the United States or establishing an

TABLE 21

R&D EXPENDITURES AS A SHARE OF GNP,
BY COUNTRY, 1963-1975

| | Government-Funded | | | | | |
	1963	1967	1969	1971	1973	1975
United States	1.9	2.0	1.7	1.5	1.3	1.3
United Kingdom	1.3	1.3	1.2	1.4	1.1	NA
Japan	0.4	0.0	0.4	0.4	0.6	0.5
West Germany	0.6	0.7	0.7	0.9	0.9	1.2
France	1.0	1.4	1.2	1.1	1.0	1.1
Canada	0.6	0.9	0.9	0.8	0.6	0.6

| | Industry-Funded | | | | | |
	1963	1967	1969	1971	1973	1975
United States	0.8	1.1	1.1	1.0	1.0	1.1
United Kingdom	1.0	1.1	1.1	1.0	0.8	NA
Japan	0.9	0.9	1.1	1.2	1.4	1.5
West Germany	0.8	1.0	1.0	1.2	1.4	1.1
France	0.7	0.8	0.7	0.7	0.6	0.4
Canada	0.3	0.4	0.4	0.4	0.3	0.5

NA: Not Available

Sources: For 1963-71, Patterns of Resources Devoted to
Research and Experimental Development in the
OECD   Area,   1963-71 (Paris: OECD, 1975),
Table V, p. 93, For 1973, U.S. International
Economic Report of the President, 1976.   For
1975, National Science Foundation, Science
Indicators, 1976.

TABLE 22

U.S. INDUSTRIAL R&D, 1977

($U.S. billions)

| | Total[1] | Percent of Total | Allocation of Funds | | |
			Basic	Applied	Develop-ment
ALL INDUSTRIES	29.9	100	$0.9	$5.7	$23.3
Aircraft and missiles	7.1	3.7	0.0	0.7	6.3
Electrical equip-ment and communication	5.9	19.7	0.2	1.0	4.7
Machinery	4.0	13.4	0.0	0.4	3.5
Chemicals and allied products	3.3	11.0	0.3	1.4	1.6
Motor vehicles and equipment	3.3	11.0	0.0	0.2	3.1
Professional and scientific instruments	1.4	4.7	0.0	0.2	1.2
Other manufacturing	3.9	13.0	0.2	1.4	2.4
Nonmanufacturing	1.09	3.3	0.0	0.4	0.5

[1] Includes federal R&D funds

Sources: National Science Foundation, Science Resource Studies Highlights, March 1979.

affiliate overseas depends on many factors, including foreign tariff rates and other political barriers to exports as well as the cost of skilled labor in the United States compared to overseas.

Many foreign countries prohibit imports to protect domestic production, or have local content or joint production requirements that virtually mandate that U.S. and foreign multinationals exploit any technological lead through direct foreign investment rather than exports. In other cases, the decision to invest abroad is dictated by the cost advantages of manufacturing, sales, and service activities in close proximity to the local market. There have also been instances where U.S. environmental laws and other government regulations have prevented domestic manufacture of potential exports and so encouraged firms to invest overseas.

Primarily, foreign investment in manufacturing affiliates overseas is concentrated in the same area as U.S. manufactured exports -- chemicals, nonelectrical and electrical machinery, and transportation machinery (see Table 24). Sales by majority-owned foreign affiliates of U.S. companies in these industries totaled over $140 billion in 1976, more than double the value of U.S. exports of these industries (see Table 25). Since 1961, the value of sales of manufactures by majority-owned foreign affiliates of U.S. firms has grown at over 15 percent per year, over 3 percentage points faster than the rate of growth of U.S. exports of manufactures over the comparable period. Sales by foreign affiliates of U.S. companies in the technologically intensive product areas such as chemicals and machinery have been among the fastest growing sectors, averaging nearly 17 percent growth per year between 1961 and 1976, just slightly below the average annual growth of exports of chemicals and machinery (17.9 percent) over this period.

Although it is frequently claimed that direct investment by U.S. firms may sometimes substitute for U.S. exports, often the direct investment itself generates a considerable volume of exports through sales by the U.S. parent company to its foreign affiliates and provides substantial domestic employment. For example, the General Electric Company estimates that 36 percent of GE's total U.S. exports are attributable to the company's foreign affiliates.

TABLE 23

U.S. TRADE BALANCE IN R & D-INTENSIVE AND NON-R & D-INTENSIVE
MANUFACTURING INDUSTRIES, 1960-1977

($U.S. billions)[a]

	1960	1965	1970	1971	1972	1973	1974	1975	1976	1977	1978
Chemicals[b]	1.0	1.6	2.4	2.1	2.1	3.3	4.8	5.0	5.2	5.4	6.2
Nonelectrical machinery[c]	3.0	4.1	5.6	5.3	5.3	5.9	10.8	14.6	14.8	13.6	18.9
Electrical machinery[d]	0.8	1.0	0.7	0.5	0.3	0.5	1.7	2.7	1.8	1.8	1.1
Aircraft[e]	1.0	1.0	2.4	3.0	2.6	3.6	5.2	5.6	5.7	5.2	8.2
Professional and scientific instruments[f]	0.2	0.4	0.7	0.7	0.7	0.8	1.3	1.5	1.4	1.5	2.4
All R&D-intensive manufacturing[g]	5.9	9.1	11.7	11.7	11.7	15.1	23.9	29.3	29.0	27.6	36.8
All non-R&D-intensive manufacturing	-0.2	-2.0	-8.3	-11.7	-15.0	-15.4	-15.6	-9.5	-16.5	-24.4	-42.7

aDetails may not add to totals because of rounding.
bIncludes drugs and related products.
cIncludes aircraft and auto engines.
dIncludes communication equipment.
eExcept engines.
fIncludes optical goods and photographic equipment and supplies.
gAll product groups included above.

Source: National Science Board Science Indicators for 1960-1976, U.S. Department of Commerce, Highlights of U.S. Exports and Imports, 1978, for 1977 and 1978 data.

TABLE 24

U.S. DIRECT INVESTMENT POSITION ABROAD
YEAR END 1978

($U.S. billions)

	All Industries	Manufacturing				Petroleum	Other
		Chemicals	Machinery	Transportation Equipment	Other		
All Countries	168.0	16.1	21.1	10.5	26.5	40.3	53.6
Developed Countries	120.7	12.2	17.8	9.1	21.1	31.1	29.5
Developing Countries	40.3	3.9	3.4	1.4	5.4	6.9	19.5
Other[1]	6.9	-	-	-	-	2.4	4.5

[1] Includes unclassified direct investment abroad and investment by official multinational institutions.

Source: U.S. Department of Commerce, Survey of Current Business, August 1979.

TABLE 25

SALES BY FOREIGN MANUFACTURING AFFILIATES OF
U.S. COMPANIES, 1961-1976

($U.S. billions)

	1961	1965	1970	1975	1976	Average Annual Growth Rate 1961-1976
MANUFACTURING	25.1	42.3	78.3	192.3	212.8	15.3%
Chemicals	3.9	6.9	12.6	37.6	43.1	17.3%
Nonelectric Machinery	2.9	5.4	12.3	32.1	34.2	17.8%
Electrical Machinery	2.2	4.0	7.7	18.8	18.4	15.2%
Transportation	6.0	10.7	16.8	38.1	44.8	14.3%
Other	10.1	15.3	28.9	65.7	72.3	14.0%

Source: Survey of Current Business, various issues and the Organization
for Economic Cooperation and Development, Trade Series B, various issues.

105

At a national level, it is estimated that sales to foreign affiliates of U.S. companies account for between 25 and 50 percent of total U.S. exports.

The sizeable U.S. direct investment overseas and the rapid growth of sales by U.S. foreign affiliates in product areas where the United States has a technological lead is not, however, regarded as beneficial by all sectors of the economy. In particular, organized labor regards this overseas investment as "the export of American jobs" by U.S. multinational corporations. Direct investment is seen as transferring advanced technology to trading partners, thereby reducing U.S. exports to these markets and encouraging the development of future trading competitors. While stopping short of demanding legislative action to restrict overseas investment, the American Federation of Labor-Congress of Industrial Organizations (AFL-CIO) has called for a closer monitoring of direct investment and for the abolition of U.S. incentives that may encourage foreign investment such as the foreign tax credit, tax deferral for unremitted profits, and insurance for foreign investment by the Overseas Private Investment Corporation (OPIC).[7] Organized labor has also raised similar objections to the recent upsurge in more direct means of technological transfer, including licensing arrangement and the provision of management services abroad, and has called for similar monitoring of such technology exports.

The issues raised by these arguments are exceedingly complex and no consensus has yet been reached on the overall impact of foreign investment on U.S. national output and employment. Although some researchers have claimed that direct investment reduces employment in the United States, other researchers have disputed these results.[8] Advocates of maintaining unrestricted international movement of direct investment capital also stress that not only do U.S. parent companies export directly to their overseas affiliates, but the additional dividend remittance generates a surplus in the services component of the U.S. trade balance, which helps offset the current U.S. deficit in merchandise trade. Moreover, by helping to increase real incomes in foreign countries, direct investment overseas stimulates the demand for U.S. exports in general.

There are also more fundamental reasons for objecting to limitations on technology transfers abroad, especially through overseas investment. Direct investment has often involved a transfer of older and more readily available technologies such as electrical goods assembly and automobile construction, although more recently an increasing amount of advanced technology is being transferred abroad. Even in the case of international transfer of newly developed technologies, however, alternative sources are usually available and any restrictions on U.S. investment is likely to lead to a substitution of foreign investment from multinational corporations of other countries in the host countries rather than increased U.S. exports.[9] This is especially true when the reason that U.S. firms locate overseas is due to high tariff barriers and other incentives used by host countries to encourage direct investment and discourage imports, or when the success of the selling effort requires close proximity between the seller and the market, such as in the service industries. Often, overseas investment represents additional investment by U.S. firms and restrictions on foreign investment would be unlikely to increase domestic investment in the United States.

On balance, direct overseas investment by U.S. firms in most circumstances is beneficial to U.S. exports and efforts to restrict or impede such investment are likely to harm the U.S. competitive position, the balance of payments, and job growth within the United States.

The Optimal Level of Exports and Government Policy Attitudes Toward Exports

There are few things on which most economists agree and there are even fewer cases where economists are in general agreement with labor, corporate, and government leaders. One of these unique cases is exports -- with one or two important exceptions most people agree that exports are beneficial to the national well-being.

If exports are generally regarded as good, the question immediately arises, "are more exports regarded as better?" In other words, does a nation derive more and more benefits as exports increase, or is a point eventually reached when further growth in exports decreases national (and international) well-being? For the most part, labor, corporate, and government leaders have had little need to address this question because practically the only time the subject of exports arises is when the United States is experiencing balance of trade or payments difficulties and then the benefits of export increases are supposedly obvious.

To economists, however, the most desirable level of trade for national (and international) well-being is the first question to be answered. Subject to qualification, the optimal level of exports is usually held to be that level of exports determined in the free competitive market. If the prices of all traded goods to consumers fully and exactly reflect the incremental costs of producing those goods, then in general the market will allocate just the right amount of society's limited resources to export production. In this happy world, the pattern of trade -- which goods and services are exported and which are imported -- will be determined by the principle of comparative advantage already discussed, and if a country's goods all become uncompetitive on international markets for some reason, then either prices and money wages in the country would fall or the exchange rate would depreciate until competitiveness was restored. This utopian economy would never suffer any trade imbalance since these adjustments of output prices and exchange rates would ensure that the value of imports equaled exports (plus the value of any net international capital inflows.) Of course, economies seldom adjust as smoothly and costlessly as in this ideal framework, but in the long run the desirable level of exports should be determined by the dictates of market forces.

The structure of international trade, however, sometimes deviates from this optimal pattern, often due to the widespread government involvement in most modern economies. The rapid pace of structural change that has characterized most industrial economies since World War II has, at times, resulted in severe adjustment problems in many traditional industries, tempting governments in almost all Western industrial countries to become increasingly involved in easing the movement of resources out of these declining industries. The acceptance of Keynesian or demand-management economics and the adoption of policy goals of the maintenance of full employment and preserving balance of payments equilibrium has strengthened this movement toward increased government involvement, even in so-called "market" economies. Governments have also intervened in their economies to preserve domestic production of certain strategic industries, including agricultural production and defense-related manufacturing for reasons of national security or prestige.

One result of this philosophy of enhanced government interventionism has been the protection of "sensitive" industries from import competition and the use of various incentives to stimulate exports. As a result, resources have frequently been encouraged to move into or remain in the production of traded goods -- exports and import competing domestic production -- and away from production of nontraded goods, often to the detriment of the nation's trading partners and competitors.

Although all countries provide an array of such incentives designed to modify trade flows, most business, labor, and government leaders in the United States feel that the United States is more sinned against than sinning when it comes to such government intervention. Needless to say, this view is not shared by similar groups in our major trading partners.

The fact that world trade is conducted in an environment of substantial government involvement raises several important issues for U.S. export policy. First, what forms does such involvement take, both in the United States and overseas? Second, is it true that foreign governments intervene more strongly to distort trade patterns than does the U.S. government? Third, what is the impact of government intervention, both domestic and foreign, on U.S. exports and domestic welfare? Fourth, if intervention by foreign governments is held to harm U.S. exports and domestic welfare, what policies should the United States adopt to countervail against them and otherwise reduce their impact?

Successive rounds of multinational negotiations have resulted in substantial reductions in tariff barriers during the postwar period. The most recent round of trade negotiations, the Tokyo Round, is scheduled to reduce average tariff rates on manufactures in the major industrial countries from around 11 percent to 7 percent by the end of the next decade. Tariff rates on a few sensitive items such as textiles and footwear, however, will still remain high in most countries. When the Toyko Round of tariff reductions is completed, average tariff levels on manufactured goods in other major industrial countries, including the European Economic Community and Japan, will be comparable with the average levels prevailing in the United States.

Because of these and past reductions in tariff levels, tariffs are no longer a major impediment to free trade for most products. Instead, a significant number of nontariff barriers has emerged as the major means of encouraging exports and maintaining international competitiveness and discouraging imports. Among the most important of these nontariff barriers are:

- import quotas, "voluntary" export restrictions and other quantitative restrictions on imports,

- restrictions on participation in government procurement contracting by nonresidents,

- the use of product standards as technical barriers to trade,

- direct government subsidies for domestic production,

- preferential tax and nontax incentives for exports,

- direct subsidies for agricultural exports, and

- preferential credit access and financing for exports.

Most international trade during the postwar period has been conducted within the framework of the General Agreement on Tariffs and Trade (GATT) which embodies an agreed code of conduct designed to limit the conditions under which governments can engage in practices that distort trade patterns. The GATT provisions, however, have been comparatively ineffective in preventing substantial government involvement in modifying trade flows. For example, although the GATT provisions explicitly prohibit export subsidies on manufactured goods, no such prohibition applies to agricultural trade. In addition, GATT does not restrict the use of domestic subsidies on production that are often as effective as export subsidies in encouraging exports. Finally, governments have been able to utilize a host of tax and financing incentives that are not covered by the GATT provisions, such as preferential access to financing for exports and the tying of bilateral aid grants to exports.

Probably the most important nontariff barrier to trade encountered by the United States is the system of border tax adjustments used by members of the European Economic Community and some other countries. Under the European system of value added taxation (VAT), an indirect tax is levied on the net output (roughly, wages plus profits) of each firm. To some degree, the VAT substitutes for direct corporate profits taxes and/or personal income taxes in most European countries using the system. While imports are subject to VAT, exports are usually exempt from the tax, effectively increasing the profitability of export production compared to production for the domestic market. Unless offset by indirect exchange rate movements, the rebate of VAT for exporters increases European exports, which not only increases U.S. imports directly but displaces U.S. exports in third country markets. Domestic production subsidies that prop up declining or inefficient industries and the common agricultural policy of the European Economic Community have also been cited as major foreign government measures that distort trade.

The United States has also instituted many measures to alter trade flows -- especially those designed to reduce imports -- that have frequently been the subject of complaint by other countries. For example, in part in an attempt to counter the European VAT system, in 1972 the United States introduced a tax provision designed to defer corporate income taxation on a proportion of profits earned through export activity (by permitting firms to form Domestic International Sales Corporations or DISCs), so raising the profitability of exporting compared with domestic sales. A considerable amount of discussion has arisen as to the legality of this measure under the GATT provisions. The United States has also been criticized for its use of customs valuation procedures (in particular, the American Selling Price system), import quotas and "voluntary" export agreements and the relatively frequent use (and/or threats) of anti-dumping and countervailing duty actions.

Since all countries engage in practices that distort trade flows, it is difficult to determine whether foreign governments do so with greater frequency and effectiveness than does the United States. A tabulation of the practices of governments of the major industrial countries shows that foreign exporters generally enjoy a greater number of government nontariff export incentives than are available to U.S. exporters (see Tables 26 and 27).

There is also some evidence that foreign export incentives may be more effective than those in the United States. For example, the U.S. Department of Treasury has estimated that the DISC provisions increased U.S. exports by between $0.6 and $3.9 billion in 1977. While this broad range of estimates has been criticized in some quarters as underestimating the impact of DISC, the figures do provide an indication of the orders of magnitude involved. In contrast, the authors calculate that, disregarding any offsetting exchange rate movements, the European VAT system may have increased European exports by as much as $15 billion in 1977, some of which represents a displacement of U.S. exports.

Similarly, based in part on estimates by Cline et al., the authors calculate that tariff and nontariff barriers to agricultural trade in the European Economic Community and Japan may have reduced U.S. agricultural exports by as much as $1.2 billion in 1978, whereas U.S. barriers probably reduced U.S. agricultural imports by $0.3 billion in the same year (again disregarding any offsetting exchange rate movements).[10]

Even foreign tariffs, while considerably reduced in importance over the postwar period, appear to have reduced U.S. exports by more than U.S. tariffs have reduced imports. Cline et al. found that at unchanged

TABLE 26

TAX INCENTIVES FOR EXPORTS, SELECTED COUNTRIES

	Belgium	France	Germany	Italy	Luxembourg	Netherlands	United Kingdom	Ireland	Denmark	Norway	Sweden	Switzerland	Austria	Portugal	Australia	New Zealand	Japan	Canada	United States
Partial or total exemption on foreign branch income	X	X	X		X				X	X			X	X	X				X
Foreign subsidiaries not subject to tax	X	X	X	X	X	X	X	X	X	X	X	X	X	X	X	X	X		
Foreign branch losses deductible	X	X	X	X	NA	X	X	X	X	NA	NA	X	NA	NA	NA	NA	X	X	X
Partial or total exemption on foreign source dividends	X	X	X		X	X			X	X	X	X	X	X	X	X		X	
Special deferrals of domestic income			X	X	NA			NA		NA	NA				NA				X
Export tax incentives						X	X	X	NA	X	X	X	X	X	X	X	X		DISC ONLY
Nonenforcement of inter-company pricing rules	X	X			NA	X	X	NA	NA	NA	X	NA	X	NA	NA	NA	X		
Border tax adjustments	X	X	X	X	X	X	X	X	X	X	X		X	X					

X indicates country has incentives, NA indicates that information was not available.

Source: "Statement of the Special Committee For U.S. Exports," in Causes and Consequences of the U.S. Trade Deficit and Developing Problems in U.S. Exports, Hearings before the Subcommittee on Trade of the Committee on Ways and Means, House of Representatives (Washington, D.C.: Government Printing Office, November 3-4, 1977), pp. 359-360.

TABLE 27

NONTAX INCENTIVES FOR EXPORTS

	Belgium	France	Germany	Italy	Luxembourg	Netherlands	United Kingdom	Ireland	Denmark	Norway	Sweden	Switzerland	Austria	Portugal	Australia	New Zealand	Japan	Canada	United States
Nontax Incentives indirectly benefiting exports	X	X	X	X	X	X	X	X	X	NA	X	X	X	NA	NA	NA	NA	X	X
Financing Assistance Rate of interest	9% 7.5%		10%	8.95%	NA	9.5% 7.8%		8%	8.5%	NA	1	NA	7%	NA	NA	NA	7.5% 8.7%	NA	8.25% 9.5%
Portion of contract value financed	90% 100%		80%	85%	NA	100%	80%		90%		100%								
Mixed Credits																	48-64%		30-55% (to buyers)
Insurance Assistance Commercial risks	X	X	X	X		X	X	X	X	NA	X	NA		NA	NA	NA	X	NA	X
Political risks	X	X	X	X		X	X	X	X		X						X		X
Production risks		X	X	X		X	X	X			X						X		
Currency fluctuations	X	X	X	X		X	X												
Performance bonds		X																	
Market developments		X																	
Exhibition expenses		X																	X
Inflation risks	X	X	X	X			X				X								

X indicates country has incentives   NA indicates that information was not available.
1 2 percent or 3 percent above discount rate.

Source: "Statement of The Special Committee for U.S. Exports," in Causes and Consequences of the U.S. Trade Deficit And Developing Problems in U.S. Exports, Hearings before the Subcommittee on Trade of the Committee on Ways and Means, House of Representatives (Washington, D.C.: Government Printing Office, November 3-4), pp. 359-360.

114

exchange rates, the complete removal of all tariffs (agricultural tariffs as well as on manufactured goods) in the major industrial countries could increase U.S. exports by over $7 billion on a 1974 base, or by $11 billion on a 1979 base. U.S. imports on the other hand would probably increase by less than about $6 billion on a 1974 base ($9 billion on a 1979 base).

Of course, there are numerous instances of implicit export subsidies that are available to U.S. exporters, but not available to those in other countries. One of the most recent and unusual cases has been the claim by many European chemical firms that the government controls on U.S. domestic crude oil prices confer an unfair advantage on U.S. chemical firms using petrochemical feedstocks, enabling these firms to "dump" their product on the European market.

For many other categories of export incentives and import disincentives, it is difficult to quantify the effectiveness of the various government incentive schemes. There are some grounds, however, for believing that the overall impact of foreign government attempts to stimulate exports may be less than implied by a simple compilation of the number of measures adopted. Even if the foreign governments were initially successful in boosting their exports (at the expense of U.S. exports) through more extensive use of incentives, in many cases this would be substantially offset by currency realignments. For example, in the long run, higher U.K. exports due to the VAT provisions would result in a stronger pound that would produce an offsetting reduction in U.K. exports. Alternatively, without these extra exports induced by the VAT provisions, balance of payments difficulties might force foreign countries into deflationary policies designed to reduce domestic demand and, ultimately, imports from the United States. These offsetting feedback effects to promote exports also apply to countries experiencing balance of trade surpluses such as Japan and West Germany.

Viewed in another way, it can be argued that the failure of the United States to intervene as heavily as its major trading competitors in promoting exports will be offset by a sufficient depreciation of the dollar compared to other currencies in the long run, effectively lowering the prices of U.S. exports to consumers of other countries.

Understandably, most business and labor leaders in the United States have been very vocal in their condemnation of the practices of foreign governments in subsidizing exports from these countries and have ignored the possibility of offsetting exchange rate movements. The direct consequences of a production subsidy are after all more immediate and obvious than an implied exchange rate movement, the exact cause of which may be disguised by a host of other unrelated factors. In the long run, however, it is true that while the overall level of exports may be relatively unaffected by foreign government practices, individual industries in the United States may be very adversely impacted. Nevertheless, the existence of compensating movements in exchange rates which offsets some of these foreign government practices is certainly an issue that should be addressed by corporate and labor leaders and tends to cast doubt on their claims that these protectionist practices are responsible for the recent U.S. trade deficits in manufactured goods. Despite these offsetting effects of successful foreign government practices of intervention, it is not necessarily true that the United States should not try to countervail against these practices nor discontinue its efforts toward dismantling them.

Adjustment to government-induced changes in trade patterns through alterations in exchange rates can be a long process and is often far from costless. For the most part, the largest costs are usually identified with the attendant inflationary impact that sometimes accompanies currency depreciations. Concern has also been expressed by some businessmen that the structure of U.S. trade ensures that currency realignments have relatively little effect on trade since exports of agricultural goods and capital equipment, which constitute a large share of U.S. exports, are very dependent on nonprice factors and are, therefore, relatively unresponsive to currency devaluation. Frequent currency realignments of substantial magnitude are also held to create considerable uncertainty in world trade, reducing the overall volume of trade and inflicting disproportionate harm on small and marginal exporters. It has also been claimed that frequent government intervention in the foreign exchange market often results in currency alignments that are not consistent with a desirable level of imports and exports.

Another infrequently raised objection to relying on the "black box" of exchange rate adjustments to countervail against foreign government practices is that even if currency realignments restore the overall trade balance, the pattern of trade for individual industries may not be the same as the desired structure under free trade as long as foreign governments continue to intervene to modify trade flows. Some industries may underexpand and others may overexpand at the end of this adjustment process. For all these reasons, many businessmen have argued for selective support of exports along the lines of present policies while at the same time stressing the need for continued efforts to reduce foreign barriers to U.S. exports.

While there is some merit in these arguments, they appear to understate the effectiveness of currency realignments in balancing trade flows (as exemplified by the recent turnaround in Japan's trade surplus) and to overstate the ability of monetary authorities to establish exchange priorities at variance with those levels dictated by market forces over extended periods of time. More importantly it is very difficult in practice to determine just which countervailing export supports are desirable and at what levels these should be applied. Countervailing against foreign export supports by the use of similar U.S. schemes raises the possibility of a nightmare collection of subsidies and tax breaks that could result in a severe misallocation of the nation's resources under the guise of improving the trade balance. Fortunately the new proposals for supporting U.S. exports most frequently advocated by the business community tend to improve market conditions or advocate only modest trade distortions and could in balance lead to an improvement in economic welfare (see Table 28).

It is also worth reiterating that is is very misleading to focus on the merchandise trade balance as the sole indicator of imbalance in the nation's external relations with the rest of the world, nor is it the most obvious measure. The United States has traditionally run a surplus on the services components of its balance of payments that usually offsets any

117

TABLE 28

NEW PROPOSALS FOR SUPPORTING U.S. INTERNATIONAL BUSINESS
ASSESSMENT BY CORPORATE EXECUTIVES

		Degree of Importance for U.S. International Business[1]		
	Very Important	Important	Not Important	Need to Know More
1. Increase in Eximbank loan authorization and more flexibility on interest rates, length of loans, "mixed credits"...............46		50	02	04
2. Greater funding of Commerce and State export promotion programs......................09		52	31	07
3. Review of U.S. antitrust laws in relation to joint ventures and trading companies.....................28		37	35	13
4. Reconstitution of President's Export Council..........06		31	33	24
5. Formation of new Cabinet Department of Trade...........17		28	31	17
6. Tax incentives to stimulate greater research and development........................48		44	04	06
7. Adoption of VAT (value-added tax) system..............14		33	31	43
8. Repeal of Jackson-Vanik Amendment tying trade to emigration policies............31		48	13	06
9. Streamlining of export controls procedures...........44		48	04	0
10. Modification or elimination of current export disincentives..................63		31	02	02

[1]Totals may add to less than 100 percent because of multiple responses or nonresponses to certain questions by some of those surveyed.

Source: International Management and Development Institute, Survey Results for June 4, 1979, Joint Council Quarterly Meeting, "Keeping Competitive in the U.S. and World Market Place" Copyright 1979.

deficits in the merchandise trade balance. On the other hand, countries that have traditionally run surpluses on their merchandise trade accounts, such as West Germany, Japan, and some OPEC countries, usually run large deficits in their balances for services, trade, and transfer payments. A thorough analysis of the external relations of the United States with the rest of the world also requires consideration of the net inflow of capital from overseas that form part of the overall balance of payments. Because of this host of influences on the overall balance of payments, claims that countervailing efforts to boost exports to eliminate the trade deficit need to be balanced by careful consideration of the implications of these measures on other items in the balance of payments.

U.S. Restrictions on Exports

Unlike the situation in many other countries, the U.S. government itself imposes many restrictions and regulations on foreign trade that adversely impinge on U.S. exports, as listed below. Since in general U.S. business leaders have felt that there is greater scope for modification of domestically imposed regulations than those enacted by foreign governments, considerable effort has been directed at their moderation or removal.

Although some of these domestically imposed restrictions on U.S. exports have been for economic reasons, most have been for political or strategic reasons and sometimes with vague, ill-defined goals in mind. This has led many business leaders to ask for a clear declaration of the trade-offs between economic goals, in terms of increased exports and political aims. In particular, businessmen have frequently asked that foreign policy export controls generally should not be used "to express displeasure with other governments' policies where treaties or other agreements have not been violated"[11] and for increased priority to be given to export expansion and a correspondingly lower priority to foreign policy aims. Importantly, business has generally requested that restrictions on U.S. exports for foreign policy or strategic reasons not be used when similar or substitute products are available to the potential export market from other industrial countries.

The difficulties of formulating a balanced and consistent policy in this area have been highlighted by the recent decisions by the administration to impose trade sanctions on the Soviet Union in retaliation for the presence of Soviet troops in Afghanistan. Although this action by the administration has received fairly wide support in the United States to date, future changes in political circumstances could well lead to a return to more normal relations with the Soviet Union and renewed calls for a removal of export controls.

Among the major U.S. government policies that are commonly held to reduce or potentially reduce exports are:

- embargoes and economic constraints on trade with selected countries such as the Soviet Union, North Korea, Vietnam, Kampuchea, South Africa, and Rhodesia,

- economic sanctions against communist countries including the failure to grant most favored nation status to most centrally planned nations, including the Soviet Union, and credit limits on loans to these countries by the Export-Import Bank of the United States (Exim bank), an official body supplying credit to U.S. export customers,

- controls on exports of nuclear materials and technology designed to limit nuclear arms proliferation,

- controls on the export of arms,

- controls on the export of strategically sensitive goods and technologies such as computers, especially to communist countries,

- requirements for environmental reviews on Eximbank loans,

- the Foreign Corrupt Practices Act, essentially an antibribery legislation,

- antiboycott laws, designed to prevent foreign boycotts from affecting U.S. trade with other countries,

- U.S. flagship requirements, which require the use of U.S. vessels for exports before Exim bank credit can be extended to foreign customers,

- Occupational Safety and Health Act requirements and Federal Drug Administration standards that require exports to satisfy U.S. standards rather than merely the standards of the export market,

- administrative delays and impediments in export licensing,

- controls on exports under the Export Administration Act designed to prevent shortages or undue domestic price increases for "essential" raw materials,

- section 911 of the U.S. tax law that increases the costs of doing business abroad using U.S. personnel, and

- the uncertainty surrounding the interpretation of the Webb-Pomerene Act, which limits the applicability of U.S. antitrust laws to export-related activities.

Even this simple listing of U.S. restrictions reveals the enormous range of issues presented. Of course it is always particularly difficult to determine the proper balance between foreign policy goals and lost export markets, particularly since such priorities will usually change somewhat with each change in administration and political and economic conditions.

Several important points, however, can be emphasized. As noted previously, American business has frequently emphasized that economic measures designed to achieve political ends require international cooperation to be successful. If alternative supplies are readily available, limiting U.S. exports is unlikely to be effective in achieving the political goals and merely benefits other nations at the expense

121

of the United States. U.S. corporate leaders have also emphasized the uncertainty regarding the application of laws is often more important than the ultimate operation of the law itself. This is particularly important when U.S. corporations must apply for export licenses. A cogent example of the effect of this uncertainty was a recent loss of a commitment for purchases of equipment worth $225 million by the Soviet Union due to export licensing delays -- French firms were awarded the contract. These delays and uncertainties make the United States appear to be an unreliable supplier in export markets.

The overall impact of these restrictions on U.S. exports is exceptionally difficult to evaluate. Certainly, the impact varies widely across products and export market. A recent survey of corporate executives found that U.S. government disincentives were particularly important for the loss of U.S. market share in the Middle East, Africa, and (of course) the communist nations (see Table 29). Delays in export licensing, controls on exports for human rights reasons, controls on nuclear exports, the income tax laws on employees overseas, and limits on Eximbank credit to communist countries were cited as being the most important impediments.

Organized labor does not share the corporate view for liberalization of Eximbank credit to communist countries. In fact, the AFL-CIO is on record as stating that no Eximbank credits should be granted to the Soviet Union, the Peoples Republic of China, or South Africa, even before the current cooling of trade relations between the United States and the Soviet Union.[12]

Organized labor's attitude to U.S. export controls differs from that of American business in at least two other respects. As noted above, the AFL-CIO is particularly sensitive about high technology exports, including those to communist countries, while generally business favors a liberalized attitude to such technology exports. The AFL-CIO also favors the use of the Export Administration Act to restrict exports of essential raw materials, ostensibly to prevent domestic inflation and a consequent loss of international competitiveness -- an unusual position considering that organized labor denies any significant inflation

TABLE 29

IMPACT OF GOVERNMENT RESTRICTIONS AND DISINCENTIVES IN SPECIFIC REGIONAL MARKETS

Regions Where Market Share Has Been Lost Over Last Five Years to Foreign Competitors	Reason For Loss of Market[1]			Magnitude of Loss		
	U.S. Government Disincentives	Lack of U.S. Incentives	Foreign Government Restrictions	Large	Medium	Small
Western Europe........	26	40	39	24	48	11
Middle East...........	69	30	24	41	33	11
Africa................	52	39	20	22	37	22
Asia..................	37	31	37	37	43	04
Communist Nations.....	63	28	24	26	37	05
Latin America.........	41	44	37	28	52	03

[1]Totals may not add to 100 percent because of multiple responses or nonresponses by some of those surveyed to certain questions.

Source: International Management and Development Institute, Survey Results for June 4, 1979, Joint Council Quarterly Meeting, "Keeping Competitive in the U.S. and World Market Place," Copyright 1979.

dampening effect of import growth.[13] In contrast, most (but not all) corporate executives are not inclined to support widespread use of such measures since their use generally results in a net reduction in export volume without appreciably affecting export or domestic prices.

Of course, much of the impact of these U.S. government disincentives to U.S. exports is offset to some extent by the same processes -- changes in prices, exchange rates, and foreign output -- that reduce the net effect of efforts by foreign governments to stimulate their exports.

V. TRADE BALANCES, PRODUCTIVITY, AND THE U.S. COMPETITIVE POSITION

The recent large U.S. trade deficits and the loss of world market shares for U.S. manufactured exports have prompted fears that the United States may be losing its overall manufacturing competitiveness. Primarily, these fears are based on the rapid growth of exports from other major industrial countries, especially Japan and West Germany, and from the newly industrialized countries of Asia such as South Korea, Taiwan, and Hong Kong.

These views are reinforced by the fact that the disturbing declines in the U.S. share of industrial country exports of manufactures are not confined to one or two major product categories, but occur in almost every manufacturing industry, even in those sectors that rely on sophisticated technology such as chemicals, electrical and nonelectrical machinery, and transportation equipment. For example, the U.S. share of industrial country exports of non-electrical machinery declined from 30 percent in 1961 to 21 percent in 1977. The share of electrical machinery trade declined even more -- from 27 percent in 1961 to less than 18 percent in 1977.

This suggests that the large and growing trade surpluses recorded in trade in these technology intensive manufactured products does not give a complete picture of the changes in the U.S. competitive position in these areas. To a substantial degree, the large trade surpluses in these products may be due to a more rapid growth in demand for these products overseas compared to U.S. demand than to increasing American competitiveness in these areas.

Frequently, the low rate of growth of productivity in the United States compared with other industrial countries has been seen as a major cause of the declining competitiveness of U.S. manufactured exports, pushing up labor costs and consequently export prices. This slower growth of output per manhour of work in the United States compared to its major trading partners is quite striking. For example, while average output per worker in the United States grew at only 2.6 percent per year between 1960 and 1978, the corresponding figure for Germany was 5.5 percent, for France, 5.6 percent, and for Japan, 8.5 percent. Moreover, U.S. productivity growth slowed to 1.5 percent per annum during the 1970s and this slow growth is forecast to continue during the 1980s. Despite this relatively slow productivity growth rate, the level of productivity per worker in manufacturing in the United States remains above that in most other industrial countries. Under this view, measures to stimulate the rate of growth of productivity in manufacturing, such as increased spending on research and development and the encouragement of faster growth of investment in more modern plant and equipment are deemed necessary to restore the U.S. competitive position.

A detailed analysis of the determinants of changes in U.S. export competitiveness will be left to another paper in this series. Nevertheless, at the aggregate level, it seems clear that the low rate of growth of productivity in the United States has not been translated into uncompetitive U.S. export prices on international markets. The relatively slow productivity growth has been accompanied by a slow growth of labor costs and a long run depreciation of the dollar, both of which have tended to keep U.S. export prices very competitive. In fact, by most measures, overall U.S. export prices were lower in 1978 compared to those of its major trading partners than at any time in the last two decades, although not all industries necessarily conformed to this overall pattern (see Table 30). Although the relatively slow growth of productivity and output in the United States has not resulted in uncompetitive U.S. export prices, this slow growth may, nevertheless, have been responsible for the decline in U.S. shares of world trade in manufactures.

As a result of the slow growth of output and productivity in the United States compared to its major competitors, the share of the United States in world output fell from over 38 percent in 1956 to about 28 percent in 1978 and is forecast to fall to 25 percent by 1985 and even lower by 1990. Over the same period, Japan's share of total world output increased from less than 3 percent to 7 percent while the share of the European Economic Community (excluding the United Kingdom) declined by less than 1 percent from about 15 percent to about 14.2 percent.

TABLE 30

INDICATORS OF U.S. COMPETITIVENESS IN MANUFACTURING
(1975=100)

	1961	1965	1970	1973	1974	1975	1976	1977	1978	1979[6]
Relative Unit Labor Costs[1]	152.8	148.2	145.0	110.2	105.9	100.0	105.2	104.6	97.0	94.9
Relative Normalized Unit Labor Costs[2]	169.7	144.0	157.0	113.2	115.0	100.0	104.9	103.5	96.1	95.0
Relative Wholesale Prices[3]	120.7	116.5	118.2	98.0	99.8	100.0	103.1	100.7	93.8	93.2
Relative GNP Deflators[4]	151.0	140.8	141.0	108.1	106.2	100.0	105.6	104.9	95.9	92.8
Relative Export Prices[5]	106.5	105.3	112.1	95.4	96.0	100.0	106.1	103.2	99.4	98.9

Note: Each index represents the ratio of the relevant indicator of prices or costs in manufacturing for the United States to a weighted geometric average of the corresponding figure for 13 other industrial countries, expressed in terms of U.S. dollars. Higher values of each index indicate that the United States is less competitive; lower values that it is more competitive.

[1]Unit labor costs: compensation of employees per unit of output in the manufacturing sector.
[2]Normalized unit labor costs: unit labor costs adjusted for changes in productivity due to cyclical changes in the level of economic activity (but not for trend changes in productivity).
[3]Wholesale prices: producer prices for finished manufactured goods.
[4]GNP deflator: price index used to adjust nominal gross national product to account for general changes in price levels for both domestically produced trade and nontraded goods.
[5]Export prices: unit value for manufactured exports.
[6]First six months.

Source: International Monetary Fund and U.S. Chamber of Commerce, Forecast Center.

The United States also suffered a major decline in its share of world manufacturing production, falling from over 40 percent in 1963 to 37 percent in 1978, while Japan's share increased from 5.5 percent to over 9 percent and the developing countries' share rose from 11 percent to over 16 percent.[14] Again the share of the European Economic Community (excluding the United Kingdom) in the noncommunist world's industrial output declined only slightly over the period.

As other countries increased their share of total world manufacturing output, it was only natural that they should increase their share of world trade in manufactures. During the first decade following World War II, the United States enjoyed considerable advantages in terms of costs of production for sophisticated manufactures over her European and Japanese competitors. A large, homogenous domestic market assured domestic manufacturers of stable demand for their products and allowed U.S. manufactures to reap most of the available cost savings stemming from large scale automated operations. More importantly, the United States possessed a considerable advantage over her competitors in terms of a large supply of skilled labor and the world's largest reservoir of technological and entrepreneurial knowledge. The postwar recovery in Europe and Japan, in part, aided by the transfer of American capital, technology, and entrepreneurial techniques through U.S. investment abroad reduced the U.S. advantage in most of these areas. By the mid to late 1960s, most large European and Japanese firms were easily capable of competing on an equal, or sometimes more than equal, footing with their American counterparts, both at home and abroad.

Of course, this increased European and Japanese share of world output was itself partially attributable to the success in penetrating world markets and the increasing share of these regions in world trade in manufactures. Causality, however, ran mostly in the opposite direction; increased output -- or rather, the increased ability of Europe and Japan to produce sophisticated capital and/or technology-intensive products at comparable costs to those in the United States -- allowed these regions to displace U.S. exports in their own markets and to increase penetration of markets overseas, including the United States. The successful formation and expansion of the European

Economic Community played a vital part in this increase in European productive capacity.

Although the U.S. share of manufactured exports fell dramatically between 1956 and 1978, the Japanese share increased from 3.4 percent to over 11 percent and the European Economic Community (excluding the United Kingdom) increased its share of manufacturing trade from 26 percent to over 36 percent over the same period. Exports of manufactured goods from the United Kingdom, however, expanded slowly and her share in manufactured exports declined as dramatically as that of the United States.

The fact that slow productivity growth has not been responsible for a decline in export price competitiveness does not imply that efforts to stimulate increases in the rate of growth of productivity are unwarranted. One of the main causes of the offsetting slow growth in wages and even the long-term depreciation of the U.S. dollar was most certainly this slow growth in productivity itself, as wages and exchange rates reacted to preserve equilibrium in the labor market and reduce the trade balance deficit.

Wages must grow slowly when productivity grows to avoid increasing unemployment in the labor market. If wages grow considerably faster than productivity, then the demand for labor will shrink and unemployment rises. Under a system of flexible exchange rates, slow productivity growth will also usually result in a long-term depreciation of the domestic currency, since slow productivity growth implies that the domestic currency cost of exports and goods competing with imports is rising faster than in trading partners. A depreciation of the exchange rate (an increase in the cost of foreign currencies in terms of domestic currency) is then necessary to ensure that exports remain competitive in foreign markets.

Since faster productivity growth results in higher real incomes for the residents of the country, it may be desirable to encourage these efforts rather than rely solely on currency realignments to prevent or reduce balance of payments difficulties. Efforts to stimulate the growth of productivity allow a larger increase in real wages, reduce pressure on domestic prices while exchange rate depreciations generally put upward pressure on prices, reduce real wages, and worsen the terms of trade.

Although there is virtual unanimity among labor, business, and government leaders that increases in productivity growth rates would be very beneficial in improving export competitiveness and reducing the trade deficit, there is certainly no such unanimity about the means by which this should be accomplished. The AFL-CIO tends to regard foreign direct investment by U.S. multinationals as a substitute for domestic investment. Place restrictions on foreign direct investment, so this argument goes, and domestic investment and, therefore, productivity will increase. Most corporate leaders feel that this is a very shortsighted policy, and favor measures such as accelerated depreciation allowances, increased investment tax credit rates, and lower corporate tax rates as the means of increasing investment and labor productivity. Most corporate leaders also favor government support for increased research and development activity as a way of stimulating productivity in the long run.

Increasingly, Congress seems also to be moving toward the use of fiscal policy to stimulate investment, and several bills are now pending whose aim is to increase investment and thereby productivity in the 1980s.

The Impact of Newly Industrializing Countries on U.S. Exports of Manufactures

Competition from the newly industrializing countries, especially South Korea, Taiwan, and Hong Kong, is also regarded as a major cause for the comparatively slow growth of U.S. manufactured exports and burgeoning imports into the United States. Despite the rapid increase in exports of manufactured goods of newly industrializing countries, the overall share of these countries in world trade remains limited in many categories of products.

As shown in Table 31, these countries have quickly achieved a very large penetration of industrial country markets for clothing, leather, footwear, wood

TABLE 31

GEOGRAPHICAL DISTRIBUTION OF DEVELOPED COUNTRY
IMPORTS BY COUNTRIES AND BROAD COMMODITY GROUPS, 1963 AND 1977
(percentages)

COMMODITY GROUP	Year	Brazil and Mexico	Far Eastern NIC [1]	Total OECD	U.S.	Japan	France	Germany	Eastern bloc	other Developing Count.
Clothing	1977	1.3	29.9	51.9	1.7	1.6	6.5	7.8	5.1	8.2
	1963	0.0	15.3	78.5	1.9	7.1	7.2	7.8	1.7	3.0
Leather, footwear, travel goods	1977	3.9	17.7	64.5	2.2	1.3	5.8	5.9	3.9	7.8
	1963	0.5	3.3	83.7	6.0	7.6	10.3	9.6	3.4	7.6
Wood and cork manufactures	1977	2.4	15.9	69.8	11.7	2.6	5.0	7.8	3.2	7.4
	1963	1.1	3.6	80.1	3.1	13.9	5.1	6.9	4.0	8.7
Electrical machinery	1977	2.2	8.4	85.8	14.4	14.6	5.8	16.5	1.0	2.0
	1963	0.0	0.5	98.2	22.2	6.3	5.9	23.6	0.6	0.5
Textiles	1977	1.7	5.8	79.0	6.3	4.3	8.1	14.1	4.1	8.6
	1963	0.7	2.1	82.9	6.1	6.2	10.1	10.1	2.1	11.4
Rubber manufactures	1977	0.4	2.5	94.2	8.4	7.5	16.7	18.0	1.0	0.7
	1963	0.0	0.2	97.6	17.0	4.5	11.2	18.1	1.0	0.7
Manufactures of metal	1977	0.7	4.3	91.9	10.2	9.1	7.1	21.7	1.4	0.9
	1963	0.1	0.6	97.8	19.4	7.3	5.4	26.2	0.6	0.4
Nonmetallic mineral manufactures	1977	0.9	2.3	74.9	5.9	3.6	5.8	11.7	5.7	7.0
	1963	0.8	0.8	84.8	8.9	6.7	6.6	13.7	3.2	3.3
Iron and steel	1977	1.0	1.0	90.3	2.5	15.0	10.8	17.8	3.6	1.7
	1963	0.4	0.0	92.2	5.3	6.9	12.7	11.4	5.1	0.8

131

TABLE 31 (Continued)

GEOGRAPHICAL DISTRIBUTION OF DEVELOPED COUNTRY
IMPORTS BY COUNTRIES AND BROAD COMMODITY GROUPS, 1963 AND 1977
(percentages)

COMMODITY GROUP	Year	Brazil and Mexico	Far Eastern NIC [1]	Total OECD	U.S.	Japan	France	Germany	Eastern bloc	Other Developing Count.
Transport equipment	1977	0.4	0.5	97.5	16.9	15.4	10.0	19.4	1.0	0.4
	1963	0.0	0.1	98.0	19.6	1.1	10.0	30.9	0.6	0.8
Machinery other than electric	1977	0.8	0.8	96.3	21.9	5.8	7.2	22.7	1.2	0.4
	1963	0.0	0.0	98.7	28.2	0.9	5.4	26.2	0.8	0.3
Chemicals	1977	0.6	0.6	92.3	14.2	2.1	9.6	19.5	3.1	3.2
	1963	0.8	0.2	91.7	22.1	1.2	8.8	20.3	2.6	3.5
Paper	1977	0.5	0.5	97.5	8.1	1.4	5.2	10.9	1.1	0.1
	1963	0.0	0.0	98.5	7.8	0.8	2.1	4.8	0.7	0.3

[1] Newly Industrialising Countries include Taiwan, South Korea, Hong Kong, and Singapore.

Source: Organization for Economic Cooperation and Development, The Impact of the Newly Industrialising Countries on Production and Trade in Manufactures, 1979.

manufactures, electrical machinery, and textiles. Most of this rapid export growth has occurred since the early 1960s and has displaced exports from other industrial countries. In many instances, for example clothing and textiles, there does not appear to have been a substantial displacement of U.S. exports since the United States was never a large exporter in these commodities. In other cases, such as electrical machinery, displacement of U.S. exports by increased market penetration by Japan is at least equally as important as displacement by the newly industrializing countries. Even in those areas where export growth from newly industrializing countries has not been as spectacular, such as iron, steel, transportation equipment, nonelectrical machinery, and chemicals, the U.S. trade share has also significantly declined, U.S. exports again having been displaced by exports of other industrial countries.

The loss of U.S. market share in manufactured exports therefore, is mainly due to the failure of U.S. exports to expand as rapidly as those from other Western competition from developing countries. Indeed, the rapid growth of the newly industrializing countries' exports almost certainly conferred substantial benefits on the United States since these countries increased their imports of investment goods since the early 1960s at a much faster rate than industrialized countries and it is in this area where the United States' comparative advantage in trade is heavily concentrated.

Attitudes to Exports in the Private Sector

Most countries recognize that regardless of the competitiveness of the nation's goods in terms of both price and nonprice factors, a strong export performance requires substantial export awareness and orientation toward exports by domestic firms. A strong export performance also needs active participation by both government and private enterprise in expanding the visibility of the nation's goods in overseas markets through such channels as trade firms exhibits and commercial exchanges.

Generally, U.S. manufacturing concerns have not regarded exporting as a high priority activity. Only about 10 percent of manufacturing firms export at all and another 7 percent are probably capable of exporting, but currently do not. Moreover, surveys have shown that only about 60 percent of nonexporting firms who are export-capable express any interest in exploring overseas marketing opportunities. Even for most of those firms currently exporting, overseas markets generally represent secondary markets compared to domestic sales.

Primarily, the lack of export awareness among domestic firms has been attributed to the traditional dominance of the domestic market in terms of both size and location, to old fashioned notions of domestic self-sufficiency and to a paucity of information on overseas markets. There are signs, however, that the private sector is encouraging some "export consciousness raising" as the economy becomes more internationalized and the consequences of the previous lack of export awareness become more apparent. For example, the U.S. Chamber of Commerce recently outlined some recommendations for export initiatives from the private sector including:

- advocacy of more corporate research and development into ways to adapt products and services to foreign requirements,

- a greater commitment of corporate resources to efforts to promote exports and ensure that deliveries are met, service maintained and warranties honored,

- increased consideration to joint ventures for exporting such as joint marketing efforts by manufacturers in complementary lines,

- increased use of Webb-Pomerene Act associations to allow joint bids to be made for export contracts, and

- a greater concentration on export market identification and development, with greater use of the foreign market studies prepared by government agencies such as the U.S.

Departments of Commerce and Agriculture, and services provided by private firms.

The need for increased export awareness is not just confined to the corporate sector. Labor leaders, employees and the public at large all need to develop and export orientation to lay the foundations for a successful export effort.

There is also a great need, however, to avoid developing a "mercantilist" attitude to exporting. All too often efforts to increase export awareness encourage beliefs that anything that promotes exports is good (and imports always harmful) and that one sign of a healthy economy is necessarily a sizable balance of trade surplus, the larger the better. Export promotion must always be undertaken within the context of the obligations of the United States as a member of the international community and with the objective of increasing world and not just national welfare.

TABLE 32

IMPACT OF U.S. GOVERNMENT POLICIES
ON INTERNATIONAL BUSINESS
ATTITUDES OF U.S. CORPORATE EXECUTIVES[1]

	Policy's Overall Impact on U.S. International Business			Importance of Policy's Impact on U.S. International Business and U.S. Trade Balance		
	Positive	Neutral	Negative	High	Medium	Low
1. Antiboycott laws.......3		12	81	22	59	18
2. Antibribery law (Foreign Corrupt Practices Act).........0		22	75	20	42	29
3. Controls on nuclear exports........3		27	68	35	35	18
4. Embargoes and economic constraints on trade with:						
o North Korea, Vietnam, Kampuchea, (Cambodia), Cuba..........11		29	51	11	14	57
o Uganda, South Africa, Rhodesia.......3		20	66	11	46	35
5. Economic sanctions against communist countries:						
o Jackson-Vanik Amendment (re-emigration from communist countries.........0		12	77	16	48	22
o Credit limits on Eximbank...............3		14	81	24	55	9
6. Requirements for environmental reviews on Eximbank and other federal programs.......0		12	81	24	46	24
7. Controls on exports for human rights reasons...............0		7	90	42	31	20
8. Controls on exports of arms................2		29	55	12	42	27
9. Controls on strategically sensitive goods and technologies...............11		38	53	27	38	27
10. Administrative delays and impediments in export licensing, Eximbank application, etc....................0		3	90	38	44	14
11. OPIC (Overseas Private Investment Corporation)..........53		25	16	3	48	33
12 Commerce Department Export Promotion Programs..............74		25	1	14	20	59
13. DISC (Domestic International Sales Corporation)..........81		11	0	29	53	14
14. Eximbank Programs.....81		11	0	31	40	18
15. Deferral and credits for taxation of foreign source income....92		1	2	83	11	0
16. Section 911 (income tax on employees overseas).............37		6	54	50	31	9
17. Webb-Pomerene (antitrust exemption for exports)..............70		19	6	13	40	39

[1]Figures indicate the percentage of respondents who listed the given policy as having the specified impact. Totals may add to less than 100 percent due to nonresponses by some of those surveyed to certain questions.

Source: International Management and Development Institute, Survey Results for 4 June 1979, Joint Council Quarterly Meeting, "Keeping Competitive in the U.S. and World Market Place," Copyright 1979.

VI. CONCLUDING REMARKS

There is little doubt that exports will continue to grow in importance to the United States over the next decade. World trade has expanded rapidly since World War II -- much more so than most domestic markets -- and after a brief slowdown over the next few years due to recent oil price hikes, this trend is likely to continue over the latter part of this decade. This expanding market offers the United States the opportunity to achieve substantial economic gains in terms of increased employment, income, and investment. In order to do so, however, it is essential that the United States maintain competitiveness in world markets and prevent any further deterioration in its share of world trade, particularly in manufacturing.

Many reasons have been advanced for the relative decline in U.S. export shares in world manufacturing trade since the 1950s. Other major industrial countries in Europe and Japan have generally experienced a more rapid growth in industrial capacity since World War II than has the United States. As these countries increased their shares of world manufacturing output, there was a natural tendency for the U.S. export share to shrink. The over-valuation of the U.S. dollar in international currency markets and gradual acceleration in inflation in the United States during the 1960s also contributed to the decline in U.S. international price competitiveness and ultimately to a reduction in trade shares in manufactures. The relatively slow growth of wages in the United States and the depreciation of the dollar compared to the currencies of most major trading partners during the 1970s, however, has tended to arrest much of this decline in U.S. manufacturing trade shares during the latter part of the last decade. Although it is likely that the U.S. dollar may depreciate further against most other major currencies over the next five years as a result of the burgeoning growth in oil imports and the recent inflationary surge in the United States, this will probably prevent a significant long term deterioration in manufacturing trade shares over the next decade.

Many complaints have also been made in the United States that widespread intervention by foreign

137

governments has held down U.S. growth and led to a flood of U.S. imports. At the same time, the U.S. government has itself imposed restrictions limiting U.S. exports for military, humanitarian, or political reasons. These measures have led to calls for a reduction in U.S. export restrictions imposed for political reasons, especially in those areas where alternative suppliers are available, and for counter-vailing action by the United States to offset as far as possible the impact of foreign government intervention on U.S. exports. Although much of the overall impact of these measures may have been offset by compensating movements in exchange rates and foreign output, individual industries may nevertheless be harmed by this government intervention. In these cases, it may be desirable to countervail against foreign government intervention which distorts trade flows. These must be conducted, however, with the ultimate goal of decreas-ing all tariff and nontariff barriers to free trade, both domestic and foreign, that are not related to vital national security interests. In particular, it is important that U.S. export promotion (and import regulation) measures not spill over into a nightmare collection of government subsidies and quotas that maintain uncompetitive industries and artificially divert resources into exports.

If there remains a further rule encouraging exports, it lies in the areas of improving the export awareness of potential U.S. exporting firms and in action designed to stimulate domestic productivity growth, investment, and innovative activity. Export awareness among U.S. firms remains very low, primarily due to the size of the U.S. domestic market compared with domestic markets in other major industrial countries. Without active efforts to encourage awareness of the potential of overseas markets, any measures to increase U.S. exports of manufactures, in particular, are unlikely to be successful. Such efforts will, however, require a high degree of cooperation between government, business and labor leaders to be effective.

Growth in overall output in the United States, and export expansion in particular, has been hampered by the comparatively slow growth in capital per worker in this country compared to our major trading competitors. At a time of rapid expansion of the labor force in the

United States, investment growth has been comparatively slow during the 1970s forcing down productivity growth and contributing to accelerating inflation. Increases in the share of government spending in GNP have also played a major part in restraining investment. Under these conditions, measures designed to boost investment in new plant and equipment and stimulate the supply of savings in the United States could make a valuable contribution to national income and substantially improve U.S. export performance. At the same time, these efforts would reduce the reliance on exchange rate changes to restore U.S. balance of payments equilibrium.

Finally, it should be emphasized that U.S. exports are but one component of the overall U.S. balance of payments. In the post-1973 era of flexible exchange rates and sudden hikes in oil prices, large fluctuations in the trade balance, and other components of the balance of payments can be expected to occur. Therefore, before any measures are taken aimed at boosting exports, particularly because of short term balance of payments difficulties, the effects of these policies on the overall international payments position need to be considered. Moreover, care must be taken to prevent a proliferation of export promotion schemes, many of which are harder to dismantle than to introduce, with every transient downturn in the trade balance.

FOOTNOTES

[1]Many of the items that are included in the definition of exports of services in the national accounts do not represent what would normally be thought of as service exports in the sense of exports of domestic service industries. For example, under national accounting definitions, service exports include the remitted dividends of overseas branches of U.S. firms as well as interest payments on the holdings of bonds of foreign governments by U.S. residents.

[2]See D. G. Johnson, "Agriculture in the International Economy," in W. Adams et al., Tariffs, Quotas and Trade: The Politics of Protectionism (San Francisco, California, Institute for Contemporary Studies, 1979).

[3]"Value added" in the manufacturing sector, which eliminates any double counting both between and within industries.

[4]As a result of increases in investment in plant and equipment in 1979, capacity output in manufacturing increased by almost 3 percent last year. Without this expected increase in manufacturing capacity, increases in both export and domestic demand for manufactures would have resulted in a very high rate of capacity utilization, severe supply bottlenecks and an even higher rate of inflation for manufactured goods.

[5]As employers increase production and employment to meet the new demand for exports, the increased wages and salaries received by the newly hired workers and the increased profits of the firms themselves lifts the spendable income of those engaged in the production of the exported goods. These workers and employers then increase their demand for consumer goods, since they have larger incomes, which results in further increases in domestic production, further increases in employment and so on. As a result, the final impact of an increase in export demand on the nation's output level is larger than the initial increase in export demand.

[6]See J. Volpe, Assessing U.S. Competitiveness in World Markets (Washington, D.C.: Chamber of Commerce of the United States, 1979), and R. McCulloch, Research

and Development as a Determinant of U.S. International Competitiveness (Washington, D.C.: National Planning Association, 1978).

[7] See testimony by Rudy Oswald on behalf of the AFL-CIO in "Causes and Consequences of the U.S. Trade Deficit and Developing Problems in U.S. Exports," Hearings before the Subcommittee on Trade of the House Ways and Means Committee, U.S. Congress, November 1979.

[8] See articles by Horst, Frank and Freeman, and Baranson in W.G. Dewald (ed.), The Impact of International Trade and Investment on Employment (Washington, D.C.: U.S. Government Printing Office, 1978).

[9] See, for example, J. Baranson, "Technology Transfer: Effects on U.S. Competitiveness and Employment," in W.G. Dewald (ed.), ibid.

[10] W. Cline, et al., Trade Negotiations in the Tokyo Round: A Quantitative Assessment (Washington, D.C.: The Brookings Institution, 1978).

[11] See Testimony of W. R. McLellan on behalf of the National Association of Manufacturers in "U.S. Export Control Policy and Extension of the Export Administration Act," Hearing before the Subcommittee on International Finance of the Senate Committee on Banking, Housing and Urban Affairs, U.S. Congress, March 1979.

[12] See Testimony of A. J. Biemiller on behalf of the AFL-CIO before the Subcommittee on International Finance of the Senate Committee on Banking, Housing and Urban Affairs, U.S. Congress, March 1979.

[13] See Testimony of Rudy Oswald on behalf of the AFL-CIO before the Subcommittee on International Finance of the Senate Committee on Banking, Housing and Urban Affairs, U.S. Congress, March 1979.

[14] These figures exclude centrally planned countries.

SELECTED BIBLIOGRAPHY

Adams, W., et al., eds. Tariffs, Quotas and Trade: The Politics of Protectionism. San Francisco, California Institute for Contemporary Studies. 1979.

Adelman, I. "Interaction of U.S. and Foreign Economic Growth Rates and Patterns," U.S. Economic Growth from 1976 to 1986: Prospects, Problems, and Patterns, Volume 12, Economic Growth in the International Context, Joint Economic Committee, Congress of the United States. Washington, D.C.: Government Printing Office. 1977.

Amacher, Ryan C.; Haberler, Gottfried; Willett, Thomas D., ed. Challenges to a Liberal International Economic Order. Washington, D.C.: American Enterprise Institute. 1979.

Baldwin, Robert E. Nontariff Distortions of International Trade. Washington, D.C.: The Brookings Institution. 1970.

Baldwin, Robert E. "Determinants of the Commodity Structure of U.S. Trade," American Economic Review, volume 61, number 1, pp. 126-146. 1970.

Bergsten, C. Fred; Horst, Thomas; Moran, Theodore H. American Multinationals and American Interests. Washington, D.C.: The Brookings Institution. 1978.

Biemiller, A. J. On behalf of the AFL-CIO, before the Subcommittee on International Finance of the Senate Committee on Banking, Housing and Urban Affairs. March 1979.

Bhagwati, Jagdish N., ed. The New International Economic Order: The North-South Debate. Cambridge, MA: MIT Press. 1977.

Cline, W., et al. Trade Negotiations in the Tokyo Round: A Quantitative Assessment. Washington, D.C.: The Brookings Institute. 1978.

Cornell, R.A., "Trade of Multinational Firms and Nation's Competitive Advantage," in Boarman and

Schillhammer, eds., Multinational Corporations and Governments. New York: Praeger Publishers. 1975.

Deardorff, Alan V.; Stern, Robert M.; Greene, Mark N. "The Sensitivity of Industrial Output and Employment to Exchange-Rate Changes in the Major Industrialized Countries." in Martin and Smith, eds., Trade and Payments Adjustment under Flexible Exchange Rates. London: Macmillan. 1978.

Dewald, W., ed. The Impact of International Trade and Investment on Employment. Washington, D.C.: U.S. Department of Labor. 1978.

Export Policy. Committee Print. Hearing before the Subcommittee on International Finance of the Committee on Banking, Housing, and Urban Affairs Jointly with the Subcommittee on Science, Technology, and Space of the Committee on Commerce, Science, and Transportation of the United States Senate. Washington, D.C.: Government Printing Office. 1978

FATSR, U.S. Foreign Agricultural Trade Statistical Report, Fiscal Years 1974 and 1977. Supplement to the monthly Foreign Agricultural Trade of the United States (April 1978). Washington, D.C.: Economics, Statistics, and Cooperative Service, U.S. Department of Agriculture.

FATUS, Foreign Agricultural Trade of the United States. 1976, 1977, 1978, 1979. Washington, D.C.: Economic Research Service, U.S. Department of Agriculture.

Horst, Thomas, Income Taxation and Competitiveness. Washington, D.C.: National Planning Association. 1977.

Horst, Thomas, "American Multinationals and the U.S. Economy," American Economic Review: Papers and Proceedings. Volume 66, Number 2. May 1976. pp. 149-154.

Hufbauer, Gary C. "Technology Transfers and the American Economy," in The Effects of International

Technology Transfers on U.S. Economy.   Washington,
D.C.: National Science Foundation. 1974.

Hufbauer, Gary C. "The Multinational Corporation and
    Direct Investment," in Peter B. Kenen, ed.,
    International Trade and Finance. New York:
    Cambridge University Press. 1975.

Hufbauer, Gary C., et al. U.S. Taxation of American
    Business Abroad.   Washington,   D.C.:   American
    Enterprise Institute. 1975.

IMF, Directions of Trade Annual 1972-1978. Washington,
    D.C.: International Monetary Fund. 1979.

Kelly, R. The Impact of Technological Innovation on
    International Trade Patterns, U.S. Department of
    Commerce, Bureau of International Policy and
    Research, Office of Economic Research, Staff
    Report OER/ER-24. Washington, D.C.: Government
    Printing Office. 1977.

Kravis, I. B.; Libsey, R. E. Price Competitiveness in
    World Trade.   New   York: National   Bureau   of
    Economic Research. 1971.

Lowinger, Thomas C. "The Technology Factor and the
    Export Performance of U.S. Manufacturing Indus-
    tries," Economic Inquiry.   Volume 13, Number 2.
    June 1975. pp. 221-236.

McCulloch, Rachel. Research and Development as a
    Determinant of U.S. International Competitiveness.
    Washington, D.C.: National Planning Association.
    1978.

McLellan, W.R. On behalf of the National Association of
    Manufacturers in "U.S. Export Control Policy and
    Extension of the Export Administration Act."
    Hearing before the Subcommittee on International
    Finance of the Senate Committee on Banking,
    Housing and Urban Affairs. 1979.

Mitchell, Daniel J.B. Labor Issues of American
    International Trade and Investment. Baltimore:
    Johns Hopkins University Press. 1976.

National Foreign Trade Council. The Case for Deferral. New York: National Foreign Trade Council. 1978.

National Science Foundation. The Effects of International Technology Transfers of U.S. Economy. Washington, D.C.: National Science Foundation. 1974.

Neuberger, E.; Lara, Juan. The Foreign Trade Practices of Centrally Planned Economies and Their Effects on U.S. International Competitiveness. Washington, D.C.: National Planning Association. 1977.

Nolan, J.S. "Export Tax Incentives," in United States International Economic Policy in an Interdependent World. Washington, D.C.: Government Printing Office, 1971. pp. 571-578.

Oswald, R. On behalf of the AFL-CIO before the Subcommittee on International Finance of the Senate Committee on Banking, Housing and Urban Affairs. 1979.

Oswald, R. On behalf of the AFL-CIO in "Causes and Consequences of the U.S. Trade Deficit and Developing Problems in U.S. Exports," Hearings before the Subcommittee on Trade of the House Ways and Means Committee. 1979.

Surrey, S. "The DISC Proposal to Subsidize Exports," in United States International Economic Policy in an Interdependent World. Washington, D.C.: Government Printing Office. 1971.

U.S. Department of Commerce. The Government's Role in East-West Trade: Problems and Issues. Washington, D.C.: Government Printing Office. 1976.

U.S. Department of Commerce. Survey of Current Business. various issues.

U.S. Department of Labor, Bureau of International Labor Affairs. New Evidence on Trade Related Employment (unpublished study). 1977.

U.S. Department of the Treasury. Domestic International Sales Corporation: A Handbook for

<u>Exporters</u>. Washington, D.C.: Government Printing Office. 1972.

U.S. Department of the Treasury. "The Operation and Effect of the Domestic International Sales Corporation Legislation: 1972 Annual Report," (and succeeding years). Washington, D.C.: Government Printing Office.

United States Tariff Commission. <u>Trade Barriers: An Overview</u>. Washington, D.C.: Government Printing Office. 1974.

Volpe, J. "Assessing U.S. Competitiveness in World Markets," Washington, D.C.: Chamber of Commerce of the United States. 1978.

Working Group on Deferral. <u>KEEP DEFERRAL: U.S. Shareholders Should Not Be Taxed on Foreign Corporation Income before They Receive It</u>. Washington, D.C.: International Division, Chamber of Commerce of the United States. 1978.

3

THE IMPACT OF U.S. FOREIGN DIRECT INVESTMENT ON U.S. EXPORT COMPETITIVENESS IN THIRD WORLD MARKETS

Jack N. Behrman
Raymond F. Mikesell

CONTENTS

148

I. INTRODUCTION

In the recent past, the issue of U.S. export competitiveness has increasingly engaged public attention as we witness the relative decline of the United States in global markets. In 1962, the United States enjoyed a 36 percent share of all OECD manufactured exports to the less developed countries (LDCs). In 1978, that share declined to less than 22 percent. This performance has raised many questions regarding the factors influencing the competitiveness of U.S. exports in these markets.

One important issue which has been the subject of considerable debate is whether U.S. foreign direct investment (FDI) in manufacturing in the LDCs results in a net substitution of U.S. exports by production abroad, or whether such investment serves to increase U.S. exports by an amount larger than they would have been in the absence of foreign investment.[1] It should be stated at the outset that there is no general answer to this question that can be applied across the board to all industries, to all types of foreign investment, and to all foreign environments. Examples of substantial net substitution of U.S. exports and of substantial contributions to U.S. exports can be cited. We do not have sufficient information, however, to make reliable estimates of the aggregate amount of substitution or of the volume of exports induced or prevented from displacement by competitors, as a consequence of U.S. foreign direct investment in the LDCs.

In this study, we analyze the role of FDI in the context of the complex and dynamic factors determining export competition and review the findings of a number of empirical studies dealing specifically with this

---

The authors benefitted greatly from comments of Robert L. Sammons on an earlier draft of this paper.

subject.   Such an analysis enables us to reach certain tentative conclusions based on an evaluation of the evidence.

A U.S. firm may undertake FDI in an LDC market to achieve one or more of several objectives.   It may establish an affiliate to produce for the domestic market in which the investment is made.   It may make an. investment in an LDC to produce a commodity or components for the U.S. market.   Or it may establish an affiliate in an LDC to produce for export to third markets in other LDCs or developed countries.   Our principal interest in this study is in the latter. Most U.S. FDI in the LDCs is designed primarily for the market of the country in which the investment is located.   This is shown in Appendix Table 3.

II. DYNAMIC FACTORS IN EXPORT COMPETITION

Exports of manufactures are not determined simply by quoting prices and taking orders from foreign firms and government entities. Manufactured products are differentiated and each seller in the export market offers for sale products of different quality and specification, prices and credit terms, and delivery conditions, together with a variety of services, including technical assistance, repair facilities, and availability of replacement parts. Markets must be developed, and products and services must be designed for particular markets. Large-scale marketing in a foreign country usually requires a certain amount of investment in warehousing, distribution, and technical service facilities. The achievement of economies for product competition may require as a minimum local packaging and simple assembling.

U.S. competition for exports to an LDC may arise from third country exporters, from locally-owned firms in the importing country, or from affiliates of U.S. or third country firms established in that country. In the majority of cases, investments in manufacturing facilities beyond those necessary to provide basic marketing services are undertaken by U.S. firms either (a) because the government of the importing country requires such investment as a condition for selling in the country due to either domestic content requirements or of high import restrictions on the finished product; or (b) because such investment is required to maintain cost competitiveness with domestic or foreign products.[2] There are several levels of investment ranging from simple assembly of components shipped from the parent firm or from third countries, to the production of all or a substantial portion of the components within the country, to the importation of the components within the country, or the importation of the components from third countries. If there are substantial economies to be achieved by investment for domestic production, such investment may be necessary as a condition for maintaining the market. Moreover, markets are not static, and cost and price reductions achieved through FDI may be required to expand the market for a product.

In what ways may an FDI in an LDC affect U.S. exports to an LDC market? Initially, a portion of the capital, equipment, and other inputs for the investment may be supplied from the United States. The early stages of a manufacturing investment in an LDC may involve only an assembly operation, in which most of the components are likely to be supplied from the U.S. parent company. In addition, the foreign affiliate is unlikely to produce a full product line, so that some of the products will continue to be supplied by the U.S. parent company. As new and differentiated products are developed by the parent company, the foreign affiliate will serve as a distribution channel for these goods until they are produced by the foreign affiliate itself. New technology and new processes introduced by the parent company will in time give rise to the exportation from the United States of new capital equipment. U.S. affiliates in the LDCs are likely to acquire more of their components and capital equipment from the United States than in the case of foreign affiliates in developed countries, where these commodities may be available on the domestic market.

Meanwhile, the products of the foreign affiliates will substitute for those formerly exported from the United States. Whether net substitution of U.S. exports takes place as a consequence of FDI must be considered in dynamic terms. If direct U.S. exports are no longer competitive with domestic output or with imports from third countries, or if the LDC government establishes import barriers forcing foreign firms to establish local producing affiliates, U.S. exports to the LDC market may be higher with foreign investment than without such investment. In addition, lower cost domestic production by a U.S. foreign affiliate may permit an expansion of the domestic market for the product in which a certain amount of direct imports will share. These same conditions may apply to the case in which the products of a U.S. affiliate in an LDC are exported to third country markets. Thus, U.S. firms may be able to maintain or expand their markets only by shifting a portion of their production abroad.

The activities described above may be generalized by stating that over the past three decades international economic activity has increasingly been characterized by the phenomenon known as "international production." International competition requires that production of a commodity or of its components takes place in the geographical location that is most advantageous from the standpoint of cost or of serving a particular market. Approximately 50 percent of U.S. manufacturing exports are by firms that also invest abroad. A study published by Business International shows that in 1977, 124 U.S. corporations in manufacturing and petroleum accounted for 38 percent of all FDI (book value) for those two sectors, and over one-third of the U.S. exports of these sectors. Moreover, during the period 1970-1977 the exports of these 124 companies rose faster than the aggregate of all U.S. nonagricultural exports.[3] This sample of companies accounted for one-sixth of U.S. factory sales and had worldwide sales of $321 billion, of which $110 billion were to non-U.S. customers (that is, foreign sales and U.S. exports). Exports of these companies from the United States totaled $24 billion (equal to 35 percent of all U.S. manufacturing exports) of which 48 percent was to or through the foreign affiliates of these companies. This study also shows that exports of the 124 companies to their foreign affiliates grew 50 percent faster than total nonagricultural U.S. exports, and exports of finished goods to foreign affiliates for resale without processing were 63 percent of their total exports to or through affiliates in 1977.

On the basis of present knowledge, it is not possible to determine quantitatively whether U.S. direct exports would have been higher or lower in the absence of FDI by these 124 companies. From what is known of government policies in foreign countries and of competition from foreign firms either by direct exports or by affiliates of foreign firms in the LDCs, however, it appears highly unlikely that a substantial portion of the markets supplied by foreign affiliates of U.S. firms could have been supplied by direct exports from the United States.

III. SOME EMPIRICAL STUDIES OF FDI AND EXPORTS

One of the most ambitious statistical analyses of exports and foreign investment in the manufacturing industries is that undertaken by Robert E. Lipsey and Merle Y. Weiss of the National Bureau of Economic Research.[4] The authors estimated the relationship between U.S. manufactured exports to 44 countries and sales of U.S. company affiliates engaged in the production of 14 manufactured commodity groups in these countries.[5] Their study also analyzed the relationship between exports and sales of foreign affiliates of 13 other major exporting countries, and the effects of non-U.S. foreign affiliate activities on U.S. exports and of U.S. affiliate activities on the exports of the other 13 export competing countries. Multiple regression equations were estimated relating U.S. and 13 other country exports as dependent variables, to market size, measures of U.S. and non-U.S. foreign affiliate activities, and certain other independent variables.[6] All of the data were for a single year, 1970. The 44 host countries were divided into 21 developed countries and 23 developing countries, and the results of the regression analysis given for each group of countries for each of the 14 manufactured commodity classifications.[7] Their findings are summarized in the following paragraphs.

1. U.S. exports and U.S. affiliate activity (net sales) were found to be positively related, with statistically significant coefficients for nine of the 12 industry classifications for the less developed countries. According to the authors, this suggests that any tendency for overseas production by U.S. affiliates to substitute for exports from the United States was offset by factors tending to increase U.S. exports.

2. The significant coefficients for exports by the 13 competing countries showed a positive relationship with sales of non-U.S. foreign manufacturing affiliates. The analysis also suggests that U.S. exports are negatively related to sales of non-U.S. foreign manufacturing affiliates in the countries where they are located.

3.   The great majority of the market size coefficients of the LDCs are positively related to U.S. and the 13 competing country exports to those countries.   This   indicates   that   affiliate   activity variables are not acting as proxies for market size.

4.   The number of U.S.-owned manufacturing affiliates and non-U.S.-owned manufacturing affiliates are positively related. This suggests that the presence of affiliates of one country attracts those from other countries.

Conclusions   based   simply   on   a   positive relationship between U.S. manufacturing affiliate sales and U.S. exports do not provide an explanation of how either the establishment of foreign affiliates or their operations affect U.S. exports. They assume that this relationship is based on an interaction between the two variables   and   not   on   some   independent   factors   that cause both to move in the same direction. This is perhaps the major weakness in this type of analysis since critics may be skeptical of arguments based on correlations without a full statistical demonstration of the underlying casual relationships.

To a considerable degree, this shortcoming can be overcome by case studies showing exports of equipment, components, and finished products to foreign affiliates and comparing the value of these exports with exports of the product before the establishment of the foreign affiliate, or with estimates of exports that would have taken place in the absence of foreign affiliates based on certain assumptions with respect to changes in the U.S. market share given the competitive conditions. For example, a case study based on the establishment of an automobile assembly in an (unnamed) Asian LDC by an (unnamed) U.S. automobile firm, showed that an investment in an assembly plant established in 1967 resulted in a substantially larger value of U.S. exports in subsequent years with the assembly plant than would have taken place in its absence.[8] The estimates of U.S. exports in the absence of the investment were based on the sharp drop in the market share of the U.S. company in the two years prior to the investment from 28 percent in 1964 to 19 percent in 1965, to 15 percent in 1966, and the growth in production and exports of Japanese vehicles over the same period.

155

An important finding of Stobaugh and Associates that has a bearing on substitution of U.S. exports by the output of foreign affiliates in the LDCs is that in these countries, "U.S. firms compete principally with the local subsidiaries of multinational enterprises headquartered in other advanced countries."[9] This finding suggests that U.S. companies were forced to establish affiliates in the LDCs as a condition for maintaining their markets in these countries. Even in the case of U.S. manufacturing affiliates established primary to produce for export to the United States, several case studies have found net positive effect on the U.S. balance of payments.[10] Such findings must be based on a demonstration that imports from U.S. manufacturing affiliates displaced imports from other sources with which U.S. output could not compete.

The Union Carbide Corporation made an extensive study of the balance of payments effects of its foreign investments over a 20-year period ending in 1970.[11] This study found that FDI and exports were closely correlated -- the company's exports from the United States increased as foreign investment grew because the foreign affiliates required intermediate, accessory, and allied products from the parent. Over the 1951-1970 period, Union Carbide exports increased nearly sevenfold compared with an increase in production by foreign affiliates of about five times. During the same period, annual exports from Union Carbide's domestic production rose from 5 percent to 11 percent and the company calculated that over the 20-year period its exports were $517 million greater than they would have been without the existence of foreign affiliates. Moreover, 57 percent of its total exports went through or to its foreign affiliates.

A study by Lipsey and Weiss entitled U.S. Exports and Foreign Investment in the Pharmaceutical Industry found that production by U.S. pharmaceutical affiliates added to U.S. exports of both bulk and packaged pharmaceutical products to the LDCs, but reduced the exports of 13 other countries included in the study.[12] They found no evidence that the production of U.S. pharmaceutical affiliates in LDCs displaced U.S. exports to those countries, but rather displaced the exports to those countries. On the other hand, non-U.S. affiliates led to a displacement of U.S. exports.

IV. THE EFFECTS OF FDI ON THE U.S. BALANCE OF PAYMENTS

The effects of FDI on the U.S. balance of payments are even more difficult to assess than those on exports alone. Financing for establishing a foreign manufacturing affiliate may be provided from the United States or borrowed from abroad. Foreign investments earn dividends and interest, but a portion of the earnings on equity will be reinvested abroad. There are also management, licensing, and other fees that are usually paid by the foreign affiliate to the U.S. parent. If the foreign affiliate exports a portion of its output to the United States, there arises the problem of determining what portion of the U.S. imports from the affiliate replaces U.S. domestic production and what portion replaces imports from non-U.S. producers. Where it can be shown that a large proportion of the imports from a U.S. affiliate operating abroad displaces imports from other sources, the FDI could still produce a positive net trade balance for the United States since U.S. exports to the foreign affiliate might be higher than imports from the affiliate less the amount of other imports displaced.

During the 1960s, the impact of FDI on the overall U.S. balance of payments was the subject of a number of studies and of intense debate among professional economists as well as among U.S. government officials and private businessmen.[13] The policy implications of the debate as to whether U.S. foreign direct investment impaired or enhanced the overall balance of payments were heightened by the U.S. government which imposed first voluntary controls over U.S. foreign direct investment in 1965 and then mandatory controls in 1968.

A study published by the U.S. Department of the Treasury tended to support U.S. government restriction of FDI outflow by showing that the payback of funds from abroad in the form of royalties, dividend remittances, interest, and export sales would be long delayed even if they exceeded capital outflow and the substitution of foreign production for a portion of U.S. exports.[14] Other studies, however, indicate a fairly rapid payback and argue that increasing returns to investment with the growth of foreign operations would result in a net contribution of FDI to the U.S.

balance of payments. So far as the overall balance of payments effects of FDI are concerned, the results of aggregate studies are inconclusive: they depend upon assumptions relating to corporate behavior with respect to the sources of financing and the remission of earnings, the degree to which foreign investment substitutes for home investment expenditures, and the extent to which U.S. export markets could have been maintained in the absence of FDI.

As in the case with studies of the impact of U.S. foreign investment on U.S. exports, case studies of the balance of payments impact of particular U.S. investments may reach more reliable conclusions than studies of aggregate U.S. foreign investment. The majority of case studies of FDI and the U.S. balance of payments which have been prepared by competent researchers have reached the conclusion that the establishment of U.S. manufacturing affiliates abroad has had a positive impact on the U.S. balance of payments. For example, Robert Stobaugh and Associates found in the nine case studies of U.S. foreign affiliates that the affiliates had a strong positive effect on U.S. balance of payments and on U.S. employment.[15] The Union Carbide case study mentioned above found tht dividends and other income from Union Carbide's foreign affiliates exceeded the outflow of FDI by the company by $20 million in 1970 and by $246 million over a 20-year period. Altogether, the company's positive contribution to the U.S. balance of payments was estimated at $236 million in 1970 and was $805 million over the period 1965-1970.

There is considerable doubt whether the U.S. government's attempt to control the outflow of FDI from the United States during the 1960s was effective since U.S. firms were able to finance their foreign operations from other sources. The establishment of government controls on FDI led U.S. firms to borrow from the Eurodollar market for financing their foreign operations and this demand for loans stimulated the further development of the Eurodollar market. Whether financing through the Eurodollar market in the long run strengthened or weakened the U.S. balance of payments as compared with financing through U.S. institutions is difficult to judge. The growth of the Eurodollar market stimulated by the credit demands of U.S. firms operating abroad created a demand for dollars outside the United States, but the growth of the market also expanded the total volume of liabilities denominated in dollars. Therefore, some have suggested that the creation of dollar liabilities (even though they were not direct liabilities of the United States) increased the instability of the external value of the dollar.

V. THE IMPACT OF FDI ON U.S. EMPLOYMENT

Proposed legislation such as the Burke-Hartke bill
(S. 151, 3 January 1973. 93rd Congress) would discourage U.S. investment abroad largely by increasing
the tax burden on U.S. corporations with foreign operations.[16] Such legislation was designed for preventing
the "export of American jobs and technology at the
expense of our own industry" as well as for improving
the U.S. balance of payments.

A number of studies have been directed
specifically at the net effects of U.S. FDI on U.S.
employment. The effects of U.S. employment as
contrasted with U.S. exports or the U.S. balance of
payments, require assumptions having to do with the
labor-output ratio of different export commodities.
For example, even though it may be shown that foreign
investments makes a net contribution to U.S. exports,
the exports gained from, say, the shipping of industrial equipment or components may have a lower labor
content than the exports lost from production abroad.[17]
Several studies, however, have stressed the fact that
the industries that gain U.S. exports at the expense of
foreign affiliate sales tend to be more R&D intensive
industries and that the jobs created are weighted more
heavily in the professional, scientific, and skill
classes, while the industries that lose exports tend to
employ higher proportions of unskilled and semiskilled
workers.[18]

As to the overall job impact of FDI in
manufacturing, the case is far from clear in either
direction, again because of the lack of empirical basis
for the assumptions that must be made.[19] Nevertheless,
studies mentioned above by Hawkins, Lipsey, Weiss, and
Stobaugh and Associates, suggest that U.S. foreign
investment in manufactures in the developing countries
are likely to have a net positive effect on U.S. jobs,
and, in any case, favor employment in the higher skill
categories.

One of the arguments made for restricting the
outflow of FDI from the United States is that funds
otherwise invested abroad would be invested in projects
within the United States, thus adding to U.S. employment and income. This implication is not supportable.

For the U.S. firms responsible for most U.S. foreign investment, capital has not been a major constraint on making investments either in the United States or abroad. In the assessment of alternative investments, market opportunities, human resource availabilities, and government polices are more important than the source of capital for most large companies. Given the opportunity of raising capital funds all over the world for investment either in the United States or abroad, the hypothesis that foreign investment reduces investment in the U.S. economy cannot be supported. Moreover, U.S. investments not made in foreign production as a consequence of U.S. government controls will not necessarily go into U.S. investment for the export sector.

A final point might be made regarding restricting U.S. foreign direct investment. To the extent that firms do not invest for direct production abroad they may be encouraged to transfer technology through licensing, technical assistance, and management contracts to foreign companies over which they have little control. The disadvantage here may be that while U.S. manufacturing affiliates operating abroad will acquire their capital equipment and components from the United States, nonaffiliated companies operating abroad are less likely to do so. Jack Baranson has expressed great concern regarding the export of U.S. technology through licensing and other forms of technology transfers not involving FDI. He has suggested that U.S. joint ventures with industrial enterprises in developing countries to which the United States can export engineering services and capital equipment as well as manufactured products may provide significant competitive advantages. He points out, however, that this will intensify the U.S. shift to capital intensive manufacturing and relinquish the more labor intensive segments of production to lower wage countries.[20]

VI. U.S. EXPORT COMPETITIVENESS AND
THE INTERNATIONAL TRANSFER OF TECHNOLOGY

It is well known that most of the new products and technology for producing them that have come to dominate international trade over the past several decades were initially developed and marketed on a large scale in the United States, but that in the case of a large number of these products the bulk of the world's export markets have been taken over by Japanese, Western Europeans, and for some commodities, by newly industrialized countries (NICs), e.g., Brazil, Mexico and South Korea. The standard explanation for this phenomenon has been called "the product cycle." A U.S. firm develops a product, then exports that product first to the developed countries and then to the rest of the world. After a market has been established abroad, it becomes more advantageous to move production abroad to plants near markets and where there are lower cost labor and materials. U.S. firms are in fact forced to establish manufacturing affiliates abroad because of competition from foreign firms that soon acquire the technology to produce the new products in competition with U.S. exports. Depending upon the degree of sophistication of the production process, affiliates may be established in the developed or developing countries, or both. In time, the product begins to be exported from abroad to third countries and eventually to the United States, in which case the product cycle is completed.

It is often concluded that the only way the United States can maintain or expand its exports is to continue to develop new products and new and cheaper methods of producing them. Efforts to negate the product cycle by restricting FDI from the United States are counterproductive, since foreign firms in developed countries will either acquire the technology from the U.S. firms that have it, or they will develop parallel technology. From this analysis it is sometimes concluded that the only hope for U.S. export competitiveness is to be found in a continual stream of innovations in products and production processes which will result in a temporary export advantage, followed by the inevitable loss of the market to foreign producers. This pessimistic conclusion is not warranted by either international trade theory or by empirical studies. It is simply not true that the United States has a comparative advantage in manufactures _only_ in newly developed, high-technology commodities.

A number of studies of international competitiveness and lagging U.S. exports have pointed to the relative decline in R&D expenditures in the United States compared to Japan and Germany as a reason for their having surpassed the United States in competitiveness.[21] They also point to a shift of U.S. technology abroad through FDI and licensing which reduces U.S. relative competitiveness. Also, less R&D in the United States reduces the injection of new products into the market and supposedly makes it more attractive to invest abroad to produce existing products as markets expand overseas.

The relationship between R&D and U.S. export competitiveness is much more complex and inferences from aggregate information on U.S. R&D expenditures are not warranted. Data on R&D must be disaggregated to the product-market level to be able to say anything constructive about the effects of R&D on international competitiveness. Military-related research must be specified as to its contribution to military exports and nonmilitary research to innovations must be identified among the various industrial sectors. Some sectors are not competitive internationally, so that research expenditures would not be relevant. Others are highly competitive domestically and in foreign markets, but levels of R&D expenditures are relatively low as in the case with textiles.

In his study of British FDI, Dunning found that high technology industries gained the most by investment in Britain; low technology industries gained the most by investment outside Britain in other countries.[22] Those industry sectors with strong import competition and low ability to export -- tobacco and textiles -- tend to have a high outflow of funds in investment abroad from Britain. The exports to and through affiliates of U.K. firms were correlated directly with R&D intensity of production of products. The fact of R&D meant that the parent company was generally in advance of the affiliate and exports were demanded in order to get "parent company products," even when there was foreign production by affiliates. (Exports from the parent are also significant when there are substantial economies of scale, requiring that production be located in a few centers to achieve low costs.)

Another study found that large firms tend to have greater exports relative to their output than smaller companies in each industry sector -- save in the low technology sectors (tobaccos, chemicals, food products, and packaging). In the low technology sectors, the large company has no particular advantage in export competition. Consequenty, the study concludes, R&D intensity is a better explainer of exports than is size of a particular company. In addition, intra-firm exports (which frequently are half of a company's exports abroad), depend on the degree of integration of the companies, with the high-technology products being exported in final form and others often in intermediate form for further processing. High R&D companies were found to have a much larger percentage of internal exports (sales from parents to affiliates and among affiliates) than did low R&D intensive firms -- 50 per-cent compared to 18 percent -- reflecting a desire to internalize intermediate stages and appropriate the benefits of R&D and technological advances.[23]

The location of R&D activities in a firm says nothing necessarily about where the inventions are utilized in production or where and how they are com-mercialized. Research undertaken in Britain can be employed by a German firm or in Latin America. The transfers may occur through intra-firm (inter-affiliate) activities, or by means of licensing and technical and management contracts. Where and how R&D is commercialized is determined by company objectives, market characteristics, organizational structures, management styles, abilities to absorb technology, factor endowments, and government policies.

Japanese firms acquired Japan's domestic market for products developed by U.S. R&D with the aid of imported technology, and later Japanese industry became the principal source of world exports of the commodity, first to the LDCs and then to the developed countries. When foreign production made possible reduced costs, the Japanese established plants in countries such as Taiwan and South Korea and produced not just for the domestic markets in these countries, but for the entire world. This is well represented by the color television plants in Taiwan and South Korea which were established by Japanese industry to supply world wide markets.[24] Japanese industry has also been quite adept in using foreign investment in manufacturing affiliates to expand Japan's export of components and related products, both to the countries in which the manufacturing affiliates were established and to third country markets which their foreign manufacturing affiliates penetrated. U.S. firms might well learn important lessons from the Japanese in this regard.

It is not, therefore, possible to state that higher R&D expenditures will necessarily lead to greater competitiveness for any one country in a particular product. There is also a signficiant difference in the effect on competitiveness of the objectives of R&D expenditures as among (a) the creation of new products; (b) modifications of existing products; and (c) the development of cost-reducing processes. The largest portion of R&D expenditures apparently goes into modifications of existing products, with new products following behind, and new processes having the smallest share. Even these expenditures are not the full story because the largest costs are incurred in scaling-up manufacturing and in marketing efforts. Therefore, what is included in "R&D" alters the effect of R&D on competitiveness. For example, a country could spend virtually nothing on research, a small amount on development, and a substantial amount on engineering, and thereby achieve considerable competitiveness. This is the story of Japan for the past two decades, and it has succeeded admirably. Japan has only recently moved into larger developmental expenditures and into basic (but industrially oriented) research.

On the other hand, European countries, notably Britain, have made substantial expenditures for basic research, but have not followed through in innovation and commercialization. Therefore, it is not possible to conclude that stimulation of R&D or even of engineering will necessarily improve export competitiveness. This will depend on the way in which the full process is brought to fruition in each product market, and this in turn will depend on whether the efforts are directed to specific industrial sectors or product lines in which success can be achieved.

R&D may be applied to achieve one or more of several objectives in expanding markets. It may be employed to achieve an increased share of an existing market for an existing product, an increased share of a market resulting from a new product, the development of an entire new market with a new product, an increased share of a market resulting from cost reduction, the expansion into new geographic markets through licensing for export, the development of a new production base for sales in many markets, increased domestic sales substituting for former imports, or the maintenance of a market position in the face of increased efforts on the part of the competitors. Each of these possible results must be evaluated to determine wether R&D activities have achieved comparative success in particular product markets.

R&D expenditures tend to be highest in high-technology sectors, and these tend to be dominated by the companies in which substantial FDI activities create a network of interrelated affiliates trading with each other. Consequently, there is a correlation between R&D expenditures and an inrease in intra-company sales across national boundaries, as compared to sales or exports to independent companies. The R&D sequence creates differential technologies, applied by managers who are differentially motivated. Industrial production moves internally into new locations and these new locations serve one another through an intricate network of intra-company trade. Therefore, international competitiveness is not necessarily increased for the country undertaking the R&D. International companies, however, are often induced by a number of factors -- not the least of which is government policy -- to keep a rough equilibrium in their imports and exports, despite the underlying competitive forces.

The only way to determine whether or not R&D efforts lead to increased international competitiveness would be to examine a single set of product markets within an industrial sector, tracing the innovation decisions, manufacturing scale-up, and commercialization to determine the net impacts of R&D in the process of reaching market success. Simply injecting funds into R&D at some stage in the process will not necessarily produce greater competitiveness. In fact, there is a large mount of duplicative R&D in the United

166

States since many companies are seeking only minor modifications by which to obtain a greater share of the market (domestic or foreign), and shifting relative positions among themselves without increasing U.S. exports.

The extent to which different industrial sectors are integrated across national boundaries through both trade and foreign investment is a significant factor in determining international competitiveness. Some sectors are essentially domestic industries, with exports a means of getting rid of surpluses or achieving economies of scale. This is the case with iron and steel and, to some extent, aircraft. These two industries are highly specific geographically, with such large economies of scale that it is not feasible to split them up geographically; therefore, international integration occurs through exports, that is production occurs where there are comparative advantages (modified by governmental intervention), and markets are served from these centers. At the other end of the continuum, the food industry is one which is highly specific to the markets where the food is sold, so the international structure is one of production close to the markets with relatively little international trade in final products. For automobiles and electronics, there are substantial economies of scale in production of components or even models, but a significant advantage lies in being close to the market as well; there is a separation of production locations with a high volume of international trade. Pharmaceuticals are somewhat in between, with a substantial volume of trade in actives, but local manufacture of compounding materials and local processing into final dosages.

To increase U.S. competitiveness in steel would require a larger volume of exports in competition with local suppliers abroad. This sector, however, is highly sensitive to national interest and, consequently, it is unlikely that a substantial volume of steel could be exported from the United States, though increased U.S. competitiveness might reduce the volume of imports. Increased competitiveness in aircraft is not likely to raise significantly the relative share of U.S. suppliers in markets where there is domestic production, given the concern of other governments for maintaining some part of the aircraft industry. Greater U.S. exports in this sector are likely to result from an expansion of the worldwide aircraft market. Increased efficiency in the food industry is also not likely to lead to export competitiveness. The structure of industry in a country is critical in determining whether increased competitiveness in terms of greater productivity, improve R&D, and cost reduction will, in fact, improve U.S. export positions.

Many countries, particularly the newly industrialized countries, have recognized that it is possible to shift the location of industry through governmental policies, thereby significantly affecting the flow of trade. This is well illustrated by the use of "local content requirements" to force the establishment of FDI affiliates in key sectors in the host country. Brazil, Mexico, India, Argentina, and even Canada have used this technique. This rule has not only limited U.S. exports, but is gradually developing new centers of production which will later be integrated back through new patterns of international industrial location.

Adjustments must be made in the advanced countries to these shifts in production location and trade patterns. Industries where these adjustments are most significant are called the "mobile industries," those in which the factors of production are relatively mobile, seeking to combine with a factor which is less mobile, but is significantly cheaper. Evidence of this mobility is found in electronics, textiles, chemicals, rubber, automobiles, and even pharmaceuticals. Segments of these industries have been moved to countries with low wage costs, but relatively high labor skills, and they will move again as this advantage disappears through economic growth in the host country. This mobility alters the location of markets and the sources from which they are served. FDI, therefore, is continually changing the competitive picture, and substantial efforts will need to be made on the part of the advanced countries to adjust to these shifts. International competitiveness from this viewpoint is in part a matter of raising productivity in existing lines (though this might slow the outward movement of industry), but it is even more a matter of staying at the leading edge of technical advance, creating new products, or new uses of existing products. Unfortunately, from the standpoint of U.S. competition, this conclusion has also been reached by other leading countries, such as Japan and Germany.

VIII.   CONCLUSIONS

Although the subject warrants considerably more empirical research than has been done thus far, we draw the following conclusions from our analysis:

1.   Information is not sufficient to determine with confidence the net effect of U.S. FDI in the LDCs on total U.S. exports, the U.S. balance of payments, or employment. Nevertheless, there are stong indications from the case studies and other empirical investigations that these effects are either positive or at least not significant negative.

2.   U.S. FDI has undoubtedly changed the commodity composition of U.S. exports and imports in favor of relatively technology intensive and professional and skill intensive commodities and services.

3.   U.S. foreign investment and trade reflect the process of international industrial integration from which the United States cannot withdraw (or reverse) if it is to perform effectively in the international economy. Within this world structure, U.S. export competitiveness will be determined by the productivity and financial stability of the U.S. economy, and the degree to which U.S. government policies encourage innovation and productive capital investment.

4.   Foreign direct investment probably contributes more to U.S. export competitiveness than technology transfers through licensing and technical and managerial contracts.

5.   There is no theoretical or empirical basis for advocating U.S. government restrictions on U.S. FDI in the LDCs.

STATISTICAL APPENDIX

At the end of 1978, total U.S. foreign direct investment in the manufacturing industries of the developing countries was $14.1 billion, of which the largest category was chemical and allied products ($3.9 billion), followed by machinery ($3.4 billion), transportation equipment ($1.4 billion), and food products ($1.3 billion). U.S. investment in manufacturing was heavily concentrated in Latin America ($11.6 billion), followed by other Asian and Pacific countries ($2.0 billion) (see Table 1). It is worth noting that the U.S. market share of exports to the LDCs was also highest in Latin American as compared with any other LDC region. In 1977, the U.S. export market share was 61 percent in Central America, 32 percent in South America (excluding OPEC countries), and 54 percent in the Caribbean, as contrasted with 19 percent in South Asia and the Far East, and 19 percent for the OPEC countries.

In 1977, capital expenditures in manufacturing by majority-owned foreign affiliates of U.S. companies in the LDCs totaled $1.8 billion, of which nearly $1.5 billion was in Latin America. The largest capital expenditures were in chemical and allied products ($382 million), machinery, except electrical ($289 million), food products ($201 million), electrical machinery ($193 million), and transportation equipment ($183 million) (see Table 2).

In 1976, total sales by majority-owned foreign manufacturing affiliates of U.S. companies in the LDCs were $32.9 billion, of which $26.3 billion were by Latin American affiliates. Of total sales for the developing countries as a whole, $29.8 billion were to the countries in which the manufacturing affiliates were located. Only $1.2 billion of the sales represented exports to the United Sates, and the remaining $1.9 billion in sales were to third countries (see Table 3). In 1976, exports to the United States by these affiliates were led by machinery, followed by food products and transportation equipment.

171

TABLE 1

U.S. FOREIGN DIRECT INVESTMENT POSITION ABROAD, BY INDUSTRY AND COUNTRY, 1978
(millions of dollars)

| | ALL INDUSTRIES | MINING AND SMELTING | PETROLEUM | MANUFACTURING | | | | | | | TRANSPORTATION, COMMUNICATION, AND PUBLIC UTILITIES | TRADE | FINANCE AND INSURANCE | OTHER INDUSTRIES |
				TOTAL	FOOD PRODUCTS	CHEMICALS AND ALLIED PRODUCTS	PRIMARY AND FABRICATED METALS	MACHINERY	TRANSPORTATION EQUIPMENT	OTHER MANUFACTURING				
ALL COUNTRIES........	168,081	7,020	33,302	74,207	6,303	16,097	4,218	21,137	10,509	15,943	3,693	17,585	24,065	8,210
Developed Countries..	120,741	4,670	26,415	60,135	5,043	12,176	3,166	17,785	9,069	12,896	1,216	12,666	11,108	4,532
Canada..............	37,280	3,030	8,247	17,625	1,599	2,896	1,148	3,580	3,026	5,377	1,061	2,448	3,882	987
Europe..............	69,669	41	14,719	36,426	2,864	7,953	1,774	12,104	5,349	6,382	113	8,692	6,576	3,103
European Communities (9)...	55,283	18	12,202	32,182	2,433	7,219	1,321	11,016	4,741	5,452	45	4,643	4,148	2,044
Other Europe........	14,386	23	2,516	8,244	431	734	453	1,088	608	930	68	4,049	2,428	1,059
Japan...............	4,963	0	1,646	2,317	134	490	5	1,269	(D)	(D)	40	613	233	114
Australia, New Zealand and South Africa..	8,829	1,599	1,803	3,766	446	836	240	832	(D)	(D)	2	912	417	329
Developing Countries....	40,466	2,349	4,525	14,071	1,260	3,921	1,052	3,352	1,439	3,046	646	4,243	11,085	3,546
Latin America.......	32,509	1,664	3,661	11,644	1,037	3,229	878	2,564	1,343	2,594	308	3,029	10,243	1,960
Latin Am. Republics..	21,336	1,267	2,005	10,855	991	2,895	(D)	(D)	1,343	(D)	(D)	2,677	2,655	(D)
Argentina..........	1,658	53	259	983	59	235	74	174	241	200	(D)	163	106	(D)
Brazil.............	7,170	268	424	4,684	285	1,143	237	1,392	558	1,068	26	580	668	552
Chile..............	230	(D)	(D)	71	5	32	(D)	-3	(D)	29	10	52	2	26
Columbia...........	769	9	85	490	50	143	19	78	(D)	(D)	(D)	69	92	(D)
Mexico.............	3,712	97	41	2,752	229	785	244	512	370	612	(D)	563	112	(D)
Panama.............	2,385	1	68	180	14	128	1	7	4	27	26	707	998	406
Peru...............	1,429	(D)	(D)	159	40	25	21	12	(D)	(D)	-1	57	9	47
Venezuela..........	2,015	(D)	290	1,059	152	278	62	142	135	291	26	321	186	(D)
Other Central Am....	797	26	49	285	90	93	17	(D)	-1	(D)	70	93	75	200
Other..............	1,170	43	(D)	192	66	33	29	14	(*)	49	(D)	72	405	109

TABLE 1 (continued)

| | ALL INDUSTRIES | MINING AND SMELTING | PETRO-LEUM | MANUFACTURING | | | | | | | TRANSPORTATION, COMMUNICATION, AND PUBLIC UTILITIES | TRADE | FINANCE AND INSURANCE | OTHER INDUSTRIES |
				TOTAL	FOOD PRODUCTS	CHEMICALS AND ALLIED PRODUCTS	PRIMARY AND FABRICATED METALS	MACHINERY	TRANSPORTATION EQUIPMENT	OTHER MANUFACTURING				
Other Western Hemisph...	11,173	397	1,656	789	46	334	(D)	(D)	(*)	(D)	(D)	352	7,588	(D)
Bahamas...	1,792	(D)	(D)	66	(D)	57	0	-2	0	(D)	12	(D)	1,264	(D)
Bermuda...	7,191	0	(D)	(D)	3	190	0	(D)	(*)	(D)	54	168	6,105	(D)
Jamaica...	(D)	264	(D)	210	(D)	15	(D)	2	0	(D)	-25	(D)	(D)	23
Other...	(D)	(D)	(D)	(D)	9	72	2	5	0	(D)	(D)	47	(D)	(D)
Other Africa...	3,411	545	2,092	274	27	56	(D)	11	0	86	88	151	75	186
Liberia...	340	(D)	110	1	0	2	0	(*)	0	(D)	76	6	(D)	(D)
Libya...	473	0	457	46	0	1	(D)	0	0	0	(D)	8	1	(D)
Nigeria...	383	(*)	262	(D)	2	29	77	3	0	(D)	3	49	16	6
Other...	2,215	(D)	1,262	(D)	25	23	(D)	8	(D)	(D)	(D)	88	(D)	(D)
Middle East...	-2,105	(*)	-3,519	200	6	68	13	(D)	(D)	29	43	85	200	(D)
Iran...	389	(*)	157	83	6	37	3	51	(D)	5	30	11	(D)	(D)
Other...	-2,494	1	-3,675	117	1	31	10	(D)	(*)	24	13	74	(D)	(D)
Other Asia & Pacific...	6,651	(*)	2,290	1,954	191	568	(D)	78	0	337	207	978	569	(D)
India...	328	98	56	241	(D)	116	(D)	18	(*)	19	(D)	9	(D)	12
Indonesia...	1,245	(D)	961	103	(D)	26	0	16	3	(D)	(D)	1	(D)	53
Phillipines...	1,003	(D)	230	405	142	127	-2	(D)	(*)	120	(D)	102	115	(D)
Other...	4,076	(D)	1,043	1,205	50	299	(D)	(D)	1	(D)	(D)	866	432	(D)
International & Unallocated...	6,874	...	2,362	...	...	...	...	...	...	...	1,831	677	1,872	132

* Less than $500,000
D Suppressed to avoid disclosure of data of individual companies

Source: Survey of Current Business, Washington, D.C.: U.S. Department of Commerce, August 1979, Table 14.

TABLE 2

CAPITAL EXPENDITURES BY MAJORITY-OWNED FOREIGN AFFILIATES OF U.S. COMPANIES, 1977
(millions of dollars)

	ALL INDUS-TRIES	MINING AND SMELT-ING	PETRO-LEUM	MANUFACTURING										TRADE	OTHER INDUS-TRIES
				TOTAL	FOOD PRODUCTS	PAPER AND ALLIED PRODUCTS	CHEMICALS AND ALLIED PRODUCTS	RUBBER PRODUCTS	PRIMARY AND FABRI-CATED METALS	MACHINERY EXCEPT ELECTRICAL	ELECTRI-CAL MA-CHINERY	TRANSPOR-TATION EQUIP-MENT	OTHER MANUFAC-TURING		
ALL COUNTRIES	27,507	628	9,317	12,730	862	702	2,435	265	695	3,648	979	1,840	1,304	1,762	3,070
Developed Countries	20,443	502	5,856	10,905	661	612	1,054	176	507	3,359	786	1,657	1,094	1,399	1,780
Canada	6,169	371	1,832	2,800	173	443	706	63	82	367	188	583	195	203	962
Europe	12,399	8	3,619	7,132	402	142	1,228	93	414	2,601	549	922	780	1,000	639
European Communities (9)	10,666	5	3,074	6,590	350	127	1,133	81	381	2,479	486	796	757	715	282
Other Europe	1,733	4	545	541	52	15	95	12	33	122	63	126	23	286	357
Japan	1,762	1	101	552	32	11	49	2	3	(D)	(D)	16	75	67	40
Australia, New Zealand and South Africa	1,112	122	303	421	53	16	70	18	8	(D)	(D)	136	44	128	137
Developing Countries	5,575	126	2,690	1,825	201	90	382	89	188	289	193	183	210	363	571
Latin America	2,564	81	412	1,464	145	77	329	80	147	260	113	174	138	281	327
Latin Am. Republics	2,278	60	261	1,448	145	77	318	80	147	260	110	174	137	272	237
Argentina	219	4	64	81	44	26	11	11	12	13	4	12	15	31	39
Brazil	970	12	33	736	(*)	(*)	186	17	22	177	85	113	67	122	67
Chile	17	2	4	6	6	(*)	1	1	3	0	(*)	(D)	(D)	1	4
Columbia	138	1	42	86	11	11	24	12	3	12	4	(D)	(D)	8	1
Mexico	339	5	2	263	50	31	54	19	14	56	8	21	8	54	15
Panama	22	2	3	5	3	0	(*)	1	0	(*)	0	0	2	2	1
Peru	90	(D)	(D)	8	2	0	4	0	1	2	(*)	(*)	(*)	1	9
Venezuela	335	(D)	13	225	24	4	33	19	88	(*)	6	22	27	45	9
Other Central Am.	84	0	31	26	8	5	3	1	3	(*)	2	0	6	4	52
Other and Unallocated	66	(D)	(D)	12	4	(*)	2	0	2	(*)	1	0	3		17

TABLE 2 (continued)

	ALL INDUSTRIES	MINING AND SMELTING	PETROLEUM	MANUFACTURING										TRADE	OTHER INDUSTRIES
				TOTAL	FOOD PRODUCTS	PAPER AND ALLIED PRODUCTS	CHEMICALS AND ALLIED PRODUCTS	RUBBER PRODUCTS	PRIMARY AND FABRICATED METALS	MACHINERY EXCEPT ELECTRICAL	ELECTRICAL MACHINERY	TRANSPORTATION EQUIPMENT	OTHER MANUFACTURING		
Other Western Hemisph....	287	21	151	17	(*)	(*)	11	(*)	(*)	(*)	4	0	1	9	89
Bahamas..............	93	1	9	(*)	0	0	(*)	0	0	0	0	0	(*)	(*)	82
Bermuda..............	2	0	1	1	(*)	0	(*)	0	0	0	0	0	0	1	0
Jamaica..............	16	2	(*)	11	(*)	0	9	(*)	0	0	1	0	1	2	1
Other and Unallocated..	175	18	140	4	1	0	1	0	(*)	0	3	0	(*)	6	6
Other Africa........	749	3	644	41	0	(*)	7	1	21	0	8	(*)	3	15	43
Liberia.............	55	6	21	(*)	0	0	0	(*)	0	(*)	0	0	1	1	30
Libya...............	77	3	77	0	(*)	0	0	0	0	0	0	0	0	(*)	0
Nigeria.............	104	0	84	13	1	0	4	0	(*)	0	(D)	0	(D)	4	3
Other and Unallocated..	513	3	461	28	(*)	0	3	1	21	(*)	(D)	0	0	10	11
Middle East.........	1,417	1	1,222	39	(*)	5	14	1	(*)	(*)	16	1	0	13	141
Iran................	79	(*)	58	9	(*)	0	6	1	(*)	1	2	0	0	1	11
Other and Unallocated..	1,337	(*)	1,164	30	(*)	5	9	1	0	(*)	15	1	0	13	130
Other Asia & Pacific..	845	39	413	280	55	7	31	7	20	28	55	8	69	53	60
India...............	24	0	1	21	(*)	0	9	(D)	(*)	3	(D)	0	0	2	(*)
Indonesia...........	236	11	195	13	(*)	0	1	0	0	0	4	(*)	4	5	11
Korea...............	83	0	26	47	(*)	(D)	3	0	13	1	(D)	0	40	(D)	(D)
Phillippines........	106	0	22	69	42	(*)	4	4	(*)	(*)	2	(*)	2	(D)	(D)
Other and Unallocated..	397	28	169	129	12	1	14	1	13	23	44	6	22	39	31
International & Unallocated..	1,489	---	771	---	---	---	---	---	---	---	---	---	---	(*)	718

* Less than $500,000
D Suppressed to avoid disclosure of data of individual companies.

Source: Survey of Current Business, Washington, D.C.: U.S. Department of Commerce, vol. 59, no. 3, March 1979, p. 34.

TABLE 3

SALES BY MAJORITY OWNED FOREIGN MANUFACTURING AFFILIATES OF U.S. COMPANIES BY DESTINATION, 1974-76
(millions of dollars)

Affiliate Area and Industry	Total Sales			Local Sales[1]			Exports to the United States			Exports to Other Foreign Countries		
	1974	1975ʳ	1976	1974	1975ʳ	1976	1974	1975	1976	1974	1975	1976
ALL AREAS, TOTAL.............	175,703	192,388	212,793	134,705	148,092	160,950	11,228	11,371	14,114	29,770	32,975	37,729
Food Products...............	17,001	18,277	20,739	15,488	16,727	18,349	334	227	313	1,179	1,324	1,717
Chemicals & Allied Products.	36,206	37,552	43,135	27,876	29,819	33,741	451	445	562	7,879	7,288	8,831
Primary & Fabricated Metals.	12,514	12,602	14,400	10,316	10,411	11,837	394	383	555	1,804	1,808	2,008
Machinery[2]................	44,888	50,926	52,599	32,579	36,435	37,155	2,377	2,248	2,768	9,932	12,243	12,675
Transportation Equipment....	32,665	38,094	44,811	22,954	27,053	30,409	5,637	5,885	7,365	4,074	5,156	6,955
Other[3]....................	32,427	34,886	37,469	25,494	27,647	29,377	2,033	2,184	2,550	4,902	5,056	5,542
Canada, Total...............	40,725	43,598	49,347	30,594	32,725	36,311	7,692	8,164	10,407	2,439	2,709	2,629
Food Products...............	4,189	4,475	5,090	4,008	4,288	4,863	117	84	107	64	103	120
Chemicals & Allied Products.	4,491	4,814	5,408	4,080	4,432	4,918	188	208	290	223	174	200
Primary & Fabricated Metals.	2,221	2,251	2,528	1,766	1,766	1,907	264	272	383	191	213	237
Machinery[2]................	7,841	8,376	8,860	6,674	7,080	7,707	703	677	803	465	618	350
Transportation Equipment....	12,044	13,264	15,737	6,760	7,455	8,350	4,898	5,280	6,864	386	529	523
Other[3]....................	9,939	10,419	11,724	7,305	7,704	8,566	1,521	1,644	1,959	1,111	1,072	1,198
Europe:												
European Communities(9) Total[4]	83,051	91,345	100,956	58,823	64,593	69,529	2,012	1,861	2,021	22,216	24,891	29,405
Food Products...............	6,845	7,268	7,851	5,989	9,359	6,681	(D)	17	26	(D)	892	1,144
Chemicals & Allied Products.	17,978	17,479	20,264	(D)	11,188	12,476	(D)	159	180	(D)	6,132	7,609
Primary & Fabricated Metals.	7,165	7,135	8,338	6,080	5,967	7,069	47	43	96	1,037	1,125	1,172
Machinery[2]................	25,749	30,051	30,561	16,944	19,368	18,966	(D)	990	1,197	(D)	9,694	10,397
Transportation Equipment....	(D)	15,154	18,816	(D)	10,514	12,615	669	497	340	3,202	4,143	5,861
Other[3]....................	(D)	14,257	15,127	(D)	11,197	11,723	(D)	156	182	(D)	2,905	3,221

TABLE 3 (continued)

Affiliate Area and Industry	Total Sales			Local Sales[1]			Exports to the United States			Exports to Other Foreign Countries		
	1974	1975[r]	1976	1974	1975[r]	1976	1974	1975	1976	1974	1975	1976
Other Europe, Total	9,387	10,244	11,256	6,934	7,745	8,476	346	315	348	2,106	2,184	2,431
Food Products	720	800	992	697	780	926	(D)	6	10	(D)	13	56
Chemicals & Allied Products	2,298	2,310	2,542	(D)	1,906	2,116	(D)	8	9	(D)	396	417
Primary & Fabricated Metals	814	850	981	539	580	608	40	8	2	235	262	371
Machinery[2]	2,626	3,075	3,064	1,856	2,236	2,221	(D)	102	120	187	736	724
Transportation Equipment	(D)	1,185	1,558	(D)	960	1,228	9	9	12	(D)	215	318
Other[3]	(D)	2,025	2,119	(D)	1,282	1,378	(D)	181	196	281	562	545
Japan, Total	5,247	5,640	6,475	4,532	4,907	5,627	94	89	138	621	644	711
Food Products	182	241	331	182	241	331	(*)	(*)	(*)	(*)	(*)	(*)
Chemicals & Allied Products	2,316	2,482	3,133	2,034	2,217	2,807	1	1	1	281	264	325
Primary & Fabricated Metals	(D)	(D)	(D)	(D)	(D)	(D)	(*)	(*)	(*)	1	1	1
Machinery[2]	2,043	2,199	2,258	1,691	1,836	1,836	69	64	109	283	300	314
Transportation Equipment	29	33	39	29	32	37	(*)	(*)	(*)	(*)	(*)	3
Other[3]	(D)	(D)	(D)	(D)	(D)	(D)	23	25	28	57	78	69
Australia, New Zealand, & South Africa, Total	10,906	11,548	11,896	10,227	10,863	11,239	59	40	48	620	645	609
Food Products	1,075	1,023	1,041	1,001	959	957	(D)	7	9	(D)	57	76
Chemicals & Allied Products	1,754	1,814	1,996	1,705	1,769	1,946	2	4	3	47	41	47
Primary & Fabricated Metals	(D)	(D)	(D)	(D)	(D)	(D)	13	14	19	41	47	34
Machinery[2]	2,075	2,358	2,386	1,894	2,094	2,157	7	1	1	175	263	229
Transportation Equipment	3,172	3,263	3,277	2,982	3,157	3,180	(*)	(*)	(*)	190	106	97
Other[3]	(D)	(D)	(D)	(D)	(D)	(D)	(D)	15	15	(D)	131	127
Latin America, Total	20,859	24,047	26,251	19,438	22,590	24,575	509	486	633	912	971	1,043
Food Products	3,563	4,013	4,598	3,252	3,700	4,192	123	95	122	187	218	284
Chemicals & Allied Products	5,179	5,920	6,656	4,926	5,674	6,423	46	57	67	207	190	166
Primary & Fabricated Metals	1,227	1,408	1,503	1,191	1,367	1,452	1	1	1	35	40	50
Machinery[2]	3,399	3,697	4,213	3,021	3,353	3,817	206	154	200	172	190	196
Transportation Equipment	3,916	4,961	5,103	3,757	4,706	4,814	55	96	149	104	160	140
Other[3]	3,574	4,047	4,177	3,291	3,790	3,876	78	83	95	205	175	207

TABLE 3 (continued)

Affiliate Area and Industry	Total Sales			Local Sales[1]			Exports to the United States			Exports to Other Foreign Countries		
	1974	1975ʳ	1976	1974	1975ʳ	1976	1974	1975	1976	1974	1975	1976
Other Africa, total..........	521	634	696	393	503	569	32	48	52	96	83	75
Middle East, total..........	262	316	369	204	238	267	3	2	5	55	76	97
Other Asia & Pacific, total.....	4,746	4,966	5,547	3,561	3,930	4,357	480	364	461	704	672	730
Food Products...............	393	421	447	332	370	373	31	17	39	32	34	34
Chemicals & Allied Products.	1,895	2,346	2,692	1,806	2,265	2,631	6	6	7	83	75	54
Primary & Fabricated Metals.	(D)	208	(D)	198	(D)	199	(*)	(D)	3	(D)	(D)	(D)
Machinery[2].................	1,053	1,053	1,131	416	361	337	347	261	338	290	431	455
Transportation Equipment.....	220	210	257	211	204	243	5	3	(*)	4	3	14
Other[3].....................	(D)	729	(D)	597	(D)	574	91	(D)	72	(D)	(D)	(D)

r   Revised to reflect additional information received after previous publication.
*   Less than $500,000.   (D) Suppressed to avoid disclosure of data of individual reporters.
1   Sales by an affiliate in the country where it was located.
2   Includes both the electrical and nonelectrical machinery industries shown separately in tables 5A-D.
3   Includes the following industries shown separately in tables 5A-D: Paper and allied products, rubber products, and "other manufacturing."
4   Consists of Belgium, Luxembourg, France, Germany, Italy, the Netherlands, Denmark, Ireland & the U.K.

Source: Survey of Current Business, Washington, D.C.: U.S. Department of Commerce, vol. 58, no. 3, March 1978, p. 36.

[1]U.S. exports in the LDCs may be affected by foreign investment in the LDCs themselves or in developed countries where the U.S. affiliates export to the LDCs. This study is concerned mainly with foreign investment in manufacturing in the LDCs.

[2]This conclusion is based on findings by Robert G. Hawkins, Robert B. Stobaugh, Robert E. Lipsey and Merle Y. Weiss, among others. Lipsey and Weiss found that "direct investment abroad is a method by which oligopolistic firms compete for shares in host country markets" and that "export competition is secondary to the competition via production in the market " (p. 44). This finding was confirmed in a study by Robert B. Stobaugh. See Robert G. Hawkins and Michael J. Jedel, "U.S. Jobs and Foreign Investment," in International Labor and the Multinational Enterprise, Duane Kujawa, (ed.) (New York: Praeger, 1975), pp. 47-93; Robert B. Stobaugh, Nine Investments Abroad and their Impact at Home (Cambridge: Harvard University Press, 1976), p. 196; and Robert E. Lipsey and Merle Y. Weiss, Exports and Foreign Investment in Manufacturing Industries, Working Paper No. 131 (New York: National Bureau of Economic Research, May 1976).

[3]"The Effects of the U.S. Corporate Foreign Investment, 1970-1977" (New York: Business International, Inc., May 1979).

[4] Exports and Foreign Investment, op. cit., Lipsey and Weiss.

[5]The commodity groups included drugs, soaps, detergents, etc.; other chemical and allied products; rubber and plastic products; primary and fabricated metals; other nonelectrical machinery; office machinery and computers; household appliances and electrical apparatus; radio and TV equipment; automobiles and trucks; other transportation equipment; textiles and apparel; stone, clay, glass and other concrete products; and professional scientific and controlling instruments.

[6]Foreign country affiliate activity is measured either by net sales or net local sales.

[7]In the less developed countries, two of the commodity classifications were combined and a third omitted, leaving only 12 commodity groups.

[8]Robert B. Stobaugh, Nine Investments Abroad and their Impact at Home: Case Studies of Multinational Enterpirses and the U.S. Economy (Cambridge: Harvard University Press, 1976), pp. 14-36.

[9]Ibid., p. 196.

[10]See, for example, Richard W. Moxon, "Off-Shore Production in the Less Developed Countries: A Case Study of Multinationality in the Electronics Industry," The Bulletin, No. 98-99 (New York University Institute of Finance, July 1974), p. 70.

[11]"Union Carbide's International Investment Benefits the U.S. Economy" (New York: Union Carbide Corporation, October 1972).

[12]Robert E. Lipsey and Merle Y. Weiss, U.S. Exports and Foreign Investment in the Pharmaceutical Industry, Working Paper No. 87 (Cambridge: National Bureau of Economic Research, January 1976).

[13]J.A. Hufbauer and G.C. Adler, Overseas Manufacturing Investment and the Balance of Payments, Tax Policy Research Study No. 1 (Washington D.C.: U.S. Department of the Treasury, 1968); J.H. Dunnings, "The Reddaway and Hufbauer/Adler Reports on the Foreign Investment Controversy," The Bankers' Magazine, vol. CCVII, May/June 1969 and vol. CCVIII, July 1969; Jack N. Behrman, "Foreign Private Investments and the Government's Efforts to Reduce the Payments Deficit," The Journal of Finance, May 1966, pp. 283-296; Judd Polk, Irene Meister and Lawrence Veit, U.S. Production Abroad and the Balance of Payments: A Survey of Corporate Investment Experience (New York: National Industrial Conference Board, 1966); and Nicholas K. Bruck and Francis A. Lees, "Foreign Investments, Capital Controls and the Balance of Payments," The Bulletin, No. 48-49, (New York University Graduate School of Business, Institute of Finance, April 1968).

[14]Hufbauer and Adler, Overseas Manufacturing Investment, op. cit.

[15]Stobaugh and Associates, Nine Investments Abroad, op. cit. p. 214.

[16]For an analysis of the Burke-Hartke bill, see The Burke-Hartke Foreign Trade and Investment Proposal (Washington, D.C.: American Enterprise Institute, February 1973).

[17]See Robert G. Hawkins and Ingo Walter, ed. "The Multinational Corporation: A New Trade Policy Issue in the United States," The United States and International Markets (Lexington: D.C. Health and Company, 1972), p. 186-7.

[18]See Robert G. Hawkins, "Are Multinational Corporations Depriving the United States of its Economic Diversity and Independence?" The Case for the Multinational Corporation, Carl H. Madden (ed.) (New York: Praeger, 1977), p. 133. This same point is made by Stobaugh and Associates in Nine Investments Abroad, op. cit., pp. 216-218. See also Robert C. Hawkins and Michael J. Jedel, "U.S. Jobs and Foreign Investments," op. cit. pp. 47-93.

[19]This was the conclusion of a comprehensive study prepared by the U.S. Tariff Commission, Implications of Multinational Firms for World Trade and Investment and for U.S. Trade and Labor, Committee on Finance, U.S. Senate (Washington, D.C.: U.S. Government Printing Office, February 1973).

[20]Technology Transfer: Effects on U.S. Competitiveness and Employment (mimeo), prepared for the Bureau of International Labor Affairs (Washington D.C.: U.S. Department of Labor, December 1976), pp. 49-50.

[21]See N. Terleckj, The Effects of R&D on Productivity Growth of Industries: An Exploratory Study (Washington D.C.: National Planning Association, 1974): E. Mansfield, "Returns from Industrial Innovation, International Technology Transfer and Overseas Research Development," in National Science Foundation, Preliminary Papers for a Colloquium on the Relationship between R&D and Returns from Technological Innovation,

May 21, 1977 (Mimeo); R. McCullouch, R&D as a Determinant of U.S. International Competitiveness (Washington D.C.: National Planning Association, 1978); Edward F. Denison, "Explanations of Declining Productivity Growth," Survey of Current Business, August 1979, pp. 1-24; Jack Baranson, Technology Transfer; Effects on U.S. Competitiveness and Employment (Mimeo), a Study Prepared for the Bureau of International Labor Affairs (Washington D.C.: U.S. Department of Labor, December, 1976).

[22]J.H. Dunning, "The U.K.'s International Direct Investment Position in the Mid-1970s," Lloyds Bank Review, April, 1979, pp. 18-20.

[23]P.J. Buckley and R.D. Pearce, "Overseas Production and Exporting by the World's Largest Enterprises: A Study in Sourcing Policy," Journal of International Business Studies, vol. 10, no. 1, Spring/Summer, 1979, pp. 9-20.

[24]For a discussion of Japanese and U.S. foreign investment strategy, see William D. Rapp, "Strategy Formulation in International Competition," Columbia Journal of World Business, Summer 1973, pp. 98-112.

4

GOVERNMENT FINANCIAL INSTITUTIONS IN SUPPORT OF U.S. EXPORTS

Roger E. Shields
R. Craig Sonksen

CONTENTS

I.   INTRODUCTION

Concerned in recent years about its performance in world export markets, the United States has generated a search for effective ways to stimulate export growth. Although this effort has explored and recommended export promotion activities in a number of different areas, it has become increasingly focused on activities relating to export finance.

Most U.S. exports are financed by commercial banks. And even though special techniques not needed for domestic transactions are required because cross-border sales may involve such things as more complicated assessments of credit worthiness, considerations relating to the need to deal with foreign exchange, and two or more national sets of commercial law, these techniques are used routinely and are highly developed. They are, of course, well known internationally by those for whom export-import transactions are an important part of business. This is as true for financial institutions and other businesses involved in export trade in the United States, where exports play a comparatively minor role in terms of relative contribution to GNP, as it is for businesses in countries where exports have a much greater value relative to GNP. Even though the United States exports only 8.5 percent of its GNP compared with 22 percent for West Germany, for example, the value of U.S. exports is greater than that of any other country in the world. Thus, although a large segment of the U.S. business community involved primarily in domestic activities may know little about customary international financial and other trade practices relating to overseas sales, there is little reason to believe that those U.S. businesses that export or support imports are any less knowledgeable in this aspect of their work than their foreign competitors.

Export promotion efforts in the United States, however, have generally not been concerned with the customary and usual methods routinely used to finance most U.S. exports. They have focused instead on considerations of official credit support for exports.[1] It is particularly in this area of export financing that U.S. practice has not matched either the techniques or levels of support found in some of its chief industrial country competitors for third country markets.

There are a number of reasons why official credit support for exports has become increasingly regarded as a key element in many national export programs among the industrial countries. Increased emphasis on exports of long-term capital equipment with high values per unit of volume has placed greater importance on methods of financing exports at fixed interest rates and with long loan maturities, a combination of characteristics difficult to obtain solely from private financial markets. The increased importance of export markets in developing countries, where foreign exchange availability from external sources is often critical to a successful export sale and where credit risks are often perceived to be relatively great, has also laid stress on a greater role for official export credit support.

The U.S. experience with official credit support for exports is not of recent origin. The Export-Import Bank (Eximbank), the principal agency of the U.S. government involved in official credit support programs, received its initial charter in 1934. Despite its history of more than 45 years with official credit support programs, however, the United States has never fully reconciled this activity with the other elements of its economic system and foreign policy. As recently as October 1980, Eximbank stated in a report to Congress, "The United States is presently revising its philosophy and practice toward government support for exports. Both the Executive Branch and the Congress have conceptually moved to a stage of much greater government support...."[2] The report continues by stating, however, that neither the executive branch nor Congress have "...been able to take the next step of funding that support with adequate budgetary resources."[3]

The Eximbank may be correct in its assessment of government support for exports in a broad sense, but it is clear that no consensus has yet been reached concerning the narrower issue of government promotion of exports through official support of export credits. This appears to be true in a conceptual sense as well as in budgetary resources.

The fundamental issue today in the United States concerning official support of export credits is not what agency or agencies of the government should be included in the program or whether direct loans or credit guarantees are most effective; the central and still unresolved issue concerns the appropriateness of government involvement in the financing of exports. The questions that surround this issue are particularly important; they are directly linked with the critical issues of economic efficiency and philosophy. Direct government financial support of specific products or industries in private markets are an anachronism in the U.S. economy. This is especially true for official credit support for exports, where the primary purpose of government intervention in the market place is to provide an overseas buyer of U.S. exports with more credit and at more favorable terms than he could obtain from private financial institutions. This type of activity by the government appears, at least on the surface, to violate deeply held, basic tenets of the U.S. free market economy. Moreover, the beneficiary of official support of export credits in the United States is often seen as big business. Eximbank programs in support of U.S. exports are frequently described in simple terms, in fact, as subsidies to U.S. businesses.[4]

Those in the United States who believe that official credit support has a vital and appropriate role in the financing of exports would prefer to discuss the amounts and types of support to be provided by specific programs, but find that they must still come to grips with the basic question of why these programs are desirable in the first place. With those opposed basing their opposition on a belief that government financing of private exports is first of all an unwarranted intrusion in international and domestic markets, it is certainly difficult, and probably impossible, to focus on the former set of issues if the latter question is not resolved.[5] Those who believe the government has no role to play in the financing of exports are understandably not interested in how the Eximbank's discount loan program can be made more attractive to commercial banks. Nor, for that matter, is the Eximbank itself interested in this question, if it has no clear charter to enlist greater commercial bank participation in support of the expansion of exports. A recent critic of the Eximbank, and by implication of official credit support programs in general, stated this proposition in plain terms:

> The Export-Import Bank continues to make headlines and generate controversy, but nobody in Washington, D.C. -- at least nobody who makes headlines -- seems to be asking the right question about this remarkable institution. The question is whether the bank should be put out of business.[6]

II. THE CASE AGAINST OFFICIAL EXPORT CREDIT SUPPORT

The case against official credit support programs has many variants, but the principal arguments contend that these programs are in essence subsidies funded by taxpayers that primarily benefit exporters and may well do little to expand exports. The result is interference with free markets that results in an inefficient allocation of resources for the benefit of a few at the expense of many. If they are correct, these agruments leave little room for government participation in the financing of exports.

The Subsidy Element in Official Export Credit Programs

Official credit programs of the United States provide three basic types of financial support for exports. First, direct loans are made to finance exports either as buyers' credits or suppliers' credits, depending on the arrangement made between the U.S. exporter and the importer. The loan is made at a fixed interest rate at a level below then-current market interest rates.

The second type of program involves insurance, covering a major portion of the principal and at least some of the interest of an export loan made through commercial channels. In the United States the basic coverage is for political risk and/or commercial risk, and a fee is charged for the insurance coverage. Some of the official export credit programs of competitor countries include other types of coverage, such as exchange rate risk and inflation insurance, in their export insurance programs.

The third type of program provides guarantees for a major portion of the export financing provided by commercial banks under the program. The residual risk in lending then lies with the government agency providing the guarantee. In return for providing the guarantee, the agency charges the bank a fee.

None of these programs result in a direct production subsidy that would enable exporters to charge lower base prices for their products, and for this reason it has been argued that official export credit programs do not constitute a subsidy to exports.[7] That, however, begs the question. If government participation in the financing of exports provides nothing that cannot be obtained in private sector markets, is there justification for a government role in export financing? Under these conditions, the very existence of government export credit programs represents an unnecessary intrusion in the marketplace and puts government enterprise in direct competition with private enterprise with no obvious public purpose being served.

No one argues, however, that official export credit programs are a duplication of financial terms available in private sector financial markets. These programs all have the effect of making credit available at terms more favorable than could be provided in their absence. The Eximbank, for example, would be operating in violation of its charter were its programs to do otherwise. The subsidy element is present in the difference between the cost and availability of credit in the presence and absence of official export credit programs.

The subsidy element is clearly seen in a direct loan at a below-market rate of interest. The subsidy element is not so clearly visible when private credits are insured or guaranteed. If all transactions operate smoothly, no insurance or guarantee payments will have to be made because of default by the importer. Moreover, in the case of insurance for commercial risk, the insurer is the Foreign Credit Insurance Association (FCIA), which is privately owned by 51 U.S. insurance entities. And in the case of both insurance and guarantees, as has already been noted, fees are paid by those desiring the protection they afford. In the case of insurance, however, the maximum liability of the FCIA itself is limited, and the residual liability for claims in excess of the limits is the responsibility of the Eximbank. In the case of guarantees, the involvement of the Eximbank or the Commodity Credit Corporation (CCC) is based on the presumption that the risks involved could not or would not be borne by private enterprise for the fees charged (the roles of both the FCIA and the CCC in export support are discussed more thoroughly later in this paper). In both cases, services are received by those associated with private sector exports at a lower than free market cost, and the difference represents the amount of the subsidy provided by official participation in credit insurance and guarantee programs.[8]

Distortion of the Allocation of Resources

The U.S. economy is predicated on the belief that, as a general rule, free markets provide the most efficient allocation of resources possible. Government intervention in free markets in the form of taxes, subsidies, and regulation of commercial activity is hardly unknown in the United States. Such interference, though, is generally believed to be justified only where the private sector cannot or will not organize activity so that the parties involved pay for the costs, both social and private, which their activities generate, or where such interference captures sufficient benefits to cause the government to undertake an activity that is on a net basis deemed to be in society's interest.

Critics of official credit support programs in the United States claim that the subsidies provided for exports represent a diversion of resources from higher, more efficient uses, to lower, less productive uses.[9] They claim this can be seen clearly in the case of direct loans made by the Eximbank. The charter of the Eximbank requires it to be financially self-sustaining, but to fund exports it borrows from the Federal Financing Bank through the Treasury, and thus borrows with the full faith and credit of the U.S. government at a lower rate than a private commercial bank could secure. The Eximbank in turn makes its direct loans at lower than market rates. Even if the lending spread between its cost of borrowing and the rate at which it lends is the same as for private sector financial intermediaries, the practice, so the argument goes, represents an inefficient use of financial resources. An efficient use of resources would require the Eximbank to lend at market rates, where the funds would be allocated for better uses.

The argument is also made that not only does the Eximbank divert funds to less productive uses, but in so doing it adds to the demand for loanable funds and drives all interest rates higher. This implicity assumes that official export credit programs are effective in promoting exports, that these programs result in additional exports over what would occur in their absence (the concept of additionality). If the assumption is made that official export credit programs do not result in significant additional exports, as many critics of these programs argue, then these programs only substitute for credit demands that would otherwise be made by private sector financing of exports.

In any case, the validity of the argument that official export credit activities represent an ineffi- cient use of resources depends on the perceived return from these activities. If no additionality results from these programs, then it is indeed hard to argue that such activities do not represent an inefficient use of resources. On the other hand, an acknowledge- ment that additionality does exist, even to a significant extent, does not prove the reverse. Real income depends on the goods and services available for consumption, and exports and the resources used to promote them are used efficiently only if they buy more than they would if used at home.

The question of just what exports "buy," or what can be considered as the return from exports, is a crucial one. This question, along with the question of how much additionality is derived from official export credit programs, must be answered before any calcula- tion about the total yield of these efforts can be made.

Government assistance to an activity is recognized as appropriate and even necessary for an efficient allocation of resources when a divergence between private and public benefits accruing from an activity causes too little of it to be done by private enter- prise. If the benefits derived from exports accrue primarily to the exporter, and international markets are otherwise free of market interference (an heroic assumption), then market forces lead exporters to export until at the margin benefits equal costs, and until subsidies to expand exports beyond that point result in a loss from a national standpoint. If, though, there are significant benefits to the nation that exporters cannot capture, reliance on private market incentives alone results in a cessation of exports below the national optimum level.

A Narrow View of Benefits from Exports

It is extremely difficult to justify on grounds of both equity and economic efficiency the use of government funds in direct support of narrow business interests that fail to pass on these benefits. One of the most serious criticisms of official export credit programs, if it is valid, is that they benefit only the exporters. In his State of the Union message, President Reagan asked for a substantial reduction in the loan authority of the Eximbank, calling it a "business subsidy." "We are doing this," he said, "because the primary beneficiaries of taxpayer funds in this case are the exporting companies themselves -- most of them profitable corporations."[10] According to another critic, "Exporters generally raise prices and capture part of the Eximbank subsidy for themselves. Eximbank may be viewed largely as a welfare agency, handing out largess to export industries."[11]

Export industries unquestionably do benefit from official credit support programs. The total cost of the product is the effective price to the importer, and this consists not only of the direct price tag on the product, but the cost of financing it as well. If the official credit support package makes possible a sale that would not otherwise be made, then the exporter benefits in the same way he would have had the sale been to a domestic buyer. A normal profit would be made. If, on the other hand, the success of the export sale is not sensitive to the price or availability of credit, the exporter is foolish to pass the reduced price of the credit package on to the foreign buyer when he could capture all or a part of the credit savings by raising his own price.

It would be extremely difficult as a practical matter to determine whether or not exporters are charging higher prices on sales involving official export credit support than on similar sales financed entirely in the private sector. The ability of an exporter to do this depends on such things as the price sensitivity of his product, which in turn is affected

194

by such factors as the degree of competition he faces from others selling the same product, the availability of substitutes, and the financial condition of the importer, among other factors.

Additionality

One of the best indicators of the extent to which exporters could capture the government export subsidy comes from an assessment of the additionality element present in official export credit support programs. In simple terms, additionality is a measurement of the change in value of U.S. exports that results from official export support programs. If it can be demonstrated that a substantial portion of export sales that use government credit support would not be made in its absence, then it is reasonable to assume that at least some of the benefits of the government's concessionary finance package are passed on to the importer.

It is difficult conceptually, as well as practically, to determine the degree of additionality of government export credit programs with any precision. There are few cases where it can be said with certainty what would have happened, or what will happen, if something else does or does not happen. It is important, nevertheless, to try to assess additionality because it is crucial to arguments both opposing and favoring official export credit programs. To repeat, these programs can hardly be justified on the grounds of enhancing the profits of exporters or providing financial breaks to importers, with no resultant increase in exports. The purpose of these programs, after all, is to promote U.S. exports. If little or no additionality results from official export credit programs, then the question of who captures the export subsidy becomes more relevant. In general, it can be assumed that some greater subsidy element in export financing would result in greater export additionality if it were passed on to the importer. If the subsidy is captured by the exporter, then a greater subsidy element will only enlarge the exporter's profits.

Two primary methods have been used to measure additionality. The first method involves a survey of

195

export transactions that asks whether the official credit support or its absence was decisive in the ability or failure to export. The second method involves the use of sophisticated quantitative procedures, including econometric analysis. Both methods, however, have inherent weaknesses, which make their results less than conclusive.

There are many factors other than the terms of the financing package that enter into the competitiveness of a country's exports. The base price, the quality of the product, availability, the ability to support the export with spare parts and service after a sale is made, the nature of foreign competition and the willingness or ability to provide such things as coproduction, foreign exchange offsets, and transfers of technology may all be critical to the success of a proposed export.[12] A lack of competitiveness in these areas can, to some extent, be compensated for by the terms of the export finance package. Thus any given set of official credit terms might be decisive in one successful export effort and unnecessary to overcome other aspects of noncompetitiveness in another.

Additionality and competitiveness, although related, are not the same concept, however. Surveys of individual case histories are also used to determine the competitiveness of official export credit programs. In a review of 140 cases offered direct loan support and concluded between 1 April 1978 and 31 March 1979, the Eximbank determined that of the 55 export sales that U.S. firms did not win, 7 sales were lost because of insufficient competitive financing. The General Accounting Office (GAO), however, identified through 86 responses to a questionnaire it administered that during 1978, 10 sales worth $434 million, all of which the Eximbank had offered to support, were lost because of uncompetitive financing.[13] Additionality can only be present, to whatever extent, in export sales actually financed with official credit support assistance. Financing that uses an official credit support component, on the other hand, can be competitive even though other aspects of competitiveness may result in a failure to make a sale. Thus, although additionality requires competitive financing, the reverse may be true -- but does not have to be.

In any event, surveys of case histories can only give an indication of the degree of additionality that exists in official export credit support programs in the United States. It would be impossible to conclude from the Eximbank survey or the GAO questionnaire that all of the successful export sales whose financing had an official credit support component would not have been made in the absence of that official support.

In an attempt to overcome some of the difficulties involved in measuring additionality mentioned above, quantitative analyses that attempt to isolate the effects of export credit terms have been undertaken. In one such study by the U.S. Treasury, Dean DeRosa and William Nye examined the additionality of Eximbank programs for fiscal year 1976 (see Table 1).[14] They concluded that some degree of additionality existed for all three of the major types of Eximbank programs (direct loans, guarantees, and insurance). The greatest degree of additionality, they claimed, existed for Eximbank loans and was almost twice as great in relative terms as the additionality associated with guarantees, which in turn was only slightly higher than the additionality coefficient associated with insurance. For direct loans, the amount of additionality was greater than the direct loan component itself (only a portion of the export is financed by Eximbank credit). This was not the case with guarantees and insurance.

DeRosa and Nye concluded that "This study suggests that Eximbank's loan program has largely succeeded in fostering new U.S. exports in recent years, while its guarantees and insurance programs have been less effective." They cautioned, however, that "These results must be interpreted carefully. In particular our estimates of Eximbank additionality are based on popular beliefs about the limitations of private financing for U.S. export sales....Hence, these results cannot entirely dispel doubts about the ability of Eximbank to foster U.S. exports."[15]

DeRosa and Nye based their analysis on an assumption that certain types of loan characteristics generated additionality. For example, they assumed that some types of export loans, such as those with long maturities and fixed rates, were not available at all or were available only to a lesser extent from

197

TABLE 1

ADDITIONALITY OF EXIMBANK FY 1976
EXPORT CREDIT SUPPORT PROGRAM

(dollar amounts in millions)

	Loans	Guarantees	Insurance
Total Authorized Amount	$2,091.0	$ 591.9	$534.3
Total Export Contract Value	5,244.8	1003.8	707.9
Aggregate Addition- ality Coefficient	0.64	0.31	0.27
Total Additional Export Value	3,372.1	307.6	191.0

Source: See Dean A. DeRosa and William W. Nye, "Additionality" in the Activities of the Export-Import Bank of the United States, Hearings on Export Policy before the Sub-Committee on International Finance of the Senate Committee on Banking, Housing and Urban Affairs, 20-21 March 1978, 7 April 1978, 13 April 1978, Part 4, pp. 58-76.

private sector sources because of market imperfections. Exports receiving this type of Eximbank support thus involved some degree of additionality.

The analysis of DeRosa and Nye should, as they point out themselves, be used with caution. The validity of their estimates rests on the accuracy of their assumptions about what financing characteristics generate additionality, and it is impossible to make any definitive statement about the validity of these assumptions, other than, as DeRosa and Nye point out, they are "popularly" held.

Another quantitative study undertaken by the Congressional Research Service (CRS), disputes the Treasury findings.[16] Jane Gravelle found the additionality generated by the Eximbank's FY 1976 direct loan program to be only about half a billion dollars, or about eight times smaller than the Treasury estimate for aggregate additionality. If Gravelle's estimate, which was for direct loan programs only, is compared with DeRosa and Nye's estimate for direct loan component of Eximbank programs, the gap is narrowed, but only slightly.

Gravelle's methodology assumes that the subsidy component of the Eximbank loan program is in effect a lowering of price to the importer. She then attempts to measure the response of importers to that cut in price. It is for this reason that her analysis makes no attempt to include the additionality that might come from the guarantee and insurance programs run by Eximbank. The reduction in the price of the export cannot be calculated in the case of the guarantee and insurance programs with the same precision as it can be in the case of direct loans, where the market and subsidized rates of interest are known.

It is difficult to reconcile Gravelle's estimates of additionality with those of DeRosa and Nye. Central to the accuracy of Gravelle's numbers are the relevant responses of export sales to the lower cost of financing resulting from official credit support. There is no general agreement on what that response is, or how constant it is over time. These responses (price elasticities), moreover, are more appropriate for marketwide demand than for the sales, in the case where the market covers the world, of a single nation.

Increased additionality for U.S. exports in a given year might have no effect at all on world exports. If that were the case, the increased additionality due to official export credit support programs would result in increased market share for U.S. exports. Gravelle's methodology does not deal directly with the issue of market share as opposed to aggregate demand. It is clear that the elasticity of demand for an individual seller's product is not the same as the elasticity of total demand for the product. In some cases, a slight cut in price by an individual seller might result in a large increase in sales, with the increase coming at the expense of other producers who fail to match the price cut.

It is also difficult to determine the precise conditions of supply and demand for capital goods with long lives and high unit value. Production and demand are likely to be dominated by a few sellers and buyers. Conventional elasticity analysis is difficult to use under these circumstances even when there is no concern about market share.

Estimates of additionality attributable to government export credit programs must be used with extreme caution. There is general agreement, however, that these programs do generate some degree of additionality. It is also clear that the degree of additionality present depends on the nature of the program, i.e., loan, guarantee, or insurance, and further depends on the specific provisions applied in those programs. Direct loans at lower rates should generate greater additionality than those at higher rates, other things being equal.

Additionality is a variable that can change. If it is only additionality that is the concern, new programs with greater subsidy elements could conceivably be devised to produce the greater additionality, unless all of the subsidy is captured by the exporter. Even in this case, the greater profits would be likely to result in incentives to export more. Additionality at any cost, however, cannot be desirable. The additionality issue thus becomes a comparison of costs against benefits. This issue is, of course, central to the cases both for and against official credit support programs.

Other Arguments Against Official Export Credit Support Programs

Exchange Rate Depreciation. Opponents of official
credit support programs also maintain that if there is
a real need to expand U.S. exports to alleviate balance
of payment weakness, this will be accomplished easily
and efficiently through the market by a depreciation of
the dollar. Exchange rate depreciation makes exports
more price competitive than they would be otherwise.
As the magnitude of the record U.S. trade deficit in
1977 became apparent, it was suggested by senior
government economic policymakers that depreciation of
the dollar was the appropriate remedy for what had
become by then a persistent weakness in the U.S.
balance of payments.

An especially steep decline of the dollar in 1977
and subsequent continued weakness of the dollar finally
led to the strong Federal Reserve Bank support measures
of October 1979. There can be little doubt that U.S.
exports have benefitted from the enhanced price
competitiveness provided by that depreciation. After a
prolonged period of stagnation, U.S. export growth
accelerated at the end of the first quarter 1978 and
continued strong through March 1980. From the first
quarter 1978 to the first quarter 1980 exports rose
72 percent -- impressive by any standard. Exports
since that time, however, have increased little, if
any, probably as a result of a strong dollar and slower
growth overseas.

Exchange depreciation strengthens the balance of
payments not only by making exports more price competitive, but also by making imports more expensive. It
might be argued that it would be better to use government support to expand exports sufficiently to provide
the needed balance of payments support and avoid the
need to reduce imports and accommodate a rise in import
prices. That is exactly what needs to be done to
correct an overvalued currency, however. It would be
foolish in the extreme to try to sustain a basically
overvalued currency by boosting exports through
government subsidies.

The issue, however, is not so clear cut.
Intervention in foreign exchange markets is sanctioned

by International Monetary Fund guidelines when it is necessary to prevent "disorderly markets." In fact, intervention in exchange markets is a common feature of our international monetary system today. And even though the disorderly market criterion provides no definitive standards for judging market intervention, it seems safe to say that much of the intervention is designed to bridge periods of exchange strength or weakness. Under these circumstances, exchange rates may not reflect conditions of basic supply and demand for a currency.

This seems especially true when heavy international capital flows in response to national interest rate differential and concerns over international political developments are considered. Exchange rates are determined by supply and demand situations with respect to individual currencies. Demand for a currency resulting from capital flows has the same impact on exchange rates as demand for export-import transaction purposes. It is not clear that the exchange rate set by total supply and demand conditions will reflect rates that would be determined by supply and demand conditions for exports and imports. A country with heavy capital inflows, caused, for example, by its status as an international haven country, might see its exports, otherwise competitive in international markets, suffer as a result. Official export credit could be seen under these circumstances as a measure restoring exports to the position that their basic competitive position would give them in world markets.

In the case of the United States, currency depreciation involves another factor that most other nations would not have to consider. Because of the relatively small size of the international sector, a decline of the foreign exchange value of the dollar may have a relatively mild effect on U.S. domestic trade flows and inflation. Because of the role of the dollar as the world's major reserve currency, however, that dollar depreciation may have a major impact on another nation's international reserve position, as much of the world trade is denominated in dollars. Occupying the role that it does in world trade and in the international financial system, the United States, in the pursuit of its own narrower interests as well as global peace and prosperity, has an obligation to coordinate its international economic policy with its foreign policy much more closely than it has in the past.

Lending in Inflationary Times.   Another   issue related to the legitimacy of official export support concerns the appropriateness of extending loans at lower than market interest rates during a time of high inflation such as the United States is in now. The real rate of interest to a borrower or lender is equal to the nominal rate minus the rate of inflation. Borrowers repay their loans in dollars of lower value because of the effects of inflation. Nominal interest rates are driven up with inflation to reflect this relationship.   Because of the need to maintain a predictable relationship between the costs of funding a loan and the proceeds of the loan on the lender's side, and the cost of the loan and the earnings from the use of the loan on the borrower's, loans with any substantial maturity usually carry variable interest rates expressed as a percentage spread over a variable interest rate such as the prime lending rate of commercial banks.

International export credit competition, however, has resulted in generally fixed interest rates for long-term loans (over five years) at below market interest rates from official credit agencies. In 1979 the average rate on these loans charged by the Eximbank was 8.6 percent. The U.S. consumer price index rose 11.3 percent in 1979 and 13.5 percent in 1980. If the pace of inflation continues at near the same rates, that would reflect a negative real rate of interest of 3-5 percent over the life of those loans.

Should the U.S. finance exports through the government at a negative real interest rate? Here again, the answer depends on the perceived benefits from the financed exports in comparison with the costs. In the case of a negative real interest rate, the appropriate costs for comparison purposes are the opportunity costs, or the difference in the return (or minimization of real loss) achieved by using the funds for other purposes. The answer thus depends crucially on the perception of additionality and the value of the additional exports resulting from official credit support programs.

<u>Exports and Tight Monetary Policy</u>.   A   related
issue concerns the appropriateness of exempting exports
from the effects of tight monetary and fiscal policies.
The call for a lower Eximbank profile by the Reagan
administration has been justified on a number of
grounds, one of which is the need for austerity in
government programs in general and a feeling that
export programs should be no exception to this
requirement.[17]

Is this argument valid? The answer is not an easy
one.   In purely domestic markets, all buyers and
sellers face the same general economic policies,
although they may not all be affected equally by them.
To some extent, though, the constraints imposed by
these policies apply to all in the market. A general
reduction in demand does not necessarily cause a seller
to lose market share during an economic downturn and
perhaps in his future market share as well.

In the case of U.S. exports, third country
competitors may face easier credit conditions. If not,
they may be helped by their own government export
credit agencies. If one exporter has steady and
reliable access to concessionary financing, then
importers will find him more predictable and easier to
deal with. This constitutes a major advantage in
export markets. The first exporter may well find his
market shut off even when he is able to provide
competitive financing in the future. In the case of
domestic markets, what one seller is unable to regain
in market share after a period of tightness is likely
to be gained by another, and there is no loss to the
country. In the case of exports, the loss of market
share may be to another country.

As Table 2 demonstrates, U.S. market interest
rates have generally been higher than those of its
primary industrial-country competitors in recent years.
Market interest rates, of course, reflect many interrelated variables, including domestic inflation rates
and monetary policy. If all export financing reflected
interest rates as determined by market conditions, then
the priority a country attached to its export competitiveness would be reflected by its broad economic and
financial policies. Higher interest rates in a country
that made its exports less competitive would be a
matter of national policy.

The interest rate differentials that affect exports financed with the assistance of official credit support programs, however, are not those shown in Table 2. The existence of these subsidized programs in competitor countries would, of course, widen those differentials in the absence of matching programs in the United States. Under these circumstances the cause of a country's lack of competitiveness may not be due to fundamental economic factors. Even though it would be appropriate in general terms for market rates to widen in times of tight monetary policies and high interest rates in the United States, the differential as influenced by foreign officials export credit support programs might have unacceptable effects on U.S. exports that could be neutralized only by general economic policies that may be unacceptable on other grounds. The United States might find it desirable to increase support for its official credit support programs even during periods of tight monetary and fiscal policies.

TABLE 2

INTEREST RATE COMPARISONS*: 1970-1980
(annual average)

	1977	1978	1979	1980
U.S.	5.8%	8.8%	11.3%	13.1%
France	9.2	7.8	9.7	12.2
Germany	4.2	3.7	6.7	9.4
Japan	6.1	4.6	6.2	11.5
U.K.	7.4	9.7	13.8	16.5

*Three-month commercial deposit rate for U.S.; three-month interbank rate for all others.

Source: International Unit, Economic Research Department, Chemical Bank.

III. THE CASE FOR OFFICIAL EXPORT CREDIT SUPPORT

Business Week, expressing its concern over official U.S. export credit policy in a recent issue, said, "the President must decide once and for all that exports shall have top priority, not only in the Administration's rhetoric, but in the resources it devotes to promoting U.S. products in world markets." It further stated that, "It will take strong leadership to persuade Congress and the nation that exports are crucial to U.S. strength."[18]

Are Exports Important?

There is no question that the Eximbank is limited by a fundamental lack of commitment to its role by Congress. This attitude reflects the broader skepticism noted earlier about the role exports and agencies like the Eximbank should play in the private commercial life of the United States. This lack of commitment demonstrates that, apart from those who benefit most directly from official credit support activities, many individuals remain unconvinced that broader benefits are received from these activities.

There are undoubtedly many economic benefits that come from a strong U.S. export performance.[19] Most economic activities, however, provide obvious benefits. The employment in export industries is often cited as a reason for supporting U.S. exports through official programs.[20] But, again, all economic activity provides employment. Exports can make no unique claim on government financial resources on this basis. In fact, if this were an important objective of government expenditure programs, funds would be spent on industries that were most labor intensive, and export industries in the United States would not likely qualify. As a practical matter, shifting labor out of declining export industries would not be costless, especially if those export industries would be competitive in a free trade environment, which does not exist today. On the other hand, the long-run cost of trying to maintain employment in fundamentally uncompetitive export industries would be far higher than the costs of shifting labor and other resources away from those industries to areas where they would be more productive; and in the long-run, those shifts would take place anyway.

Other commonly cited reasons for supporting exports through government programs relate to concerns with U.S. balance of payments performance, depreciation of the dollar, and inflation, all of which are inter-related. It needs to be emphasized again, however, that exports must have a special beneficial role to play to have a valid claim on special government support through export credit subsidies.

The Special Role of Exports. Exports in fact do have a claim to a special role in the U.S. economy. It is in the role of an earner of foreign exchange that exports are unique. Although the production of an export may provide no more employment or have no different impact on technology than the production of a good for the domestic market, it is different from the good sold in the domestic market because, in addition, it earns foreign exchange, the foundation on which a strong balance of payments must ultimately rest.

The claim on support by government programs must rest on more than the role of exports as a source of foreign exchange, however. As a fundamental proposition, public programs should benefit the public, not just the direct beneficiaries of the program. They should be imbued with the public interest. Exports must be not only beneficial in a private sense, but they must also create a substantial element of social benefit. Furthermore, these benefits must meet the criterion mentioned earlier, that is, they must be such that existing market conditions cannot provide adequate incentives to induce the private sector to export in socially optimal amounts. Exports, or at least certain categories of exports, must create significant externalities.

Finally, government export credit programs must involve additionality and must be more efficient in boosting exports than other methods of export promo-tion. If, for example, the most efficient way to promote exports is through the maintenance of enhanced productivity in a low inflation environment, then that is, of course, vastly preferable to government export credit programs.

Export Performance and Its Importance to the United States

U.S. export performance affects a number of factors that have other than economic benefits. The strategic role of exports in U.S. foreign policy is one such factor discussed in an earlier paper in this series, Dr. Penelope Hartland-Thunberg's "The Political and Strategic Importance of Exports." As noted in that study, a country's ability to compete successfully in world markets and control its external payments situation is taken as a reflection of the economic strength and managerial competence of that country. The same is true of the international position of the country's currency over time. Persistent large trade and current account deficits accompanied by persistent depreciation of the national currency in foreign exchange markets is not taken as a sign of techno-logical leadership and strong management. It raises questions, instead, about the future influence of that country not only in international economic affairs, but in international political and military affairs as well. For many countries, in fact, international economic strength provides a source of power and influence that would not be warranted by military strength.

The United States especially needs to pay closer attention to its international economic position than it has during at least the past few years. Despite the fact that U.S. imports are relatively small in compari-son to GNP (9.5 percent in 1980), the United States is still the world's largest importer. And even though U.S. exports in 1980 comprised only 8.5 percent of GNP, the United States is also the world's largest exporter. Developments in the international sector of the U.S. economy that seem comparatively insignificant in aggregate to the United States often generate extremely important consequences overseas, affecting the United States as serious issues in other areas.

If exports are important to the United States in general, and not just to those who export, what is the best way to promote sound long-run export growth? First, and most important, is a sound competitive position regarding the basic criteria of price, quality, service, and availability. There are reasons for believing, however, that this may not be enough in international markets as they exist today to ensure a sound export position. In their study on U.S. export competitiveness, Raymond Mikesell and Mark Farah conclude that "the loss of U.S. shares in the LDC market over the 1970-1978 period cannot be attributed to a decline in U.S. overall price and cost competitiveness."[21]

A failure of exports to meet standards of high quality, for example, can nullify cost competitiveness, but there are other factors that seem especially important now which could also have this result. International markets today are characterized by a significant element of state intervention. Governments almost by definition are motivated by factors beyond the traditional profit motive. (See Appendix I.) This is one of the primary reasons for the development of extensive official export support programs.

Official Export Credit Competition

Although many techniques are used by the major industrial country competitors of the United States to support export sales, including direct subsidies or tax relief to industries that hold promise of becoming export oriented, primary reliance has been placed on export financing supported by government programs. The importance of financing to an export sale, particularly when high-value items with long lives are involved, can hardly be over stressed.

The price of the export itself may vary considerably depending on the terms of financing. The nominal price attached to the export itself is only the point of departure in many cases. If the terms of the loan are attractive enough, shortcomings in product quality may be overlooked. In many instances, the financing has more to do with the affordability of the export than any other single variable. Even when no competition for the sale exists, the availability of financing may well determine whether the sale will be made. Many developing countries have a desire and particular need to conserve scarce foreign exchange and condition their purchase of exports on the availability of an adequate package to finance them.

Official Export Credits. Accordingly, many of the various government institutions supporting export sales have developed large, comprehensive programs. Today these institutions can provide export credits that offer substantial advantages over anything that can be obtained in commercial financial markets. Some of the advantages are more constant credit availability, longer terms, greater flexibility with regard to export payment terms, and lower interest rates.

The attractiveness of official export credit support has made such institutions as the Export Credits Guarantee Department (ECGD) in the United Kingdom, the Export-Import Bank of Japan, Hermes of West Germany, and the Compagnie Francaise d'Assurances pour le Commerce Exterieur (COFACE) in France central figures in export sales competition. The competition is centered around medium and long-term export credits and a wide variety of financing techniques -- ranging from direct loans at subsidized rates to insurance for short-term credits -- are utilized by these institutions.

Official subsidization of export financing is an established custom. The Eximbank was created in 1934, and the ECGD is more than 60 years old. Over the years, these organizations have exhibited great flexibility and ingenuity in adjusting their financing techniques to changes in export markets and national policy.[22] Table 3 gives some indication of the various programs offered.

There are many factors that should be taken into account in determining the relative competitive position of a country's official export support programs. Basically, however, they can be divided into three basic elements: (1) the number and variety of programs used, (2) the effectiveness of the way in which programs are administered, and (3) the quantitative measures of support that concern the size of the programs, fees for guarantees and insurance, and interest rates charged on loans. In a survey of U.S.

210

TABLE 3

EXPORT CREDIT AND INSURANCE PROGRAMS
IN THE MAJOR TRADING NATIONS

	Canada	France	Germany	Italy	Japan	U.K.	U.S.
Preferential Medium And Long-Term Fixed-Rate Export Credits	X[1]	X	X	X	X	X	X
Financial Guarantees	X	X	X			X	X
Commercial and Political Risk Insurance	X	X	X	X	X	X	X
Inflation Risk Ins.		X				X	
Exchange Rate Risk Ins.	X	X	X	X	X	X	
Mixed Credits[2]		X	X		X	X	X
Performance and Bid Bond Guarantees/Ins.	X	X	X	X	X	X	X[3]
Local Cost Support	X	X	X	X	X	X	

[1]Long-term export credits only.
[2]Although the countries indicted have used mixed credits, the extent of this usage has varied widely.
[3]Offered through the Overseas Private Investment Corporation (OPIC).

Source: Report to the U.S. Congress on Export Credit Competition and the Export-Import Bank of the United States, October 1980, and Financing Exports and Imports - A Guide for the Use of World-Wide Banking Services in International Trade, Chemical Bank.

bankers and exporters, the Eximbank was compared with similar institutions in France, Germany, Italy, Japan, and the United Kingdom regarding the effectiveness of short, medium, and long-term programs in 1978 and 1979. The United States' highest ranking was fourth, and its overall position was higher only than that of Italy.[23]

As Table 4 illustrates, the Eximbank also ranked low in 1978 and 1979 in terms of official export support authorizations. For official credit support relative to total country exports, the Eximbank ranked last in both years. Tables 5 and 6 demonstrate that effective interest rates, which are a blend of the rate charged by Eximbank and the privately financed portion of the export credit, were also generally higher than those charged by their foreign competitors.

Interest rates charged are of special importance to an assessment of competitiveness. As noted earlier, DeRosa and Nye found that the additionality associated with loans was almost twice that associated with insurance and guarantees. Interest rates charged by Eximbank have clearly not been competitive in terms of nominal levels.

Is it valid to use nominal interest rates when assessing the competitiveness of programs across country lines? It is claimed that this involves an element of interest rate illusion, since movement in exchange rates can add to or offset the nominal cost of interest.[24] Table 7 contains some measures of movements in some industrial country currencies in 1980. In all but the case of the Canadian dollar, the variation from the currency highs against the U.S. dollar to their lows was 15 percent (14.8 percent for the pound) or higher, although most of the currencies depreciated against the dollar for the year as a whole. The appreciation of the U.S. dollar in 1980 was in sharp contrast to its performance in 1977, 1978, and 1979.

Given this kind of volatility in foreign exchange markets, with official intervention a key factor in determining at least the extent, if not the direction of the movements, an exporter is faced with great uncertainty and difficulty in making exchange rate forecasts. Under these circumstances a significant nominal interest rate differential represents an

TABLE 4

OFFICIAL EXPORT SUPPORT AUTHORIZED[1]

($ millions)

	1978	1979	% Change
Canada	4,030	3,535	(-) 12.3
France	30,660	32,155	4.9
Germany	14,960	14,505	(-) 3.1
Italy	8,705	8,020	(-) 7.9
Japan	31,810	39,355	23.7
United Kingdom	35,115	33,430	(-) 4.8
United States	7,375	9,490	28.7

[1]Official agencies in the European countries and Japan require cover for all transactions receiving financing support. Thus the figures for these countries represent only insurance and guarantee authorizations. Data for Canada and the United States, countries where this requirement is not imposed, reflect both financing support and insurance/guarantee cover.

Source: Report to the U.S. Congress on Export Credit Competition and The Export-Import Bank of the United States, October 1980, p. 4.

TABLE 5

COMPARATIVE LONG-TERM (OVER 5 YEARS)
OFFICIALLY-SUPPORTED INTEREST RATES
(percent)

Average Rates: Country[3]	Face Rate[1]		Fees/Insurance[2]		Effective	
	1978	1979	1978	1979	1978	1979
France	7.50	7.50	0.85	0.85	8.35	8.35
Germany	8.00	8.20	0.70	0.70	8.70	8.90
Italy	7.80	7.80	0.50	0.50	8.30	8.30
Japan	8.00	7.85	[4]	[4]	8.00	7.85
United Kingdom	7.50	7.50	0.60	0.60	8.10	8.10
United States	8.70	8.60	--	--	8.70	8.60

[1] Actual rate charged for nonair, nonship and nonnuclear transactions in selected countries.

[2] Standard insurance premium and banking fees, excluding commitment fees, for public sector buyers in selected countries.

[3] Except for the United States, the rate shown is the rate charged on the officially-supported portions. For the United States, the rate shown is the "blended" cost for the financed portion.

[4] Fees and insurance are included in the "face" rate for Japan.

Source: Report to the U.S. Congress on Export Credit Competition and the Export-Import Bank of the United States, October 1980, p. 15.

TABLE 6

MEDIUM-TERM FIXED EXPORT CREDIT INTEREST RATES
(percent)

	1978		1979	
	Face	Effective[1]	Face	Effective[1]
France	7.25	8.00	7.25	8.00
Germany	7.00	7.80	7.50	8.30
Italy	8.60	9.00	8.60	9.00
Japan	7.25	7.85	7.25	7.85
U. K.	7.25	7.85	7.25	7.85
United States[2]	9.05	9.25	10.95	11.20

[1] Includes the average insurance premium for a medium-term sale to public buyer in an upper-tier developing country such as Brazil.

[2] Discount loan program rate plus 1.0 percent.

Source: Report to the U.S. Congress on Export Credit Competition and the Export-Import Bank of the United States, October 1980, p. 25.

215

TABLE 7

SELECTED CURRENCY RANGES IN 1980

(in currency units per U.S. dollar)

	High	Low	Percent Change 1/2/80 to 12/31/80	Average	Percent Variations High - Low
Mark	1.703	2.018	-12.4	1.814	15.9
Date	1/3/80	12/11/80			
Yen	201.8	259.3	+17.8	225.2	22.2
Date	12/30/80	4/18/80			
Pound	2.4530	2.1370	+ 7.0	2.3273	14.8
Date	1/4/80	4/4/80			
Canadian	.8767	.8249	- 1.9	.8556	5.1
Date	7/7/80	12/16/80			
French Franc	3.998	4.675	-11.4	4.218	15.9
Date	1/3/80	12/16/80			
Italian Lira	799.4	955.1	-13.6	854.0	16.3
Date	1/3/80	12/16/80			

Source: International Unit, Economic Research Department, Chemical Bank.

element of certainty and may well be the decisive factor in an importer's analysis of the cost of credit. In periods of lower exchange rate volatility, less massive official intervention in foreign exchange markets and less variance in economic performance parameters among key currency nations, differences in nominal interest rates among countries are expected to be less important in calculations of the real cost of credit.

In any case, the Eximbank's credit programs are neither as varied in qualitative terms nor as competitive in quantitative terms as those of its chief overseas competitors. These differences caused the Comptroller General to conclude that the Eximbank cannot consistently offer interest rates to U.S. exporters competitive with that offered by other official credit institutions to their own exporters. He concluded that on an average loan, interest rate differentials can mean as much as $5 million in additional cost to the purchase of U.S. exports.[25]

Efforts to Limit Export Credit Competition.
Almost from the moment that official credit support institutions were created, it was recognized that there existed a potential for expensive credit wars between nations. Although believing that some subsidization of exports was worthwhile, nations recognized at the same time that there was a limit beyond which the return did not justify the cost. To avoid credit wars, the Berne Union was formed more than 45 years ago to bring these institutions together for the purpose of exchanging information on credit practices and to formulate nonbinding credit guidelines.

These provisions worked reasonably well until the early 1970s when, for reasons at least partially related to the turbulence that occurred in the international monetary system, export credit competition began to heat up. Persistent attempts have been made since that time to limit international export credit competition, including an informal gentlemen's agreement in 1974 and negotiations that led to unilateral declarations in 1976 by the United States, West Germany, France, Italy, Switzerland, Canada, and Japan about the export credit guidelines they would follow. These unilateral declarations, in turn, led to the

Arrangement on Guidelines for Officially Supported Export Credits agreed to at the Organization for Economic Cooperation and Development (OECD) headquarters in February 1978.

The arrangement attempted to set limits on export credit competition in three areas: minimum down payments, minimum interest rates, and maximum credit maturities. The minimum down payment was set at 15 percent. Minimum interest rates were determined for three loan maturity groups and for three classes of countries. The maturities, country groups, and interest rates set in 1978 were as shown below:

Borrowing Countries	Maturities		
	2-5 Yrs.	5-8.5 Yrs.	8.5-10 Yrs.
Relatively Rich	7.75%	8.0%	No Credit Provisions
Intermediate	7.25%	7.75%	No Credit Provisions
Relatively Poor	7.25%	7.5%	2.5%

Credit with maturities under two years was excluded from the agreement, and credit with a maturity of more than ten years was prohibited. Excluded from the coverage of the agreement were military items, aircraft (the subject of a separate "understanding"), nuclear power plants, agricultural commodities, and shipping.

The 1978 arrangement was only an interim step that represented progress in the drive to avert an export credit war. It left many nations, particularly the United States, unsatisfied, and subsequent negotiations have taken place within the OECD to bring export credit policies more closely into line with market conditions. In April 1980, a draft of a study on official export credit rates was presented to the OECD Export Credit Group. The study proposed that basic interest rate guidelines be changed and offered two proposals for consideration as possible replacements. One proposal, favored by the United States and referred to as a differentiated rate system, calls for different interest rates for various currencies. These rates would be tied to market rates of interest in each country and would be changed periodically to reflect changes in market rates. The second proposal, the uniform moving matrix system, called for a uniform interest rate for all member country currencies.[26]

It was hoped that agreement on one or the other of these proposals would be reached at the May 1980 meeting of the OECD credit group. Participants at the meeting were unable to reach agreement, and after agreeing on a 75 basis point increase in rates for relatively rich and intermediate countries and a 25 basis point increase for relatively poor countries, the group adjourned, stipulating that a new agreement should be reached by 1 December 1980.

Another series of meetings was held during Autumn 1980, but produced no agreement. In a letter to the chairmen of the Committees on Banking, Finance, and Urban Affairs in the House and Senate dated 31 October 1980, John L. Moore, Jr., chairman of the Export-Import Bank, wrote that "there is reason for guarded optimism regarding the possibility that international negotiations may yield significant long-run budgetary and/or financial relief. While several major obstacles to final agreement have yet to be resolved, there is near-unanimous international agreement that the level of export credit rates should be raised quite considerably and kept more in line with money-market trends."[27]

Despite the feeling that a new agreement was close, negotiations failed to reach that goal during 1980. Although some progress has been made to limit export credit competition, there are reasons for believing that the major industrial nations may not abolish these practices to any sigificant extent. Past agreements, official or otherwise, have often been honored in the breach. At the same time, the nonoil developing nations are entering what will be another difficult period for them in the wake of the latest and what is likely to be a continuing round of oil price increases. The subsidy element that official export credits provide will be eagerly sought by this important group of countries as they try to maintain import programs essential to their continued economic development.

For their part, it is not yet clear to what extent the industrial nations, apart from some notable exceptions, really desire to limit export credit competition. If one nation extends more liberal credit terms and its practices are not matched by its competitors, it may well increase its export market share. Although it may not increase its share of world exports if its terms are matched by its competitors, more liberal credit terms by all industrial nations will lead to greater exports for all countries than would otherwise be the case. It is not obvious at this point that the major industrial countries will conclude that this is not worth the cost of the subsidies, especially since interest rates in these countries are or shortly will be coming down from their recent high levels. This decline in interest rates will lower the absolute cost of these subsidies. At the same time, the growth of world trade is slowing, and exports have not become less important to countries like Germany and Japan, which traditionally have had strong current account surpluses but now find themselves in heavy current account deficit.

IV. U.S. OFFICIAL EXPORT CREDIT POLICY

What Should It Be?

Official export credit policy of the United States should be designed to support and complement U.S. international economic policy. It is, or should be, an integral part of that policy. As such, the overriding objective and top priority of the United States in the area of official credit policy should be to continue to seek to reduce the subsidy elements in a national export credit programs permitted by the OECD Arrangement on Guidelines for Officially Supported Export Credits. As noted earlier, the United States has pursued this through negotiations, but with only limited success up to the present time. These negotiations should continue. The United States, however, should not reject out of hand other methods that might achieve its goals. The U.S. Treasury Department has suggested that a willingness by the United States to increase the competitiveness of its official credit programs in the absence of an agreement that would bring these programs closer to market conditions would exert sufficient pressure on other parties to the arrangement to achieve U.S. aims. This idea should be carefully explored and not casually rejected. Again, as noted earlier, a policy of more closely matching the competition by increasing the depth and breadth of U.S. official credit programs might prevent other nations from increasing their export shares but might still result in an overall increase in exports. What the reactions of the other parties to the agreement would be is conjectural.

In any case, the United States should recognize as a guiding general principle that present circumstances in international markets are characterized by active market intervention by governments. The United States cannot by itself enforce free market principles in international trade markets. Furthermore, its efforts to intervene in international markets on behalf of U.S. exporters has produced an official credit system that is neither as broad in terms of coverage nor as deep in terms of the subsidy element as those of most of its primary industrial world competitors. Given these facts, and with concern over its long term export performance, the United States is confronted with a basic policy choice. Should government and industry in the United States seek a new and innovative relationship that would preserve the basic features of the private enterprise system but provide U.S. exporters with a more equitable basis on which to compete in international markets? Is this in fact possible?

U.S. official export credit policy should not have as its ultimate goal the matching of its foreign competition. There is no reason to seek imitation for its own sake. There is not much to be said in support of a program that would allow a key element of U.S. international trade policy to be made in foreign capitals. U.S. trade policy should be designed to meet U.S. trade goals in the most cost effective way possible. U.S. trade goals, in turn, should be carefully and completely integrated with U.S. domestic and foreign policy. Not unless this is done can the magnitude and character of U.S. official export credit support programs be developed appropriately.

Sound Basic Economic Policy. Before proceeding further, though, it needs to be stressed that export credit policy cannot substitute for attractive products in stimulating exports. Although competitive prices and high quality may not be sufficient in many cases to export successfully in today's markets, they certainly are necessary.

Also of overriding importance is a basically sound economy that achieves strong growth in productivity and keeps inflation under control. Without control of inflation, interest rates cannot be maintained at levels that would allow U.S. financial institutions to offer export financing rates comparable to those offered overseas in countries like Germany and Switzerland, where inflation rates and interest rates have been far below those in the United States.

V. OFFICIAL EXPORT CREDIT PROGRAMS
IN THE UNITED STATES

Despite the lack of a consensus about what their roles ought to be, or even whether they have an appropriate place in the U.S. export structure, there is at least a general reluctance in the United States to abolish the central export credit programs that presently exist. This ambivalence has produced programs of an off-again on-again nature. Nevertheless, the major official export credit programs of the United States are well developed and mature. The key elements of these programs are described below.

The Export-Import Bank of the United States

The central position in the U.S. official export structure is filled by the Eximbank. Although it is not a formal requirement of its charter, the Eximbank has been run as a financially self-supporting institution. Its charter does require it to be competitive with its sister institutions overseas in terms of the support it offers U.S. exports. These principles may prove to be mutually incompatible. Between June 1979 and June 1980, the Eximbank's funding costs moved above the average interest rate charged on its loans. Even so, the nominal interest rates offered by the Eximbank did not in general match the rates charged by its competitors. (See Tables 5 and 6.)

The Eximbank does not receive appropriated funds from Congress. It funds its activities by borrowing from the Treasury or the Federal Financing Bank and repays these borrowings from the proceeds of the repayments of the loans it makes and the charges for the insurance and guarantees that it issues. (At one time, the Eximbank relied upon debentures and participation certificates to meet its needs for long-term funds. At least for the present, that practice has been discontinued.) Far from having operated at a loss in the past, the Eximbank has paid more than $1 billion from its earnings to the Treasury since it was chartered 47 years ago. It is obvious, though, that it cannot continue to make loans at a rate below its own funding costs and continue to remain self-sustaining.

223

The Budget. Even when there is a positive funding spread between the rate at which it borrows and the rate at which it lends, the activities of the Eximbank show up in the federal budget on the expense side. The Eximbank's activites can be separated into the three main components mentioned earlier: loans, both direct and discount loans to banks, guarantees to banks that finance exports, and insurance, which is administered jointly with the FCIA.

Congress exercises control over Eximbank activities in these areas through the budget process. Because it receives no appropriated funds, Congress sets limits on the extent of Eximbank activities in each of its three main programs. Rather than placing limits on its liabilities owed to the Treasury or the Federal Financing Bank, limits are placed on the assets that Eximbank can create. In recognition of the difference in the nature of its lending programs on the one hand and the credit guarantee and insurance programs on the other, loans count against Eximbank authorizations on a one-for-one basis, while 25 percent of guarantees and insurance authorizations are counted against its limits. Each fiscal year a new ceiling or new authorization is imposed by the Congress on the Eximbank. In addition, the Export-Import Bank Act sets an overall ceiling of $40 billion for Eximbank authorizations.

In any given year, the Eximbank's authorization in any of the three areas does not necessarily reflect an actual disbursement of funds. Funds are disbursed in accordance with the conditions attached to the various transactions, and in some cases the lag between the date of authorization and actual disbursement of funds is considerable. Budget figures for the Eximbank thus do not necessarily reflect the disbursement of funds, nor do they necessarily reflect the impact of actual Eximbank borrowing from the Treasury or the Federal Financing Bank. Moreover, repayments of loans are not counted against the ceiling on new authorization in any given year.

Given the special circumstances of the Eximbank's budget, special federal budgetary treatment would seem justified. The Eximbank authorization, nevertheless, is treated in the federal budget as if it were another ordinary line item that relied on appropriated funds.

224

A budget is far more than a record of planned financial transactions. It is, or certainly ought to be, a document used for planning and control. Congress must be aware of Eximbank plans and activities, and to this extent the Eximbank should occupy a place in the federal budget document.

From 1971 to 1974, Eximbank was afforded off-budget treatment. The advantage of this status is that charges in authorizations have no impact on formal federal budget expenditures. According to one line of reasoning, a return to an off-budget position for the Eximbank would allow the debate over its authorizations to be removed from the annual debate on the size of the federal deficit. Some fear, however, that this might also reduce an important element of control over Eximbank activities. Beyond the debate over whether Eximbank authorizations should be in or off budget, it is important that the process used to determine the level of authorizations convey a factual image of the total impact of Eximbank activities. For this reason it does not seem appropriate that Eximbank should be included as an integral part of the federal budget. It might, instead, be included as a special exhibit. It is not that Eximbank activities should have a higher priority than other budget items when the need to cut expenditures and balance the budget is paramount, it is simply that a consideration of the budget along these lines is a red herring. Present budgetary treatment of the Eximbank conveys a false sense of the impact of its activities on the federal budget or on macroeconomic aggregates in the U.S. economy.

The Budget and the Competitive Position of the Eximbank. To fulfill the obligation under its charter to be competitive, the Eximbank certainly does not have to match the amount and terms of support offered by its competitors on an item by item basis. There is no strict standard that can be used to define competitiveness, and even though it was noted earlier that U.S. exporters and banks do not consider the Eximbank very competitive relative to its sister institutions, there is proof of a sort that Eximbank has been competitive in at least a limited way. Eximbank authorization limits have been fully utilized. In FY 80, the ceiling on guarantees and insurance became restrictive for the first time. Loan ceilings, in contrast, have placed serious constraints on the Eximbank for some time. By definition, then, Eximbank programs have been fully utilized, and it is difficult to describe a fully used facility as noncompetitive so far as actual transactions are concerned. That describes an ability to compete only to the limits of the authorizations, however.

The limits on direct loans have been especially restrictive. Eximbank has had to select carefully the uses of its limited funds. It describes the results of the procedure it uses in allocating its scarce resources as making Eximbank "selectively competitive."

LOAN AUTHORIZATIONS
($ billions)

FY 78	FY 79	FY 80	FY 81*	FY 82*
3.4	4.5	4.6	5.1	4.4

*proposed by the Reagan administration.

Because no foreign aid appropriations bill was ever passed for FY 81, the $5.9 billion loan authorization was set in a continuing resolution. The proposed reduction in the direct loan ceiling for FY 82 of almost one-third comes at a time when demand for Eximbank credit is growing rapidly.

Because it is going to be faced with tight lending constraints regardless of how the current FY 82 budget problems are resolved, how can the Eximbank best use the funds that it will have available? It is in the intermediate term loan area in which the Eximbank appears to be least competitive.[28] More emphasis in this area, however, would only come at the expense of long-term programs.

The question of how direct loan authority should be distributed between programs of different maturities involves issues about what industries and what size businesses should be the recipients of direct loan support. Aircraft have traditionally been the area of greatest concentration of Eximbank loans. They are high value per volume items and thus provide some economies in the costs of loan administration, while the intermediate loans are usually smaller in value.

The producers of aircraft and other big ticket items are themselves large corporations but utilize large numbers of small businesses as subcontractors.

The question of additionality is also important. As mentioned earlier, the additionality associated with loans was about twice that of guarantees and insurance. (See Table 1.) Since the Eximbank direct loans have an immediate and specific subsidy component while the subsidy element in guarantees and insurance is more obscure, greater additionality might thus be expected from the loan program; but there seems to be little basis for expecting different degrees of additionality from long as opposed to intermediate term loans.

Since the Eximbank's competitors receive direct subsidies or are generally able to borrow at lower rates, the Eximbank has been unable to match the subsidy element in the loans offered by the competitors. Because the rate charged by the Eximbank is a blend of its own lower rate with higher private sector financing, one way for the Eximbank to increase the competitiveness of its financing would be to increase its portion of the credit. Since the Eximbank will still have to ration its credit selectivity even without an increase in the attractiveness of its financing, any increase in the subsidy element might well only lower the additionality associated with its loans.

The answer to increased competitiveness for the Eximbank thus seems to be larger authorizations, particularly for the loan component. Without an increase in authorizations, it is doubtful that the Eximbank will be able to do any more than follow its present policy of offering selective competition. Since the Eximbank does not receive appropriated funds, the level of authorizations, as already noted, is technically separate from its funding mechanism. There have been suggestions, however, that reliance on the Federal Financing Bank for its funding operations results in a lower ceiling being placed on Eximbank authorizations because of concern about the aggregate level of government borrowing. As a result, alternative funding mechanisms have been proposed for the Eximbank. One proposal, for example, would provide for direct borrowing in private financial markets through the sale of tax-exempt securities.

227

The problem, however, does not seem to be so much with the mechanics of the funding operation, i.e., a belief that the Federal Financing Bank mechanism is inefficient or disorderly, but rather a fundamental lack of conviction that a greater Eximbank role and mission in supporting U.S. exports is appropriate. Given a change in these views, a move toward greater autonomy and flexibility in its funding operations might prove useful.

A more serious problem concerns the widely held view, supported by past and current practice, that the Eximbank should be financially self-sustaining. Unless economic policy succeeds in bringing down interest rates in the United States to more moderate levels, or Eximbank's counterparts abroad raise their own official export credit rates, the Eximbank will face the prospect of either incurring an out-of-pocket loss in its operations or of becoming substantially less competitive than it is at the present time in its direct loan programs. And while it can incur a loss for a short time without jeopardizing its financial soundness, the Eximbank cannot incur losses on a sustained basis. With its current loan programs already lacking in some aspects of competitiveness, there may shortly be no way for the Eximbank to fulfill the terms of its charter without appropriations from Congress. Although economic conditions may change and make the issue academic, a discussion of the implications of a financially self-sustaining Eximbank needs to begin soon.

Potential Changes in Budget Procedures. There are several changes in budgetary procedures that, although they cannot do much to overcome the Eximbank's basic budget constraint, might at least represent positive developments in terms of a more orderly and objective analysis of Eximbank activites. The Eximbank's budget is now part of the foreign aid appropriations process. There seems to be little justification for this. Foreign aid has been a controversial area in recent years and, with the Eximbank's activities controversial in their own right, there is no reason to add this burden to the Eximbank's load. Eximbank authorization should be considered with other international trade legislation.

As noted earlier, at the present time Eximbank receives an annual authorization. This creates uncertainty about the cost and availability of credit in the minds of exporters and importers who must have multi-year time horizons. Table 8 shows the sharp buildup in total Eximbank authorizations from 1970-1974 and the subsequent decline from 1974-1977, particularly in the sensitive direct loan component. Although authorizations should reflect current policy, longer-term multi-year authorizations could provide a more efficient basis for planning. To provide for greater certainty on the part of exporters and importers and more continuity in its programs, Eximbank authorizations should be for multi-year periods, with annual review by Congress.

TABLE 8

EXIMBANK AUTHORIZATIONS: 1970-1980*

($ millions)

	Total	Loans	Guarantees & Insurance
1970	3,968.1	2,208.8	1,759.3
1971	5,396.5	2,362.1	3,034.4
1972	7,230.3	3,284.6	3,945.7
1973	8,514.3	4,053.5	4,406.8
1974	9,099.5	4,904.6	4,194.9
1975	8,314.9	3,812.6	4,502.3
1976	8,619.9	3,488.8	5,131.1
1977	5,599.6	1,220.6	4,379.0
1978	7,376.4	3,424.6	3,951.8
1979	9,491.2	4,474.9	5,016.3
1980	12,609.2	4,577.8	8,031.4

*Fiscal Years.

Source: Eximbank Annual Reports: 1970-1980.

The Discount Loan Program. The discount loan program is the basic source of intermediate, fixed-rate credit for U.S. exporters. Under the discount loan program, U.S. commercial banks can expand their own export financing activities by discounting export notes carrying fixed interest rates for up to 100 percent of

the note's value. Maturities of up to five years are
eligible for the discount loan program. The FY 82
budget proposals of the Carter administration recommended that the discount loan program be abolished.
The Reagan administration proposed that authorizations
for FY 82 be continued at a level of $400 million.

Despite its potential for extensive use, the
discount loan program has been little used by U.S.
banks. As administered by the Eximbank, the minimum
rate at which banks can discount their notes is equal
to the discount rate of the New York Federal Reserve
Bank at the time the credit commitment is made, with a
spread of no more than 1 percent allowed between the
rate carried on the note and the rate at which the note
is discounted. With the Federal Reserve discount rate
at high levels during 1980, the rates at which bank

DISCOUNT RATE, FEDERAL RESERVE BANK OF NEW YORK, 1980 (percent)

Feb. 15	May 29	June 13	July 28	Sept. 26	Nov. 17
13	12	11	10	11	12

loans would have to have been made to insure
profitability under the discount loan program were
essentially noncompetitive. There seems to be little
reason why discount loan rates should not match other
direct lending rates. The profit from these loans
accruing to commercial banks could still be controlled
by the spread between the fixed rate financing offered
by the banks and the rate at which those loans could be
discounted. Discount loan programs are used exten-
sively by the foreign branches of U.S. banks to finance
exports in some of the countries in which they are
located because of the attractive terms that some of
Eximbank's competitors provide. With the original
detailed export loan credit analyses performed by the
commercial banks, discount loans are advantageous from
the standpoint of utilizing the export loan
administration of the private sector.

<u>Commercial Bank Guarantee Program</u>. The commercial bank guarantee program is designed to encourage greater participation by U.S. commercial banks in supporting U.S. exports by providing guarantees on medium-term export loans made by U.S. banks. Such guarantees cover up to 90 percent of the commercial and 100 percent of the political risk on medium-term transactions financed by U.S. banks. In addition to a cash payment of at least 15 percent, the Eximbank generally requires an exporter to retain for commercial and political risks 10 percent of the financed portion of the sale, while the commercial bank is also expected to assume a share of the commercial risk as well. Although the Eximbank does not specify an interest rate to be charged, guaranteed coverage of interest rate repayment is limited to 6 percent by the Eximbank. The Eximbank charges the participating bank a fee for this guarantee based on the repayment terms of the obligation and the amount of risk retained by the exporter.

The relative importance of the commercial bank guarantee program in total Eximbank guarantee authority has been declining over the past several years. Eximbank guarantee authority has been allocated primarily to long-term guarantees related to direct credits. Whereas the commercial bank guarantee program accounted for almost 60 percent of Eximbank's total guarantee authority in FY 78, in FY 80, the share dropped to 19 percent. At the same time, the portion accounted for by long-term guarantees climbed from 39 percent to 75 percent. It is not clear what impact this shift in emphasis has had on Eximbank's overall competitiveness.

<u>Human Rights and Foreign Policy</u> Involvement. Eximbank credits have been linked to human rights goals of the United States as in the Jackson-Vanik amendment, which withholds Eximbank credit to the Soviet Union until that country affords certain basic rights to its ethnic minorities. They have also been linked to foreign policy goals of the United States. This linkage has been strongly criticized.[29] Some argue that U.S. exports that might contribute to a potential adversary's military capability are already controlled by the Export Administration Act and there is thus no reason for Eximbank involvement in foreign policy: Human rights objectives and foreign policy goals should be left to other areas.

231

Far from being exempt from foreign concerns, U.S. export policy, including Eximbank's activities, should become an integral part of domestic policy. A strong U.S. export position supports and strengthens U.S. foreign policy. As for human rights, U.S. domestic commercial and economic policy routinely and regularly aims at objectives involving human welfare. There is no reason that international economic policy should be different.

With regard to foreign policy, the denial of exports for military purposes says nothing about the consequence of actively assisting a potential adversary in the nonmilitary area. To the extent that a potential adversary is able to divert domestic resources from a nonmilitary to a military area because of Eximbank credits, this military effort has been helped. Beyond that, the United States has invoked significant economic and financial measures twice in the recent past (in the case of Iran and of the Soviet Union) on behalf of foreign policy goals. It would be naive in the extreme to believe that international economic policy and foreign policy can or will be separated in the future.

The appropriate question is not whether Eximbank activities should be linked to U.S. national foreign policy and human rights goals but how? How can it best be used in a productive, effective way, and what ways are inappropriate, useless, and likely to damage our pursuit of these goals? It should be remembered that, just as with U.S. exporters, on-again-off-again Eximbank credit policies may well lose their effectiveness with foreign borrowers. It should also be remembered that one of the most fundamental human rights of all is the right to better one's economic status. It may be that Eximbank credit policy can be used far more effectively in support of human rights in a positive way than in a negative mode.

Mixed Credits. Policy regarding mixed credits is really an issue that belongs in a discussion of the foreign policy and human rights aspects of Eximbank policy. Official U.S. policy is opposed to the mixing of export credits with foreign aid. Many countries routinely used mixed credits to finance large, high-value projects at very low rates over long periods.

232

The resulting rate and maturity are generally much more favorable than what could be obtained under the export credit alone. It has been estimated that 10 percent of French exports are financed with mixed credits. In recent months the Eximbank has made greater efforts to match these practices by its competitor export credit institutions. Without access to foreign aid funds or an official mechanism to coordinate with U.S. foreign aid programs, it will be extremely difficult for Eximbank to make more than a token effort at matching foreign mixed credit deals.

The U.S. opposition to mixed credits stems from the unquestionable fact that this is not the most effective way to supply foreign aid in terms of the recipient country's development. The recipient country is frequently obliged to use the foreign aid component of the loan for one purpose when, without any strings attached, it would be used in another way. The aid is also tied to exports from the country offering the mixed credit, when similar exports might be purchased under better terms elsewhere. These drawbacks of mixed credits may give rise as well to resentment of the donor country by the recipients.

On the other side, it may be that the alternative available to the recipient country is not mixed credits or the most efficient aid package, but mixed credits or no aid package. The Development Assistance Committee (DAC) countries of the OECD are nowhere close to their foreign aid target levels. In the United States, foreign aid programs have steadily been losing support in recent years. Mixing foreign aid with export credits would be a way to link foreign aid with a program that could show concrete benefits in terms of employment generated and foreign exchange earned through export sales. Moreover, the United States should seek to maximize the return of its foreign aid program. It is certainly proper to have as an objective of foreign aid the progress of developing countries. Is it any less honorable, though, to seek to establish new commercial relationships and support for U.S. foreign policy and human rights objectives through foreign aid?

There is no problem in finding recipients for foreign aid. The problem is in the maintenance of adequate aid levels. The U.S. government should consider the use of mixed credits as a device for both export promotion and the provision of foreign aid. The use of mixed credits would in a sense only be recognition of the fact that a subsidized Eximbank loan already contains an element of aid in the subsidy.

Foreign Content and Local Costs. Until recently, Eximbank policy opposed the financing of the local costs or foreign content associated with U.S. exports. Its approach to these subjects has been more flexible in recent times. The Eximbank should continue with a more flexible approach with regard to the funding of exports with foreign content or local costs associated with export projects. Its competitors routinely finance exports that have foreign content. Although arbitrary specific guidelines could be used to determine what the absolute or relative limits of foreign content should be, a case by case approach that would examine all aspects of the export would be a better approach. The objective, of course, is not to subsidize foreign sales, but U.S. exports. Fulfilling that objective might, under some circumstances, require the financing of exports with some degree of foreign content.

Local cost funding decisions would profit from the same approach. If the local cost component is small and is the key to the export sale, there is little reason why the Eximbank should not fund it. The decision, too, should be made on a case-by-case basis.

Both of these areas are sensitive and require good judgment. The Eximbank cannot and should not take on the role of financing any U.S. export that applies for funding assistance. It should have the discretion, though, that it needs to fulfill its role. Local cost and foreign content funding decisions are areas where that discretion should be applied.

Foreign Competition for U.S. Exports. There has been much discussion over the extent to which the Eximbank should finance U.S. exports that have no apparent overseas competition (long-range commercial aircraft are often cited as an example, although the European-manufactured airbus is certainly a competitor for a certain segment of this industry and a potential

234

competitor for the entire area). Strict adherence to
the guidelines of meeting the foreign competition for
export financing would result in no Eximbank support
for these exports. In the case of high-value exports
with long useful lives, however, the presence of the
concessionary Eximbank participation might be essential
to the sale. The absence of Eximbank participation and
the failure to make a sale may also be an invitation to
future competition. The U.S. should certainly be
concerned about the future competition to its exports
as well as present competition. On the other hand,
Eximbank programs should not simply be directed at
opening up new markets for subsidized U.S. exports.
The Eximbank should use its discretionary authority,
with close Congressional and Executive Department
oversight, to determine the appropriateness of its
support in cases where no actual competition exists.

Foreign Credit Insurance Association

The Eximbank coordinates its export insurance
activities with the Foreign Credit Insurance Association (FCIA). Formed in 1961 at the urging of the U.S.
government, the FCIA today is composed of 51 leading
private marine, property, casualty, and reinsurance
companies with a paid-in capital of $14 million. Under
a cooperative arrangement, the FCIA administers the
U.S. export credit insurance program on behalf of its
51 companies and the Eximbank. With the Eximbank
acting as its reinsurer on excess risks, the FCIA
generally covers normal commercial credit risks in
export transactions, while the Eximbank assumes
liability for political risks.[30] The FCIA's normal
operating expenses are covered through the fees and
premiums it collects on its insurance coverage.

Just as the U.S. Congress sets Eximbank ceilings
on its insurance activities, the Eximbank sets limits
on FCIA insurance commitments. These limits are
established in an annual reinsurance agreement between
the Eximbank and the FCIA. Such limits are a function
of several factors, including the Eximbank's own
insurance authorization level and the degree of private
insurers' participation in export-related insurance
syndications in earlier years. Moreover, the Eximbank
can set guidelines on how the FCIA authority is

used -- i.e., short or medium-term, specific country limits. The FCIA also uses the same country rating system as Eximbank. Although the FCIA does not offer insurance without Eximbank participation, the Eximbank can and does provide coverage without FCIA involvement. In such cases, the Eximbank still funnels such projects through the FCIA.

Between them, the Eximbank and the FCIA offer a wide range of export insurance programs that are generally very flexible and competitive with overseas competitor programs. Under these programs, insurance coverage is available for short and medium-term commercial and political risks with various options. Table 9 briefly describes the primary features of these programs. The master policy essentially provides a blanket protection for large-volume exporters that allows for flexibility and quick action, while the deductible makes for lower premiums. The short-term comprehensive policy is attractive to exporters that deal in, and to banks that finance, commodities characterized by a quick turn over. The medium-term policy is used largely for case-by-case insurance for capital or quasi-capital goods. The combined short and medium-term policy is designed for exporters selling equipment and parts to distributors and dealers where short-term coverage is appropriate during a "floor plan" period, after which the medium-term coverage is needed.[31]

Eximbank/FCIA export insurance programs traditionally have been cost competitive. Table 10 demonstrates that the U.S. short-term insurance programs in 1978 and 1979 were more competitive in terms of cost and coverage than similar programs in France and Germany, although not as competitive as programs in Japan and the UK. Moreover, one could argue that since coverage, not cost, is the major consideration in short-term financing, Table 10 actually understates U.S. competitiveness in this area.[32]

Reflecting this competitiveness, over the past three fiscal years Eximbank/FCIA export credit insurance has supported nearly 5 percent of total U.S. nonagricultural exports. In FY 80, $5.5 billion in official export credit insurance supported $8.1 billion in U.S. exports. To the extent that comparable export

TABLE 9

EXIMBANK/FCIA EXPORT INSURANCE PROGRAMS

POLICY	TERM	POLITICAL COVERAGE	COMMERCIAL COVERAGE	SPECIAL FEATURES
Master	Short/Medium term with repayment up to 5 years	100%	Optional 90%	A first-loss deductible on commercial risk; substantial discretionary authority for exports. Lowest premium of insurance policies
Short-Term Comprehensive	Sight draft to 180 days	100%	Optional 90%	Large discretionary limit
Medium-Term	181 days to 5 years	100%	Optional 90%	Advance cash payment of 15-20%. Includes machinery, plant equipment and other income producing capital goods
Combined Short-Term/ Medium Term	Parts & Acces. up to 180 days; inventory financing to 270 days; receivables financing up to 3 years	100%	Optional 90%	

Source: U.S. Department of Commerce, A Guide to Financing Exports, May 1980.

TABLE 10

COST AND COVERAGE OF SHORT-TERM INSURANCE PROGRAMS

		1978	1979
France:	Average Fee ($/100) Cover -- Commercial Political (%)	0.70 85/95	0.70 85/95
Germany:	Average Fee Cover	0.76 85/90	0.76 85/90
Italy:	Average Fee Cover	N/A 90/100	N/A 90/100
Japan:	Average Fee Cover	0.20 60/90	0.20 60/90
UK:	Average Fee Cover	0.34 90/95	0.34 90/95
U.S.:	Average Fee Cover	0.70 90/95	0.70 90/100

Source: Report to the Congress on Export Credit Competition and the Export-Import Bank of the United States, October 1980, p. 30.

insurance coverage could be obtained in the private market, it could probably be obtained only at a higher cost. As noted earlier, there is some evidence that the additionality associated with export insurance is significantly smaller than that associated with loans. In the case of insurance, however, the distributed effects must also be considered particularly when placing official export credit programs in the broader context of the general U.S. international economic policy and its relationship with foreign policy. It is questionable, for example, whether private markets today would be willing to provide insurance coverage at other than prohibitive rates for U.S. exports that are sold to some less developed countries (LDCs) (exports to LDCs account for about 35 percent of total U.S. exports) -- particularly at a time of increasingly difficult economic conditions in those countries related to rising oil costs and slower worldwide growth.

The recent experiences of the major official export insurance agencies highlight the risks associated with exporting to LDCs -- risks that could discourage private markets from participating. Because of adverse political and economic developments, as well as a reluctance to boost premiums to match risks, official export insurance agencies recorded unprecedented losses in 1980. West Germany, for example, recorded a loss of an estimated $47 million, its first since 1949. In France, COFACE's loss in 1980 is expected to surpass the previous year's record $308 million loss. Meanwhile, Britain's ECGD announced an underwriting loss of $265.4 million in 1980, against a deficit of $61 million in 1979.[33]

Official export credit insurance programs are obviously not expected to operate as if they were run by private companies; but neither should they be allowed to ignore losses. Export credit losses which are made good by export credit insurance do not earn foreign exchange, and far from enhancing a country's position in the market where the loss occurred, they are likely to make commercial relations, at least, more difficult.

There is certainly no need for U.S. export credit insurance programs to compete for foreign credit insurance programs which experience unacceptable losses. The competitiveness of U.S. export credit insurance programs, in fact, cannot be judged in terms of a comparison of coverage or costs of competiting programs whose loss experience would be unacceptable to the United States. It may be that the loss experience of other countries will result in a change in the structure of their export insurance program. The fact that official export insurance agencies have been so reluctant to raise premiums commensurate with risks or refuse coverage, however, is an indication that governments are hesitant to burden their exporters with such additional costs -- particularly in a period of sharp export competition. It appears that thus far governments are comfortable with providing this type of subsidy as a means of supporting exports.

Thus, in the current environment Eximbank/FCIA insurance programs have a key role to play in supporting U.S. exports. The competitive coverage and rate structure these programs offer should be maintained at appropriate funding levels.

Private Export Funding Corporation

The Private Export Funding Corporation (PEFCO) is closely associated with the Eximbank. Established in 1970, PEFCO is a private corporation owned by 54 commercial U.S. banks, 7 U.S. industrial firms, and 1 U.S. investment banking firm. PEFCO's principal purpose is to provide medium and long-term fixed rate financing to public and private overseas borrowers for the purchase of U.S. goods and services. The Eximbank guarantees unconditionally the principal and interest of all PEFCO loans. For its lending operations PEFCO raises funds in the private capital markets by selling its own debt obligations, which carry the Eximbank's guarantee. In addition, the Eximbank has made available to PEFCO a $50 million revolving line of credit. The Eximbank exercises a broad measure of supervision over PEFCO's major financial management decisions and Eximbank's approval is required for individual export loan commitments and for the rate structure and maturity of PEFCO's long-term debt obligations.[34]

Since it was organized as a supplemental lending source, PEFCO makes loans only when necessary funds are not available from traditional private sources. PEFCO's facilities have been particularly popular during periods of tight money. PEFCO generally provides loans at fixed interest rates (some floating rate loans have been made) with maturities beyond the normal range of commercial banks. The average fixed rate on PEFCO's outstanding export loans was 9 percent at the end of 1980.[35] PEFCO usually participates in export financing deals with one or more commercial banks as colenders and the Eximbank as guarantor and colender. PEFCO's share of individual loans ranges from a modest to a substantial percentage of the group's total, often taking the middle maturities between those of the commercial banks and the Eximbank.

Since its formation in 1970, PEFCO has extended over $3.6 billion in export loans. In 1980 the total of PEFCO's new loan commitments tripled to $1.5 billion. This sharp jump was largely a function of the increased availability of the Eximbank's guarantee authority in FY 80, as well as the increased attractiveness of fixed-rate loans during last year's period of high interest rates. Moreover, PEFCO's newly-introduced deferred pricing scheme, under which fixed interest rates on loan commitments are not determined until the approximate time that funds are actually disbursed, proved popular.

Obviously, any discussion of PEFCO hinges on its relationship to the Eximbank and the Eximbank's own activities. Many of the arguments concerning the proper role of export promotion already discussed in this paper are applicable to PEFCO. In terms of PEFCO's own performance, a strong Eximbank with adequate funding authority is fundamental to maintaining PEFCO's role in export credit finance. In addition, though, PEFCO has demonstrated its effectiveness by pursing innovative financing techniques such as the deferred pricing scheme. The Eximbank should be encouraged to develop and utilize to an even greater extent the export financing expertise available in the private sector.

Commodity Credit Corporation

Just as the Eximbank supports nonagricultural exports, the Department of Agriculture's Commodity Credit Corporation (CCC) supports agricultural exports. Established in the 1930s, the purpose of the CCC is to promote U.S. agricultural sales abroad of surplus goods. The CCC is separate and distinct from the Agricultural Trade Development and Assistance Act (P.L. 480).[36]

Until FY 79 the primary vehicle used by CCC to promote agricultural exports was the Export Credit Sales Program (GSM-5). Under the GSM-5 program, U.S. exporters could apply for direct CCC financing of eligible U.S. commodities at terms ranging from 6 months to 36 months and interest rates marginally above the U.S. Treasury's borrowing cost. Through the regular budget process, Congress set the CCC's annual authorization ceilings, which the CCC then allocated on a country-by-country basis.

To supplement the GSM-5 program and to encourage U.S. banks to make additional financing available for agricultural exports, the CCC in Fy 79 introduced the Non-Commercial Risk Assurance Program (GSM-101). This program provided protection for U.S. banks against noncommerical risks such as insurrection, warfare, expropriation, etc. In essence, the CCC began to assume the role of guarantor rather than lendor. The shift to guarantor was completed in FY 81 when the CCC shifted to the Export Credit Guarantee Program (GSM-102).

The GSM-102 program replaced GSM-5 program in FY 81 and expanded the GSM-101 program by extending the CCC guarantee to include commercial risks on short-term agricultural sales at market rates. The GSM-102 program guarantees 100 percent repayment on export financings. The GSM-102 program limits the interest rate guarantee to 6 percent, however, regardless of the market rate, thus leaving the U.S. lenders with a signficant interest rate risk during periods of high interest rates such as exists today. Table 11 shows the transition from the CCC's role as a direct lender to a guarantor.

As Table 11 shows, over the past three fiscal years, the CCC has provided support, either through direct credits or guarantees, for a total of $4.7 billion in U.S. agricultural exports -- about 5 percent of total U.S. agricultural exports. The argument is made that removing the CCC from direct lending has eliminated any subsidy involved in CCC financing of agricultural exports. However, although CCC guaranteed sales are at "market" rates, these sales still contain a subsidy element to both the exporter and the importer arising from the CCC guarantee. Without the CCC guarantee, it is not clear that the importer or the exporter could obtain financing. In all likelihood, the interest rate would be higher without the guarantee. The difference between the "market" rate obtained by the importer and the rate he would otherwise have to pay without the CCC guarantee can be viewed as a subsidy to the importer. On the other hand, the exporter also receives a subsidy in increased export sales that may not have been made without the CCC guarantee. Such a subsidy may arise because the importer might forego a purchase if unable to afford the higher rate, or the private U.S. bank would not have extended the financing without such a guarantee, thus making the sale nearly impossible. In today's international financial market, many U.S. banks are approaching their self-imposed country lending limits. Since a CCC guaranteed loan is ultimately a U.S. government risk, a bank may be more apt to grant the export credit since its exposure level will not be affected. In essence, CCC involvement allows banks to go beyond their country limits and provide credit that might otherwise not be provided, particularly at that "market" rate.

It is not clear whether U.S. agricultural exports in aggregate would drop without the CCC program, although the geographical pattern of exports would certainly change. It is clear, though, that U.S. exporters face stiff competition from other large agricultural exporting nations such as Canada, Australia, and Argentina in the area of official agricultural export credit support. Continued CCC support is warranted as a component of a coordinated overall economic and foreign policy. In terms of more effective utilization of the program, however, the question of 100 percent interest rate guarantee should be examined. Since the CCC allocates its export support

TABLE 11

CCC AUTHORIZATION LEVELS AND SALES
(millions)

Authorization

	FY 82	FY 79	FY 80	FY 81
GSM-5	1700	1600	800	0
GSM-101	-	-	1000	0
GSM-102	-	-	-	2000
	1700	1600	1800	2000

Sales

	FY 82	FY 79	FY 80	FY 81
GSM-5	1600	1500	718	0
GSM-101	-	63[1]	698	0
GSM-102	-	-	100	N/A
	1600	1563	1516	N/A

[1]Since both programs were begun well into the fiscal year, no authorization was set at the outset, although sales were eventually made under these programs.

Source: Commodity Credit Corporation.

on a country by country basis, interest rate coverage
could help insure greater utilization of the allocation
in countries where risks are considered extraordinarily
high.

VI. OTHER OFFICIAL U.S. PROGRAMS
THAT SUPPORT U.S. EXPORTS

There are many other official U.S. programs that in one way or another are involved in export promotion. These range from informational seminars to trade missions. This paper will briefly discuss only the major programs that are indirectly involved in financing U.S. exports.

Overseas Private Investment Corporation

The Overseas Private Investment Corporation (OPIC) is the U.S. Government's principal catalyst for stimulating U.S. private investment in developing nations. OPIC offers U.S. investors insurance against various noncommercial risks, makes direct loans to potential investors, participates in preinvestment survey financing, and provides U.S. lenders protection against both commercial and political risks by guaranteeing loans to eligible investors.[37]

Such loan guarantees often provide investors with the support necessary to obtain U.S. private loans for the purchase of U.S. goods and services. Thus, it is argued that export promotion traditionally has been a secondary benefit of OPIC's formal activities. OPIC estimates that over the previous three fiscal years OPIC-supported investments have resulted directly in $3 billion worth of U.S. exports.[38]

Moreover, OPIC plays a key role in supporting U.S. services exports and, as such, plays a complimentary role with the Eximbank in overall U.S. export promotion. OPIC offers protection for bid, performance, retention, and advance payments bonds posted by U.S. construction and service contractors against on-demand letters of credit. Through such activities OPIC is offering services that are routinely provided by official export support programs in other industrialized countries.

This type of involvement in export promotion has prompted legislative efforts to give OPIC a greater export promoting function. In the 96th Congress,

Senators Ribicoff and Javits proposed a bill that would have altered OPIC's charter to give it a formal export mission. The bill died with the last Congress, but similar legislation is likely to be introduced during the current session. A key provision in any new legislation could be the removal of restrictions on OPIC activity in higher-income developing nations.

It is debatable, though, whether or not export promotion is the proper role of OPIC. The argument that OPIC increases U.S. exports has not been proven conclusively. Furthermore, U.S. investment overseas may lead to a substitution of local production for U.S. exports. Thus, although OPIC serves a vital function in overseas investment policy, more research needs to be done on the full impact of OPIC on U.S. exports, particularly with regard to the long-term prospects for U.S. exports.

The Small Business Administration

Another program the U.S. government uses to promote exports is administered through the Small Business Administration (SBA). The SBA does not have a specific program for direct export-oriented lending. Rather, the SBA promotes small business participation in international trade indirectly, primarily through its loan guarantees program. Funds obtained from private financial institutions under the SBA guarantee may be used to purchase machinery, equipment, facilities, and supplies needed to manufacture or sell products overseas, as well as for working capital.[39]

The SBA traditionally has played only a minor role in export promotion. Organizationally, the SBA is set up to encourage overall small business activities, not necessarily exports. The SBA estimates that in FY 80 some $3 million in loan guarantees were provided to firms who derive 50 percent of their total revenues from export sales. It should be noted, however, that small business already is substantially involved in overseas sales through the many subcontractors who supply major U.S. exporting industries. For example, it is estimated that commercial jet manufacturing for export in the United States generates nearly 90,000 additional jobs in primary support areas.[40]

247

The question of whether the SBA should have a greater and more formal role in export support is a difficult one. One proper role that the SBA can and should play in export finance is that of a liaison between small business and the Eximbank. Indeed, over the past several years the SBA and Eximbank have been moving in this direction. In coordination with the Department of Commerce, OPIC, and the Eximbank, the SBA sponsors conferences designed to assist smaller firms in learning of opportunities available in foreign trade and what government services are available to help them. As far as actual export credit support is concerned, there seems to be little reason why Eximbank, with the SBA in the liaison role, could not provide all of the services needed by small business exporters. At the same time, a duplication of functions which might otherwise result in a misuse of scarce resources would be avoided.

VIII. CONCLUSION

The official export credit support programs of the United States in recent years have in general failed to match the financial terms or breadth of coverage offered by the competing programs in other major industrial countries. This is particularly true of the direct loan component of these programs. Although this reflects a valid recognition of the fact that there is no inherent reason why U.S. programs should duplicate on a one-for-one basis competing overseas programs, it also reflects a fundamental lack of consensus in the United States, both in the government and the private sector, about the role of these programs in a free market economy. Although official export credit support programs in the United States are now well established, the current debate centers at least as much on whether they should even exist as on what individual program and corresponding funding levels should be.

A key factor in the debate that is often minimized is that the international economy is not characterized by free markets. Barriers to trade are commonplace, and so are their opposites, nonmarket mechanisms designed to promote exports. Among the industrial nation competitors of the United States in third country export markets, official export credit support programs that interfere with the operation of the free market play a central role in export promotion schemes. These programs are especially important in the competition to export high value capital equipment with long useful lives to developing countries, particularly where foreign exchange availability is an especially important factor in the export sale. In these cases, base prices and product quality may be of secondary importance to the cost and availability of export credit.

Unless the United States is willing to make a long-term adjustment to a level and pattern of export production and trade that does not reflect the principle of comparative advantage, it will have to face the question of how best to offset the impact of official export credit programs overseas. Up to the present time, the response to that question has been only implied by tentative and lukewarm commitments, both within the government and the private sector, to U.S. official export credit programs.

There can be no question about the need in the United States to reestablish an economic environment characterized by a stable price level and the subsequent lowering of interest rates which that would bring. Such a development, coupled with floating exchange rates free to adjust to imbalances in the external accounts and economic programs that will enhance productivity and product quality, will do much to improve the competitiveness of U.S. exports in overseas markets. These are all items of the highest priority. They are not likely to be enough over the long run, however, to counter the specific impact of the official export credit support programs of other industrial countries that are likely to persist. Unless the United States is willing to accept passively the advantage these programs give to overseas competitors of U.S. exporters, the United States will either have to bring about a reduction in the extent of the subsidies offered by competing programs or increase the size and scope of its own official credit programs.

The United States should in any case make every effort to achieve a negotiated reduction in the subsidies offered by competing official export credit programs. This should be made a matter of the highest priority. Failing that, the United States must come to grips with the question of what kind of export posture best supports the goals of domestic and foreign policy. This demands recognition of the fact that international economic policy is an integral part of both.

With well-established programs in place that provide the basic structure for a comprehensive official export credit support program, the major issue facing the United States now is the level of support that these programs should receive in aggregate, and how that support should be allocated between the basic areas of direct loans, credit guarantees, and credit insurance. All of these programs appear to have some degree of additionality associated with them, but to significantly different degrees. Direct loans appear to be more effective in promoting exports than either guarantees or insurance in additionality per dollar of program authorization.

A more appropriate measure for allocation of resources to these programs, though, would be the value of additional exports for each dollar of cost. The cost of providing a dollar's worth of insurance or guarantees may differ significantly from the cost of a dollar's worth of direct loan. It is that cost that should be compared with the value of additional exports. This calculation has not been made.

More generally, the official export credit support provided U.S. exports must be geared to the attainment of specific goals. It is impossible now to know what the aggregate level of funding for these programs should be. There is a real cost associated with the subsidies inherent in these programs. These costs must be compared with the benefits associated with the additional exports they produce. And since the costs are borne by the public, the benefits must accrue to the public as well. Official export credit support programs should not be geared simply at meeting foreign competition.

Interim funding decisions must and will be made for these programs, but these programs will continue to drift as they have in the past until a comprehensive U.S. export strategy is formulated. Competitive financing is critical to export performance, but the United States has yet to determine what level of export performance is necessary.

Until this is accomplished, it makes little sense to make substantial reductions in U.S. official export credit programs. Among other negative effects, such reductions might seriously prejudice U.S. efforts to negotiate a multilateral reduction in export subsidies on the part of the major industrial country export credit program.

It would also make little sense to expand the number of government agencies involved in export credit programs. The Eximbank of the United States occupies the central place in U.S. programs and should continue to do so. A proliferation of programs and duplication of efforts would be confusing and wasteful. To the extent that the Eximbank has not already achieved close communication with actual or potential U.S. exporters who could benefit from official programs, closer coordination between the Eximbank and organizations

251

such as the Small Business Administration should be achieved.

STATE INTERVENTION IN INTERNATIONAL MARKETS

Greater awareness of export opportunities, enhanced price competitiveness through the depreciation of an over-valued currency, and emphasis on quality and services are all essential to a program aimed at increasing exports. In a free market economy, price, quality, ability to meet promised delivery schedules, and after-sales service are the basis for competition among private business enterprises. In the U.S. economy, which for all of its regulation by government is still a free market economy, these criteria are within the span of control of private enterprises. Government intervention in the market place is generally not direct in nature. Broad gauge fiscal and monetary policies aim at influencing the economic environment within which private enterprises operate. Individual buyers and sellers who are free within the constraints imposed by monetary and fiscal policy to make their own individual decisions to buy or sell based on market factors are thus the key to successful sales over time for entrepreneurs operating in a free market economy.

That may well not be the case in markets where direct state intervention in economic life occurs on a regular basis at the industry and firm level. In fact, the justification in government involvement at this level must go beyond considerations of monetary profit. Government intervention at this level thus introduces noncommercial criteria into the market place which can be of significant importance and heavily influence a decision to buy or sell.

Rationale for Government Intervention

Governments are responsible for the general economic health of the state. They are responsible, for example, for the maintenance of high employment, for price stability, for maintaining a sound position in the external accounts, and for economic growth in general. They are also responsible for other activities that may not be directly related to formal economic objectives but which strongly influence or are influenced by the state of the economy. National security is an example of one such area.

Governments that participate directly and pervasively in the economic lives of their citizens justify this participation in terms of the achievement of desirable collective goals that would not be or could not be achieved by private enterprise alone. This is the externality argument again; the activity of a private entrepreneur will fall short of the socially desirable level because the entrepreneur will not personally be able to capture the added benefits that accrue to society to offset the costs that he (and not society) incurs. The government, which represents all of society, is in a position to support the added costs because it can capture the benefits. A private firm operating on its own must be efficient and try to maximize profits to survive. The owners may well be concerned about aggregate unemployment in the economy, but they are hardly in a position by themselves to add workers to the payroll whose cost exceeds the revenue they contribute to the firm. As far as the owners are concerned, the firm's contribution to government welfare payments to unemployed workers will not change if they fail to add marginal workers to the payroll. The government, on the other hand, which does find that its budgetary costs for welfare payments increase in direct proportion to the number of unemployed, not to speak of the political and social costs of high unemployment, may decide that it is cheaper from an overall cost point of view to subsidize the employment of marginal workers.

The legitimate interest of a government in applying noncommercial criteria to commercial markets has been recognized by the rules of the General Agreement on Tariffs and Trade (GATT) and by the recently concluded negotiations of the Tokyo Round of the Multilateral Trade Negotiations (MTN) in certain areas of government procurement. Although both call for greater use of standard commercial criteria in government procurement practices, both note exceptions, such as national defense procurement, where other criteria may be applied.

But the reasons offered for more extensive government involvement in commercial economic activity are far from confined to government procurement practices, and to a significant extent point to an especially pronounced intervention in international markets. To some extent this can be explained by political and economic philosophy. The United States has a long standing tradition of free markets where government's primary role is to enforce competitive behavior among private business interests. The private sector-government relationship is one that requires an arm's-length relationship.

Most other countries have no such constraints on government-business relationships. The private sector-public sector distinction is blurred in most U.S. trading partners' or trade competitors' countries. Government ownership, either complete or partial, of banks, manufacturing concerns, airlines, construction companies, and virtually every other line of economic activity is commonplace in most of the developing countries. It is also true of countries like France and Germany. Government ownership is only the most direct and obvious form of state participation in the economic life of a country. Financial subsidies to firms and industries is another. More subtle but no less effective than direct ownership or government subsidies are close associations that bring government representatives and representatives of industry together for purposes of directing economic activity along specific lines. This has been used with great success in Japan.

The choice of how economic activity is organized in a country is, of course, an internal decision of that country. As far as the domestic sector of a country is concerned, the choice of economic system and the extent of government involvement in commercial activity which that entails has little impact on other countries. How a country conducts its international trade is a different case, because it is in international markets where international economic systems come together and where different countries find themselves playing the same game, while using different rules.

Obstacles to Imports

The involvement of governments in international trade is pervasive. It is the rule rather than the exception. Direct trade restrictions such as tariffs and quotas at one time were the mainstays of trade protectionism but today have been largely replaced by more comprehensive and effective devices, the nontariff trade barriers (NTBs). One of the principle thrusts of the Tokyo Round of the MTN was to reduce NTBs. Its success in accomplishing this is not yet known.

Some forms of state involvement occur for the purpose of obtaining imports under more favorable terms than could be obtained in free markets or to obtain imports that could not otherwise be obtained at all. Countertrade, in which the importing country mandates that the exporter accept goods in return as payment, is a form of barter and is especially useful for a country where foreign exchange is unavailable or particularly scarce. Because the ability to conclude a countertrade agreement depends on a mutual coincidence of wants, it is often easier to arrange countertrade agreements between governments, with the government of the exporting country guaranteeing the exporter, if he is a private entrepreneur, a market for the goods he receives as payment for the export.

Offset agreements that require that the exporter import in return for goods of his choosing equal in value to a certain portion of the export is similar in nature to countertrade but more flexible. The importing country's motive in obtaining an offset agreement is primarily to earn foreign exchange to offset its foreign exchange expenditure. Offset agreements contribute at the same time to the financial (and perhaps technological) health of export industries and simultaneously contribute to employment levels in the importing country. In contrast to countertrade, offset agreements are commonly used by some of the most advanced and sophisticated trading nations in the world. Western European nations, for example, often use offset agreements in high-value import cases involving government procurement.

Production-sharing agreements require that components of the exports or a certain number of units of the export be produced in the importing country. In addition to the creation of employment, technology transfer is involved in this kind of arrangement. The acquisition of advanced technology provides a powerful incentive for government intervention in foreign trade transactions, and not only for developing countries.

There is little incentive for a private importer who wants to maximize profits to demand countertrade, offset, or coproduction agreements. An airline is engaged in carrying passengers and cargo; a private airline presumably would be interested in purchasing the aircraft it needs at the lowest possible cost and, in a market free of state intervention, would probably do exactly that. If it had to import the aircraft, offset or coproduction requirements would only make the transaction more complicated and costly. Yet coproduction and offset requirements mandated by governments are a common feature of overseas purchases of U.S. aircraft, both commercial and military.

Incentives for Exports

The object of much of the state intervention in foreign trade that exists today is not to raise barriers to imports but to promote exports. This is really a kind of trade protectionism in reverse. It is easy to understand, however, at least on the surface, why some countries find it an attractive practice.

Exports are a component of the national product, and an increase in exports contributes to economic growth just as an increase in the output of any other sector of the economy. In economies where exports comprise a significant portion of total output, a decline in the growth rate of exports can have a major impact on aggregate growth rates and employment levels. The impact on a particular sector of the economy may be even greater. Germany, as noted earlier, exports more than 20 percent of its GNP and about half of its output of manufactures.

A large export sector also provides a country with an opportunity to maintain economic growth rates and employment levels during times of decline in the domestic economy by shifting output to the export sector.

In 1976, for example, as Germany emerged, albeit slowly, from the 1975 world recession, over 45 percent of its increase in output came from export growth. For France, about one-third of the increase in total output in 1976 was attributed to export growth. For the United Kingdom, the figure was about 45 percent. For the United States, less than 4 percent of the increase in aggregate growth came from export growth.

Production for export markets also permits smaller economies to escape the limitations imposed by their size and achieve economies of scale in production. The size of the domestic market in France would not be sufficient to support an efficient aerospace industry by itself, but successful sales to the world market minimizes that problem.

This can be an especially important consideration with respect to defense-related industries, where national requirements alone could not economically support essential production research and development capabilities. Production for export provides a way around this problem.

For these and other reasons, many countries have concluded that it is not only good to export to the extent permitted by free markets, but that the benefits provided by additional exports that require state assistance are worth their additional cost. That calculation may be wrong, but it is clear that social benefits over and above the benefits that accrue to individuals may well be associated with exports. This is a result that cannot be rejected out of hand. The calculation must be made.

The U.S. Economy and State Intervention

Examining the reasons for state participation in international trade markets, it becomes easier to see why the United States has not followed these practices. Although some individual industries might be exceptions, the vast size and affluence of the domestic U.S. market has posed no obstacle to the establishment of economies of scale in production. U.S. technology in past years has led the world; government has felt no need to demand that the importation of products be accompanied by production technology. The dollar is the world's principal reserve currency, so the United States has had no shortage of foreign exchange.

For the United States with a relatively small export sector, employment has been a function largely of domestic economic activity, which in turn can be influenced most efficiently by general monetary and fiscal policy. When shipments of oranges from California to New York decline, shipments of oranges from Florida to New York may increase. With most of its economic activity centered on internal trade, there is no net loss to the United States when the location of economic activity shifts as long as resources and labor are free to shift as well because these shifts are generally from one area within the country to another. These shifts are, in fact, desirable because they promote efficiency. For the United States these shifts are at worst a zero-sum game as long as economic policy succeeds in maintaining the same level of aggregate domestic demand.

The same is not true for a country with a relatively large export sector. A loss of exports is a national loss to another country; it does not represent a redistribution of labor and other productive resources within the country. A shift of exports from one country to another is not a zero-sum game, and where the export shifts are large, the loss may be painful.

Regardless of its impact on economic efficiency, active state participation in foreign trade markets is today a well established practice. This presents serious problems for U.S. exporters. They find themselves following rules that apply to the free market U.S. economy in an international economy that is significantly different. They depend on their ability to outperform their international competitors in such areas as price and quality and find that the presence of state intervention has introduced an additional set of criteria that also must be met.

This also presents a serious dilemma for the United States. For the reasons noted earlier, U.S. export performance must improve. It is clear that the United States has not promoted its exports to the extent done by its main competitors. Given this circumstance, it seems highly likely that on the basis of competition on equal terms, the U.S. share of world exports would be higher than it is now.

It has been argued in this paper that the decisions of individuals operating alone in export markets might well result in a lower than socially optimal level of exports. It is obvious that this conclusion has been reached by many of the nations whose exports compete with those of the United States.

[1]See, for example, U.S. Department of Commerce, Business America, "Presidential Declaration Stresses Commitment to Export Growth," 23 October 1978, pp. 13-15.

[2]Export-Import Bank of the United States, Report to the U.S. Congress on Export Credit Competition and the Export-Import Bank of the United States, October 1980, p. 94.

[3]Ibid.

[4]See, for example, Clyde H. Farnsworth, "Washington Watch" in The New York Times, 2 February 1981, p. D2 and President Ronald Reagan's State of the Union Message as reported in The New York Times, 19 February 1981, p. B8.

[5]The typical line of argument against official export credit support programs is typified by Steven E. Plaut in "Export-Import Follies," Fortune, 25 August 1980, pp. 74-77.

[6]Ibid., p. 74.

[7]U.S. Congress, Senate, Committee on Banking, Housing, and Urban Affairs, Subcommittee on International Finance, Hearings on Export-Import Bank Authorization, 95th Congress, 2nd session 20-21 March and 7 and 13 April 1978, pp. 28-31.

[8]The activity of the Eximbank or of its counterparts abroad alters the terms of financing available to importers from what they would otherwise be in free financial markets. This alteration represents a subsidy to exports. It might be argued that official export financing entities can, because of their government status, finance their export loans at lower cost than private financial institutions or the exporters themselves and that, as long as they do no more than pass these savings on to the importers and do not suffer losses as a result of their export financing activities, no subsidy element is present. But the pure cost of credit, devoid of any risk element, would be the same to any borrower. The cost of the loan to the borrower should reflect real cost plus a risk

element that would reflect the importer's risks, not the lender's. To claim that a lower than market interest rate involved no subsidy element, it would have to be argued that, somehow, the risk of an export loan is different for an official export financing entity than for a private financial institution involved in the same activity. There is no inherent presumption that the government is a better manager of risks than a well-managed private entity.

[9]Op. cit., Plaut, p. 76.

[10]Op. cit., President Reagan's State of the Union Message, p. B8.

[11]Op. cit., Plaut, p. 76.

[12]Coproduction, or the willingness to produce part of the import in the importing country, is often important in export sales for government procurement in both developing and industrial countries. Coproduction not only involves a savings of foreign exchange, but it also contributes to employment in the importing country and usually involves the transfer of technology as well. Offset agreements require that the importing country's foreign exchange expenditures be matched to a specific extent by foreign purchases of local products or services arranged by the foreign exporter. Offsets are also designed to result in a savings of foreign exchange and enhanced domestic economic activity for the importing country. Both offsets and coproduction agreements are most likely to occur when the importer is a government. Both types of arrangements, however, can also be made a condition by the government of the importing country for the issuance of a license to a private importer.

[13]Comptroller General of the United States, Financial and Other Constraints Prevent Eximbank from Consistently Offering Competitive Financing for U.S. Exports, 30 April 1980, p. 10.

[14]DeRosa, Dean A., and Nye, William W., "Additionality" In the Activities of the Export-Import Bank of the United States, in hearings before the Subcommittee on International Finance of the Committee on Banking, Housing, and Urban Affairs, United States Senate, 95th Congress, 2nd session, Part 4,

Export-Import Bank Authorization and Related Issues, 20-21 March and 7 and 13 April 1978, pp. 58-76.

[15] Ibid., p. 64.

[16] Gravelle, Jane, Impact of Eximbank on U.S. Exports, Congressional Research Service, The Library of Congress, 25 April 1978.

[17] Op.cit., Farnsworth, p. D2.

[18] See, for example, "A Weak Push for Exports," Business Week, 29 September 1980, p. 138.

[19] See Jack Carlson and Hugh Graham, "The Economic Importance of Exports to the United States," Significant Issues Series, vol. 2, no. 5 (Washington, D.C.: Georgetown University Center for Strategic and International Studies, 1980).

[20] See, for example, U.S. Congress, Senate, Committee on Banking, Housing, and Urban Affairs, Subcommittee on International Finance, U.S. Export Policy: A Report, 96th Congress, 1st session, February 1979, p. 1.

[21] See Raymond F. Mikesell and Mark G. Farah, "U.S. Export Competitiveness in Manufactures in Third World Markets," Significant Issues Series, vol. 2, no. 9 (Washington, D.C.: Georgetown University Center for Strategic and International Studies, 1980), p. 102.

[22] Op. cit., Export-Import Bank Competition Report, October 1980.

[23] Ibid., p. 39.

[24] Op. cit., Financial and Other Constraints Prevent Eximbank from Consistently Offering Competitive Financing for U.S. Exports, 30 April 1980, p. 35.

[25] Ibid., p. i. A more complete assessment of the competitive standing of Eximbank can be found in the October 1980 Export-Import Bank Competition Report.

[26] See A. Wallen, "Implications for the Arrangement of Operational Alternative to the Present Matrix," a report prepared for the Organization for Economic

Cooperation and Development on the Arrangement on Guidelines for Officially Supported Export Credits, April 1980.

[27]Op. cit., Export-Import Bank Competition Report, October 1980.

[28]Ibid.

[29]See "Special Report: U.S. Export Policy," Washington International Business Report, December 1978, p. 3.

[30]U.S. Department of Commerce, International Trade Administration, A Guide to Financing Exports, May 1980, pp. 6-9.

[31]Ibid.

[32]Op. cit., Export-Import Bank Competition Report, October 1980, p. 29.

[33]See, for example, Fowler W. Martin, "European Exporters Having Difficulty Collecting Payment Due to World Woes," in The Wall Street Journal, 4 February 1981, p. 48.

[34]See "How to Work with PEFCO," Private Export Funding Corporation, 15 September 1980.

[35] 1980 Annual Report, Private Export Funding Corporation, 2 February 1981, p. 8.

[36]Op. cit., A Guide to Financing Exports, May 1980, p. 11.

[37]Ibid., pp. 9-10.

[38]See, for example, U.S. Department of Commerce, "New OPIC Programs Promote Exports," Business America, 5 May 1980, p. 20. The $3 billion figure provided by OPIC public affairs office.

[39]See, for example, U.S. Department of Commerce, The Small Business Market Is the World, pp. 15-18.

[40]Op. cit., Senate Banking Committee hearings on Export-Import Bank Authorization, 20-21 March and 7 and 13 April 1978, p. 550.

5

HAS THE U.S. EXPORT PROBLEM BEEN SOLVED?

Penelope Hartland-Thunberg

In 1978, the then Assistant Secretary of Commerce, Frank Weil, observed "Each year, within a year or so from the commencement of a strong export program,.the financial winds change and the balance of payments problem grows less. Thus each time...there is a risk that if our current account deficit shrinks, as we hope it will, that the will behind the effort will be sapped away by other priorities."[1]

Indeed, since those words were spoken, current account deficits of about $15 billion in 1977-1978 have been replaced by a surplus of $5 billion. U.S. exports have grown by 25 percent or more during each of the past two years, and the U.S. trade gap has declined by nearly $5 billion.[2]

Today in the pressure of budget cutting in President Reagan's White House, the current healthy level of U.S. exports is being cited as evidence that money can be saved by cutting such export aids as the loan activities of the U.S. Export-Import Bank. Has the competitive position of U.S. business in world markets really shifted permanently for the better? Or was the Assistant Secretary of Commerce uncommonly prescient in 1978 when he suggested that "other priorities" might once again sap a long-range export effort?

Our examination of the basic determinants of U.S. competitiveness suggests that the sanguine explanation of the improvement in U.S. trade and payments is just that -- merely optimistic.

Basic Determinants of Competitiveness

The competitive position of a nation's exports in world markets is basically a function of its export prices and the uniqueness of its goods. There are very few goods entering world trade today that are truly unique, in the sense that no usable substitute for them exists. Although one item or one supplier may be preferred over another other things being equal, a less preferred item or supplier will be chosen if the price difference is sufficient or if some other consideration compensate for the degree of uniqueness in the preferred item. Certain of the most technologically advanced computers are truly unique for certain purposes, but the number of such truly unique products can probably be counted on one hand. Thus in the vast bulk of international transactions, the determining factor in exports and imports will be price.

The concept of price that is relevant to a consideration of the competitive position of any country is an all-inclusive one, including the time and place of delivery and the time and place of payment. Differing conditions of sale among different potential suppliers frequently are far more important than the price of the narrowly defined product alone in determining which supplier will win the order. This is especially true for "large-ticket" items like aircraft, telecommunications systems, "turnkey" projects involving factories, dams, power systems, or other custom-designed industrial enterprises or systems. Where millions of dollars are involved, differences in design among different suppliers are likely to be minor compared with differences in conditions of sale in determining which bid is accepted. In 1980 Eastern Airlines chose the European-produced Airbus over the Boeing 767, despite the fact that the American product was preferred for its purposes. It did so because the credit terms available with the Airbus made its overall price irresistible. Later Transworld Airlines was induced to order the 767 rather than Airbus because according to the (London) Economist (14 February 1981) "Boeing practically gave away" its price, thus absorbing the credit differential.

For small-ticket items the condition of sale that is probably most important in determining export competitiveness in today's world is the currency in which payment is to be made. With fluctuating exchange rates, the current strength or weakness of a currency can be the determining factor in the choice among potential suppliers. Soundly based econometric studies have demonstrated the close relationship between currency values and total level of exports.[3] For the United States, for example, it has been established that the volume of exports will rise or fall 12 to 18 months after a price change that occurs due to an exchange rate shift.

Price competitiveness in this broad sense is very much subject to the influence of differences in government policies among the trading nations of the world. Differences in financial or monetary policies, undertaken for reasons related to the level of employment or inflation within a country, affect interest rates and exchange rates. On a less aggregative level, differences in national policies regarding such internal matters as environmental controls, business taxes of all kinds, human rights regulations, labor standards and protections can in their cumulative effect have a profound influence on price competitiveness. It is now generally recognized that the competitiveness of American business in world markets has suffered a dual disadvantage of increasing intensity during the past decade or so stemming not only from the cost-increasing impact of regulations of the U.S. government but also from the cost-decreasing impact on U.S. foreign competitors of the export support programs of foreign governments.

Current Position of U.S. Export Competitiveness

Both the U.S. Congress and the executive branch acknowledge the role of U.S. government policies in depressing U.S. exports; it is therefore expected that major steps will be taken this year to remove or amend a number of the more burdensome laws and regulations. The U.S. tax burden on U.S. businessmen abroad is likely to be reduced and the antiboycott law simplified; the Foreign Corrupt Practices Act will probably be made more realistic; antitrust policy as it applies to U.S. business abroad is likely to be adjusted. In addition, the government-wide review of federal rules and regulations as they add to business costs will result in an additional source of relief for U.S. exporters.

At the same time, however, the executive branch has recommended the emasculation of the one U.S. government effort which has had the effect of helping to counter the competitive disadvantage to which U.S. exporters are subjected by foreign government subsidies of their competitors' export credit terms. The reduction in U.S. Export-Import Bank credits proposed in the 1981 U.S. budget comes at a most unfortunate time. As a recent issue of the (London) Economist noted, (14 February 1981) "A credit war has broken out among the rich exporting countries of the West." (p. 78). A four-year-old gentlemen's agreement among OECD countries to adhere to the same credit terms for certain categories of foreign buyers fell apart last year, in large part because of the intransigence of the French. Thus, just at the time when our chief competitors in Europe and Japan have declared credit warfare by making the terms of their officially-supported credits more liberal and more imaginative, the United States is being asked by the executive branch to declare "unilateral disarmament in the trade field."[4]

The forms of direct and indirect subsidies provided by foreign governments to their exporters vary greatly and recently have become increasingly difficult to identify. The important question, however, is whether other developments affecting U.S. exports favorably are likely to be sufficient to counterbalance the unfavorable effect of the credit war and U.S. "disarmament" so that overall U.S. exports will not suffer. The executive branch acknowledges that the cuts in lending could hurt U.S. exports, (Journal of Commerce, 13 February 1981) but their citing the current healthy U.S. export level implies that in their thinking other factors will compensate for the injury.

Skepticism about such claims is warranted because it is widely accepted by competent students of the international economy (e.g. Federal Reserve Bulletin, January 1981, p. 10) that the current improved competitive position of U.S. exporters is the result of the 1977-1978 depreciation of the dollar. Since late 1978, however, the dollar has risen slowly and by the end of 1980, the real effective exchange rate (its trade-weighted value allowing for differences in national rates of inflation as computed by Morgan Guarantee Bank) had returned to its 1977 level.

During the second half of 1980 the dollar rose 7 percent on the average and since then has risen even further against most European currencies. The effects of the dollar's strength will appear in trade data for late 1981 and early 1982, in a decline of U.S. exports and an increase in U.S. imports following the well-established lag of 12 to 18 months.

271

The dollar's recent strength is traceable primarily to extraordinarily high U.S. interest rates, secondarily to slower economic growth during 1980 in the United States than in our major trading partners. Slower U.S. growth depressed U.S. imports more than relatively higher (although slowing) growth rates abroad depressed our exports. The outlook for the next year or two, however, is for a combination of interest rate factors and growth factors both operating to depress U.S. exports.

U.S. interest rates are likely to remain high by historic standards as a result of continued inflationary pressures and the efforts of the monetary authorities to control them. Further, any decline in U.S. interest rates is likely to be accompanied by declining rates abroad because European governments are currently chaffing at being forced into tighter money policies than they wish because of pressures on their exchange rates. Thus the interest rate differential in favor of the dollar will probably endure, sustaining the attraction to foreigners of dollar investments and thereby keeping the dollar strong. A strong dollar, moreover, contributes to the U.S. fight against inflation by keeping import prices low. The probabilities thus favor a continuation of dollar strength and thus a sustained depressant on future U.S. exports.

High interest rates, moreover, will have serious repercussions on the most rapidly growing developing countries which have become important markets for the manufactured exports of the industrial nations and currently absorb one-third of such U.S. exports. The rapidly growing LDCs have been the big borrowers. A large part of their outstanding indebtedness is on a floating interest rate basis. The sharp rise in rates between 1979 and 1980 added 50 percent to their interest payments and contributed significantly to their financial difficulties. Their imports are already growing more slowly under the combined weight of higher prices for oil imports and interest payments; the trend toward deceleration in U.S. exports to these countries is likely to continue at least for the next year or so.

Economic growth in the major industrial countries during 1981 is expected to decline and to be lower than it was in 1980.[5] These facts imply that cyclical factors of declining growth abroad will reinforce the depressing effect of exchange rate factors on U.S. exports. Consideration of the aggregative forces affecting U.S. trade thus do not argue in support of a counterpoise to U.S. "disarmament" in the export credit war.

Despite these aggregative trends are there perhaps specific developments that might influence this conclusion? As we have noted, export credits are an important element in international competition primarily for the large-ticket items, the very expensive exports. Since most of these are custom-tailored for the requirements of the purchaser, they are less vulnerable to exchange rate changes than are consumer goods. This, however, is another way of saying exchange rate changes are usually smaller than other factors like interest rate differentials which combine to determine price bids including conditions of sale.

Relevant to a consideration of the trend in U.S. competitiveness is the change in the U.S. share of world exports of manufactures. In fact, it was persistent decline in this share from over 20 percent in the 1960s to a low of 17 percent in 1978 that sparked the original concern in the United States over a decline in U.S. competitiveness.[6] The inexorable decline in the U.S. share was finally broken in 1979 when the share rose from 17.0 percent to 17.4 percent. Available preliminary data for the first half of 1980 show a continued improvement. The change in direction, welcome as it is, however, is neither sufficiently robust nor of sufficiently long duration to indicate unequivocally that the declining trend has been reversed. In fact, there is a serious danger that U.S. "unilateral disarmament" at the onset of an export credit war could bring about a reversal of the reversal that is being so roundly welcomed.

How long are U.S. exports likely to suffer the effects of cut-throat competition from Europe and Japan in the export credit war? No one can answer the question of course, but it seems safe to conclude that the warfare will last longer if the United States is a nonparticipant than it would if this country, accounting for one-quarter of global GNP, were to be a serious combatant. The intransigence of the French, which was the reason for the failure to renew the previous international agreement on minimum credit terms, would probably evaporate quickly if they became convinced that the U.S. Congress and the U.S. Executive were serious about a threat to meet any government-sponsored credit terms offered by U.S. export competitors. Such a threat, backed by action if necessary, would probably cost the U.S. government less in expenditure than "unilateral disarmament" will in lost revenues.

Summary

History appears to be repeating itself. The Reagan White House is recommending a cut in the funding of the U.S. Export-Import Bank. Other priorities may once again sap a much needed, long-range effort to reverse the trend in the decline of U.S. exports. The reason supporting this cut is the current healthy level of U.S. exports; however, our research suggests that this approach is overly optimistic. The evidence does not support the claim that the long-term decline in U.S. exports has been reversed. Accordingly, we do not believe it wise for the United States, in the current export credit war, to disarm itself unilaterally by cutting the Eximbank funding.

274

[1]Quoted in Penelope Hartland-Thunberg, _Political and Strategic Importance of Exports_, Significant Issues Series (Washington, D.C.: Center for Strategic and International Studies, 1979), p. 18.

[2]Chase Manhattan Bank, _International Finance_, 5 January 1981.

[3]The seminal article in such studies, for example, was H. Junz, and R. Rhomberg "Price Competitiveness in Export Trade Among Industrial Countries," _American Economic Review_, May 1973.

[4]Ambassador Michael A. Samuels in speech before the Scripps Howard Newspaper Editors, Williamsburg, Virginia, 8 September 1980, processed.

[5]OECD, _Economic Outlook_, December 1980.

[6]U.S. Department of Commerce, _International Economic Indicators_, December 1980.

6

U.S. PROGRAMS THAT IMPEDE
U.S. EXPORT COMPETITIVENESS:
THE REGULATORY ENVIRONMENT

Robert A. Flammang

CONTENTS

I. INTRODUCTION

Item: The president of a large U.S. engineering
and construction firm charges that his firm lost
several major construction projects abroad because
European competitors paid off government officials.
The Foreign Corrupt Practices Act of 1977 outlaws such
actions for U.S. firms, but such payments are not
illegal in West Germany and many other countries; they
are considered an ordinary business expense and are
thus tax-deductible.[1]

Item: A Brazilian official recently noted that
"Of the first 70 nuclear reactors built outside the
United States, 63 were American built. In the last
three years, 37 more were built, two of them by U.S.
firms and 35 by European suppliers." U.S. exporters of
such equipment attribute this to the increasingly
stringent application of export controls by the U.S.
government.[2]

Item: In a letter to George Meany, then president
of the AFL-CIO, an Argentine businessman alleges that
identification of Argentina as a human rights violator
has prevented U.S. suppliers from even bidding on at
least $1 billion worth of ships and electronic
equipment the Argentine military is procuring. The
equipment is expected to be supplied by Germany, the
United Kingdom, Canada, and Israel.[3]

Item: The president of a major U.S. shipping
company argues that U.S. businesses are inhibited from
bidding jointly on foreign contracts because of
uncertainties about the legality of such actions under
U.S. antitrust laws. The Justice Department has
promised opinions within thirty days of the time it
receives "all relevant data," but "in thirty days the
French or Germans will have walked away with the
contract."[4]

Item: "After seven months, Beech Aircraft has
still to get a decision on a $3 million sale of

279

training aircraft to Algeria, although the same type of aircraft has previously been supplied to and are in service to that nation."[5]

According to a report of the Senate Banking Committee in February 1979, U.S. exporters believe that "the biggest incentive the United States Government could provide to exports would be to reduce the many export restrictions and disincentives it imposes."[6] This contention is supported by the results of an attitude survey of U.S. corporate executives in June 1979 (see Table 1): those surveyed felt that U.S. government disincentives were more important than foreign government restrictions in all markets except Western Europe. Moreover, in most market areas, the respondents felt that disincentives outweighed the lack of U.S. incentives to export as a reason for the loss of markets.

Table 2, derived from the same survey, highlights those specific disincentives that these executives felt were most restrictive: controls of exports for human rights reasons, administrative delays in export licensing and credit applications, antiboycott laws, environmental review requirements, corrupt practices legislation, economic sanctions, and controls on nuclear exports. Table 3, which specifies those courses of action that these executives felt would be most helpful to the expansion of U.S. business abroad, underlies the importance of relaxing export disincentives in general, but also suggests that appropriate tax incentives and a review of antitrust legislation are also desirable.

In this essay, the focus is on human rights controls, antiboycott regulations, legislation covering corrupt practices, environmental and health considerations, antitrust, taxation, embargoes, and national security measures. (Administrative impediments are discussed elsewhere in this series.) These measures were prompted by the highest of motives: to ease the plight of millions of subjugated people, to promote competition, to contravene bribery, to save the environment, and so forth. But all of these measures also have "by-product" effects on U.S. exports, the balance of payments, domestic employment, and even on the long-run political, economic, and strategic clout

TABLE 1

IMPACT OF GOVERNMENT RESTRICTIONS AND DISINCENTIVES IN
SPECIFIC REGIONAL MARKETS

Regions Where Market Share Has Been Lost Over Last Five Years to Foreign Competitors	Reason For Loss of Market[1]			Magnitude of Loss		
	U.S. Government Disincentives	Lack of U.S. Incentives	Foreign Government Restrictions	Large	Medium	Small
Western Europe......26	26	40	39	24	48	11
Middle East.......69	69	30	24	41	33	11
Africa........52	52	39	20	22	37	22
Asia........37	37	31	37	37	43	04
Communist Nations.....63	63	28	24	26	37	05
Latin America......41	41	44	37	28	52	03

[1]Totals may not add to 100 percent because of multiple responses or nonresponses by some of those surveyed to certain questions.

Source: International Management and Development Institute, Survey Results for June 4, 1979, Joint Council Quarterly Meeting, "Keeping Competitive in the U.S. and World Market Place," Copyright 1979.

281

TABLE 2

ATTITUDES OF U.S. CORPORATE EXECUTIVES TOWARD U.S. EXPORT DISINCENTIVES[1]

	Policy's Overall Impact On U.S. International Business			Importance of Policy's Impact on U.S. International Business and U.S. Trade Balance			
	Positive	Neutral	Negative	High	Medium	Low	Weighted Score[2]
1. Antiboycott laws.......	03	12	81	22	59	18	100
2. Antibribery law (Foreign Corrupt Practices Act).........	0	22	75	20	42	29	95
3. Controls on nuclear exports...............	03	27	68	35	35	18	105
4. Embargoes and economic constraints on trade with:							
North Korea, Vietnam, Kampuchea (Cambodia), Cuba..................	11	29	51	11	14	57	65
Uganda, South Africa, Rhodesia..............	03	20	66	11	46	35	87
5. Economic sanctions against communist countries Jackson-Vanik Amendment (re-emigration from communist countries)..	0	12	77	16	48	22	91
Credit limits on Eximbank..............	03	14	81	24	55	09	104
6. Requirements for environmental reviews on Eximbank and other federal programs.......	0	12	81	24	46	24	102
7. Controls on exports for human rights reasons...	0	07	90	42	31	20	114
8. Controls on exports of arms...............	02	29	55	12	42	27	82
9. Controls on strategically sensitive goods and technologies..........	11	38	53	27	38	27	102
10. Administrative delays and impediments in export licensing, Eximbank application, etc.	0	03	90	38	44	14	119

[1]Total may add to less than 100 percent due to nonresponse by some of those surveyed to certain questions.

[2]Weighted Score: represents the weighted average of the assessment of the importance of government policy impact on international business; 'high' importance responses were multiplied by 3, 'medium' responses by 2 and 'low' responses by 1 to obtain totals for each policy assessed.

Source: International Management and Development Institute, Survey Results for June 4, 1979, Joint Council Quarterly Meeting, "Keeping Competitive in the U.S. and World Market Place."

TABLE 3

NEW PROPOSALS FOR SUPPORTING U.S. INTERNATIONAL BUSINESS:
ASSESSMENT BY CORPORATE EXECUTIVES

		Degree of Importance for U.S. International Business[1]			
		Very Important	Important	Not Important	Need to Know More
1.	Increase in Eximbank loan authorization and more flexibility on interest rates, length of loans, "mixed credits"..............46		50	02	04
2.	Greater funding of Commerce and State export promotion programs.....................09		52	31	07
3.	Review of U.S. antitrust laws in relation to joint ventures and trading companies....................28		37	35	13
4.	Reconstitution of President's Export Council.........06		31	33	24
5.	Formation of new Cabinet Department of Trade...........17		28	31	17
6.	Tax incentives to stimulate greater research and development.......................48		44	04	06
7.	Adoption of VAT (value-added tax) system.............04		33	31	43
8.	Repeal of Jackson-Vanik Amendment tying trade to emigration policies...........31		48	13	06
9.	Streamlining of export controls procedures...........44		48	04	0
10.	Modification or elimination of current export disincentives.................63		31	02	02

[1]Totals may add to less than 100 percent because of multiple responses or nonresponses to certain questions by some of those surveyed.

Source: International Management and Development Institute, Survey Results for June 4, 1979, Joint Council Quarterly Meeting, "Keeping Competitive in the U.S. and World Market Place," Copyright 1979.

of the United States in the world at large --
detrimental effects that were certainly not intended by
either those who authored the programs or those who
administer them today.

The Age of the Specialist

At root, these unintended by-product effects stem
from the growing tendency toward specialization.
Growing populations, the increasing complexity of
modern life, and the information explosion have thinned
the ranks of Renaissance men and women and forced most
people to "know more and more about less and less." So
today the environmentalist knows little about the
economic impact of clean air laws (and, like other
specialists, is usually little concerned about matters
remote to his or her central interest), just as the
business executive knows little about the total
environmental impact of that business's operations.
The world is filled with special interest groups, each
aware of the benefits of the programs they promote and
blissfully unaware of the costs.

When there were still plentiful frontiers for
mankind, it was possible for people to be freer in
their pursuit of benefits and to forget or ignore many
of the consequences of their actions. As the world
fills up and frontiers recede, however, each person's
use of resources and general pattern of behavior will
have an increasing impact upon others. We all become
more vocal when we feel that our interests are being
hurt; the costs of our actions also become more
apparent. There is always a lag between a change and
the human recognition of that change, however, so there
will always be a tendency to overshoot in our pursuit
of a given benefit. When the costs become apparent, we
tone down our actions somewhat so that the benefits and
costs come into a better balance with each other.
Programs that impede U.S. exports need such toning
action.

The Monopoly Mentality

At the end of World War II, the United States was in the most powerful position vis-à-vis the rest of the world that it has ever attained. Politically, economically, militarily (and in our own minds, probably even morally) it was preeminent. Selling abroad was easy, if the buyer could scrape up the cash. Buying abroad was more of a problem, especially when it came to manufactures. The rest of the world needed the United States; the United States had little need of the rest of the world. A "monopoly mentality" was born in those years that is still with us. This mentality assumes that this country is the only effective source of supply and that the denial of supplies is an effective means of influencing foreign behavior. It assumes, likewise, that the U.S. market is the only one that matters, that U.S. technology is supreme, that U.S. investment and aid are alone in the world, and that all of these assumptions can be used as tools to wring concessions from other countries.

As Dr. Penelope Hartland-Thunberg points out in another publication of the U.S. Export Competitiveness Project, the United States did not in fact choose to maintain a monopoly position, but for a variety of humanitarian, strategic, and political reasons chose systematically to help rebuild the economies and polities of Western Europe and Japan and to begin to assist in the development of the less-developed countries in the late 1940s and 1950s.[7] This assistance required balance of payments deficits to supply these regions with funds for reconstruction and development, and deficits in turn led to a de-emphasis on exports and an emphasis on imports. Dr. Thunberg points out that this "Marshall Plan mentality" meant that the United States willingly accepted discriminations against its goods and currency -- nontarriff barriers, undervalued currencies, etc. -- and that mentality became institutionalized. It continues today.

We are thus left with an out of date national mental framework. Although we try to think in less monopolistic terms, there still remains enough of a U.S. monopolistic outlook to influence other countries. The reality is that we have been successful in creating strong friends who are also strong competitors. If we retain a monopoly mentality coupled with the Marshall Plan mentality, we may well end up with a much-reduced international economic stature.

Efficiency vs. Stability

Changing the way we think to make better policy requires that we discover what our goals really are. Until the last decade or so, America's chief economic goals were reasonably apparent to most observers: greater efficiency, greater productivity per man-hour, and a higher standard of living for all. Competition was promoted to encourage efficiency; tax laws were structured to promote efficiency; and environmental concerns were de-emphasized because they might retard efficiency. The monopoly mentality is not one that worries about outside competition or about security.

Growing interdependence has changed the way we behave. American vulnerability to all sorts of shocks was laid bare with the oil embargo of 1973-1974, the resignation of a president, and a unilateral withdrawal in Vietnam. Our concern for efficiency gave way to a rising concern for stability and security. "Project Independence" was one piece of evidence; lack of response to military actions in Africa by Soviet-sponsored groups was another. A cutback on space outlays, greater emphasis on home concerns, the plight of the cities and adequate health care, were others. "Me-ism" flourished -- the ultimate narrowing of our range of concerns.

Growing interdependence, although leading to pullbacks from abroad in areas where we feel we cannot control things, also leads to attempts to extend abroad elements that we do feel we can control. This, after all, also extends our security. The human rights push is an attempt to unite more people under a common moral banner -- specifically, our own conception of human rights as primarily a political and civil issue, rather than an economic and social one. Antiboycott, antibribery, and antitrust measures applied outside the United States are intended to project our notions of proper, open, arms-length business practices beyond our borders. Environmental, health, and safety rules are made to apply in foreign surroundings to convey to others our own ideas of what is ecologically acceptable behavior. We generally treat foreign-earned income the same for tax purposes as we treat domestic-earned income because we feel that it is dangerous to make moral distinctions between the different sources, and we pressure other countries to put an end to special subsidies and tax breaks afforded their exporters for this reason as well as for others. Our vigor in promoting our notions of what is right and wrong outside of our own borders has even led to the charge from some Third World leaders that we are engaging in "moral imperialism."[8]

Flexible Exchange Rates: Panacea?

One of the reasons why the United States has been able to live with the reality of economic retreat coupled with moral attack is the advent of flexible exchange rates. Academic economists have argued for decades that free market determination of exchange rates would solve balance of payments problems. Deficits would drop the value of the dollar, which would encourage exports, discourage imports, and erase the deficit. Surpluses would do the reverse. Policymakers could thus turn their attention to purely domestic matters, letting external economic imbalances settle themselves.

That, at least, is the theory. In practice, balance of payments deficits have been anything but eliminated, although there is little doubt that flexible rates do affect the adjustment process. There are a variety of reasons for the persistence of U.S. deficits, apart from the relatively benign neglect of policymakers.

First, price is not the only factor in a buyer's decision-making calculus, and often not the principal one. In theory, other factors may be held constant; in the real world, they rarely are. Quality, design, credit terms, delivery times, service after the sale, and continuity or reliability often outweigh price considerations. U.S. exporters often lose sales because of one of these nonprice factors. A buyer's expectation of future price increases may also divert a U.S.

sale to another supplier. Or, as seems to be the case with a large portion of U.S. exports, foreigners may simply be relatively insensitive to price reductions for the kinds of goods the United States sells or in the markets where it sells.

Second, U.S. price advantages may be nullified by a wide variety of trade restrictions in customer countries. Import quotas prevent price reductions from having any effect, as to variable import levies such as those employed by the European Economic Committee (EC) on agricultural products. Government purchases (a major part of total purchases in many countries) may be effectively limited to domestic suppliers. Central bank intervention to prop up the dollar may prevent price advantages from being fully expressed in the customer's marketplace. Subsidies or special loans to local competitors may prevent imports from the United States. The list can be extended "ad nauseum," but, as Dr. Thunberg notes, the Marshall Plan mentality has led the United States to accept many of these impediments to U.S. exports without installing similar impediments of its own.

Third, growth rate differences may offset price advantages for U.S. exporters. The United States grew faster than did most of its trading partners in the last half of the 1970s, consuming more imports here while exports, in real terms, stagnated. Moreover, U.S. exports are relatively "income inelastic" (insensitive to income changes) compared to its imports, particularly in the short run, so that foreign incomes would have to grow faster than U.S. incomes just to keep trade balanced.[9]

Fourth, the technology lead of the United States has evaporated in many product lines, partly because of increased research and development expenditures abroad and partly because of both a de-emphasis on U.S. R&D activity overall and a diversion of attention to environmental, as opposed to cost-reducing objectives. Both governmental and private U.S. budgets have suffered from revenue constraints throughout the 1970s, and long-term investments have generally been sacrificed for the sake of short-term consumption.

Fifth, many U.S. producers have simply not been interested in exporting. The large domestic market is lucrative and foreign markets are mystifying enough to make exporting more a luxury than a necessity. Awareness of both the threat and the promise of growing involvement in the international economy has been slow in coming; it is to be hoped that the "export or perish" syndrome so characteristic of smaller countries will begin to rub off on potential U.S. exporters before the comfortable existence heretofore enjoyed ends with a loud roar.

The Roots of Power

The panacea of flexible exchange rates has thus tended to fade in the complexities of the real world, yet we continue to deny a portion of U.S. exports in the belief it will have some beneficial effect abroad. As specialists, we still promote our favorite benefits with little realization of their associated costs. The irony of all this is that, in good Marxian fashion, we are producing the antithesis of what we want.

Power is vital to survival, and survival is the ultimate goal of the nation-state, a social organism, just as it is of physical organisms. Power in the international arena is the ability to influence other countries, and it has its roots in contacts -- trade contacts, investment contacts, aid contacts, political and social contacts, and so forth. Influence cannot be exerted unless there is some kind of contact, or perception of contact.

Of course, contact is also at the root of vulnerability -- susceptibility to influence by others. Contact itself does not mean that one country, on balance, is in a position to exercise power over another. The balance of power depends on the structure of the contact and on what is happening to that structure over time. For example, U.S. trade links with the rest of the world have been growing faster than domestic trade; by itself, this means little from a balance of payments standpoint except that we can both influence others and be influenced by others to a greater degree than heretofore. The balance of power depends on what is being exported and imported, how important these items are to the United States vis-à-vis its trading partners, what other sources of supply

289

and market outlets are available, and so forth. In other words, the balance of power depends on the structure of the contact.

Changes in the structure of the contact also affect the perceived balance of power -- this is the momentum (or trend) aspect of power. A country with growing dependence on oil imports, for example, may be perceived as losing power even though it has far less relative and absolute dependence on imported oil than another country that is freezing or reducing its dependence upon outside energy sources.

It is this momentum that most afflicts the United States as we leave the 1970s and confront the 1980s. Growing interdependence is not really the problem; rather, it is the changing structure of our contact -- especially our trade contacts -- with the rest of the world. U.S. oil dependence (and other raw material dependence) has been growing at the same time that foreign technological dependence on this country has been declining. Our survival as a nation may well depend on how well we can conserve and stretch both domestic and imported vital materials and on how well we can regalvanize our research and development efforts. Overall, we must consume less and work more.

It is common to hear references to "the U.S. defeat in Vietnam." What actually happened, of course, is that the U.S. unilaterally withdrew its forces, feeling that the costs of our involvement outweighed the benefits. With few benefits visible, we lacked commitment. Today, we tend to find ourselves with-drawing from the export arena, in part because of government policies with significant anti-export content and in part because we still think as monopolists and suffer from a woeful lack of commitment to exporting.

Our diminishing export profile thus appears to be part of a larger malaise, an unwarranted loss of confidence that stems in part from Vietnam, in part from Watergate, in part from the economic resurgence of Japan and Western Europe, and in part from our addiction to past illusions, our love of the "good life", and an ostrich-like desire "not to get involved" in anything, including an increasingly competitive world market.

Ironically, a unilateral retreat from world competition reduces contact and reduces our power to do anything abroad -- to promote human rights, fight corruption, put an end to boycotts, improve the natural environment, or whatever. We are doing the opposite of what we want to do, very steadfastly, with the best of intentions.

II. U.S. EXPORT DISINCENTIVES

The Human Rights Campaign

Human rights concerns are not new, nor are they exclusively the domain of Americans. Thomas Jefferson held in the Declaration of Independence that all are endowed "with certain inalienable Rights." The phrase was echoed 13 years later by the National Assembly in France, by most European declarations of political and civil rights of the nineteenth century, by the Charter of the United Nations, and even by the constitutions of some of today's most repressive states.

There has been, however, a notable shift in meaning for the term "human rights" in the twentieth century. From a rather narrow focus on civil and political liberties, the definition has broadened to include basic social and economic rights, including adequate food, housing, education, and medical care. In the United States, however, the older emphasis on political and civil matters still seems paramount, so that we find ourselves condemning civil rights violations in a number of countries that have made remarkable progress on the economic and social front. The Soviet Union and China are outstanding examples. These countries respond with charges that the United States is a prime human rights offender, as evidenced by its continuing discrimination against minorities and women, by its failure to meet minimum United Nations standards for prisons, and by its failure to ratify every principal U.N. convention or covenant dealing with human rights since the original charter. In the Third World, where political and civil liberties exist mainly on paper, the common view is that these aspects of human rights are luxuries that must wait until basic economic and social needs are met. So human rights advocates do not stand on common ground even with respect to definitions.

The U.S. campaign for human rights around the world has been institutionalized in several pieces of legislation. The Harkin amendments to U.S. economic aid legislation in 1975 and military aid legislation in 1976 make human rights a consideration in the allocation of assistance and human rights provisos are now

292

attached to loans from the Export-Import Bank, to investment guarantees from the Overseas Private Investment Corporation, to Public Law 480 agricultural sales under Title I, and even to the services of the Peace Corps. The U.S. government is even pressuring the World Bank to take human rights into consideration in its lending, a politicizing action drawing much flak from nearly all quarters, at home and abroad.

The score card on the effectiveness of U.S. human rights policies is mixed, at best. On the positive side, we can note releases of political prisoners and some easing in the treatment of those not released in the Dominican Republic, Chile, Morocco, Tanzania, Korea, and several other places. Elections have been held in Panama and Ecuador, Uganda is free of Idi Amin, and Nicaragua of Anastasio Somoza. The movement of dissidents from the Soviet Union increased for a time, and there is more freedom of expression in China. In many other areas, however, human rights have not been affected or have taken a turn for the worse. Argentina has simply turned to other suppliers, Guatemala has done the same, most Arab states have stood their ground, the Soviet Union has hardened its stand against its dissidents, Iran traded one dictatorship for another, and there has been no impact at all on Vietnam, Laos, North Korea, Burma, or Cambodia, the worst offenders of all. Even where human rights have improved, of course, there is no certainty that U.S. policy is the cause, even in part. In South Africa, for example, the economic position of blacks has improved, but it was improving before the U.S. human rights offensive was launched.

The fact is that most foreign observers see U.S. policies on human rights as politically naive and fundamentally unworkable. A former assistant secretary of state and director of the National Humanities Center, Charles Frankel, claims that the policies imply that "a government can insert itself between another government and its citizens," and that this is both contrary to "a functioning system of international law and reasonably peaceful relations between nations."[10] Moreover, the denied credits or supplies are normally available somewhere else: Argentina turned to Britain, Germany, France, and Israel for its arms, Ethiopia turned to the Soviet Union, Nicaragua turned to Israel, etc. The net result upon the United States may thus be negative in three ways: "U.S. credibility is reduced, the offending nation still obtains the products it seeks from other nations, and the U.S. trade balance suffers."[11]

Ironically the use of economic sanctions by the United States to promote human rights may even worsen conditions for those who are supposed to be beneficiaries. First, it often strengthens the hand of the offending government as its supporters unite to oppose U.S. efforts; Rhodesia and South Africa are cases in point, as are Chile and Argentina. Second, its effects are quite often directed particulary at the poor. If economic assistance is cut to an offending Third World country, for example, more often than not it will be the poor who will suffer most. If South Africa suffers a recession because of a U.N.-sponsored boycott, it will be mainly blacks who suffer the loss of jobs and income. Third, if U.S. export sales are lost, those who will be laid off first will be the inexperienced, the elderly, the Hispanic, the black, and the newly-employed women -- the marginal workers in this country, in other words, those who have trouble meeting their basic needs.

And are U.S. export sales lost because of the human rights campaign? The Department of State, counting denied sales and orders not bid, estimated in 1978 that the branding of Argentina as a human rights violator, along with other U.S. export restrictions, cost the United States $813,519,000 in exports, a figure that "may indeed be conservative since we cannot accurately calculate the cost of already discouraged business due to our widely known licensing and financing delays."[12] This figure, remember, is for Argentina alone. In Brazil U.S. electrical equipment manufacturers were effectively excluded from bidding on the Itaipu hydroelectric project (worth $200 million in orders) and the Itaipu high voltage transmission project (worth $900 million) because of human rights considerations. In South Africa the same group was constrained from bidding on nearly $540 million of electrical equipment for coal mines and nuclear power plants, again mainly (in their view) because of human rights considerations. There is no guarantee that U.S. exporters would have won all of these contracts, of course, but they certainly would have won some. Nor is this set of examples exhaustive. Clearly, lost sales

worldwide for all U.S. exporting firms could easily
amount to several billion dollars, and with 35,000-
40,000 jobs at stake for each billion dollars worth of
exports (a consensus of several estimates), the
employment considerations are far from negligible.

Thus, U.S. human rights policies fall short both
with respect to results and with respect to those who
pay for whatever results are obtained. We have failed
to distinguish between human rights as an objective and
human rights as a policy. No one can quarrel with the
objective, but human rights as a policy confuses ends
with means. Human rights policy reduces mainly to
preaching, since the economic weapon doesn't work.
Preaching reeks of moral imperialism, of arrogance, of
blindness to one's own shortcomings. It irritates
without yelding results. For if a country should
comply with U.S. demands that it put its own house in
order, it in effect admits that it has been a human
rights violator; its pride cannot be saved. On the
other hand, quiet diplomacy with a nolo contendere tone
may not only be more effective, but cost virtually
nothing.

The execution of U.S. human rights policies has
also been far from uniform. We have come down hard on
friendly countries like Argentina, Chile, South Korea,
the Philippines, Thailand, and Indonesia and have had
little to say about genocide in Cambodia, Vietnam, and
Laos. (In fact, when Vietnam promises to reduce the
rate of exodus of the boat people, it is hailed as a
great humanitarian nation.) Sales have been approved,
then disapproved, then approved again. Although Sandra
Vogelgesang argues that "concentration on consistency
. . . misses the point" because we apply pressure only
on those over whom we have some leverage, the appear-
ance is clearly one of a double standard of morality.[13]
Moreover, our leverage is mainly over friendly nations,
those with whom we have a degree of economic and
political contact. Selective application of human
rights policies thus means we must alienate those
closest to us, give them every reason to reduce their
contact with us, and leave us with no leverage at all.
Far from missing the point, selective application of
human rights policies can be nothing less than a
blueprint for failure.

Intentions are one thing. Effects are another.

Antiboycott Regulations

The Export Administration Act of 1979 (Public Law 96-72) presently prohibits "any U.S. person" from taking actions "with intent to comply with, further, or support any boycott fostered or imposed by a foreign country against a country which is friendly to the United States and which is not itself the object of any form of boycott pursuant to United States law or regulation."

The purpose of this prohibition is to prevent U.S. exporters from cooperating with the Arab states' boycott of Israel. The boycott, which began in 1946, was initially a primary boycott wherein the participating Arab states agreed not to deal with Israeli companies or nationals. In 1951, the boycott was extended to the secondary stage, in which the cooperating states agreed not to do business with any firm that did business with Israel. It has since moved to the tertiary stage, which prohibits firms doing business in Arab countries from doing business with any firm (regardless of nationality) that does business with Israel, and has even required that firms doing business in Arab countries supply information regarding the religious affiliations of their owners and managers. The United States does not condemn primary boycotts, but has outlawed cooperation with secondary and tertiary boycotts since 1977 on the grounds that no U.S. firm should be barred from dealing with a friendly country or with another U.S. firm because of a foreign boycott.

As a principle, this and other antiboycott regulations of the United States stand on firm ground. If Arab states choose not to deal with Israel, we are saying, fine. If their pressure, however, carries to the second and third remove, it interferes with the rights of others and may even prevent one U.S. firm from dealing with another.

In practice, the Arab boycott of Israel had little effect until the oil blockade of 1973-1974 and the multiplying of prices during the same period. Not all countries held to the agreement, and those that did, often did so sporadically. With the surge of petro-dollars into the Middle East and the rapid expansion of

exports to Arab countries, however, the boycott began
to bite. Many U.S. exporters found themselves
effectively restricted and complied with the Arab
boycott. The response in this country was so strong
that earlier encouragement not to comply was replaced
with mandatory noncompliance provisions.

U.S. exporters in general support the concept
behind U.S. antiboycott legislation, but argue that
diplomatic negotiations are a more preferable way to
settle boycott questions. They point out that antiboycott regulations only anger Arab countries at a time
when the push for peace in the Middle East is most
pronounced. Moreover, competing countries have not
imposed antiboycott measures of their own, allowing
their firms to enjoy greater business at the partial
expense of U.S. firms. It is also alleged that large
firms with sizable legal staffs have found ways to work
within the antiboycott rules, while small firms find
themselves shut out.

The amount of U.S. export sales lost due to
antiboycott legislation is, of course, not known.
Shortly after U.S. mandatory antiboycott reglations
took effect, however, the London _Times_ noted that U.S.
firms began to lose more business in traditionally
friendly Saudi Arabia: a $953 million industrial
project at the port of Jubail went to a Korean company;
a $300 million contract for the construction of the new
Jeddah international airport was lost by Brown and
Root, a U.S. firm, to Hochtief of West Germany; the
British edged out Americans on a $200 million hospital
construction contract; a $163 million port development
project went to a Greek company; and Westinghouse, who
wrote into their bid that they would not comply with
the Arab boycott requirements, lost a $1 billion water
desalinization contract to a Japanese firm. Certainly
these were not necessarily lost just because of the
antiboycott regulations, but one observer felt that a
"certain wariness" had been introduced between Americans and Saudis by the legislation.[14] Additionally,
the U.S. heavy electrical equipment industry estimates
that antiboycott legislation has cost them almost $800
million in export sales in only two years, including a
$400 million steam power plant project in Kuwait, a
similar $200 million project in Iraq, and a $170 million one in Syria. Moreover, Deere & Company
reportedly was prevented from bidding on a contract to

supply $18 million worth of tractors to Iraq by the legislation, according to testimony before the Senate Banking Committee in October 1978.

The official position of the Carter administration, however, is that few, if any, sales to Arab states have been lost because of the antiboycott provisions. Former Secretary of Commerce Juanita Kreps, in testimony before the Senate Banking Committee regarding the extension of the Export Control Act in March 1979, argued that a satisfactory balance had been struck between resisting boycotts and minimizing adverse effects on exports.[15] She noted that exports to the Middle East had risen 16 percent since the regulations took effect, with exports to Saudi Arabia up 22 percent and to Kuwait up 36 percent: "So clearly the impact on our trade has not been disastrous as some predicted it would." Secretary Kreps also reported that fewer questionnaires are now required of U.S. firms doing business with Arab states and that some businesses report that having the backing of the law has allowed them to resist boycott demands without losing particular sales.

If the antiboycott regulations of the United States have in fact cost few exports, we can, of course, be pleased. There is no way to firmly establish this at the macroeconomic level, however, because the rising incomes of the Arab oil states are a powerful magnet for any country's exports. This, however, is not really the point. As with the case of human rights, the question really is "are measures of this type appropriate to the end desired?" Do they, in other words, help to end the situation that gave rise to the boycott in the first place -- the hostilities between Israel and its Arab neighbors? Granted there may be fewer demands for cooperation from U.S. firms exporting to the Middle East, but, is this really the test of success? The root of the problem is not the existence of secondary or tertiary boycotts; if this were so, the United Statees itself could not engage in secondary boycotts. The facts are that the United States secondarily boycotted Switzerland during World War II (and Switzerland was a neutral country) and today blacklists 203 ships owned by a variety of nationalities because those ships have made at least one call in Cuba. The test of success has to be whether it can affect the economic warfare between

Israel and its Arab neighbors or not. It clearly cannot. So the tool is inappropiate to the task, serves to undermine contact with a group of countries with whom contact is very important in any sense to the United States, strengthens our competitors and does virtually nothing to either strengthen Israeli security or satisfy Arab claims for justice.

Why, then, do we have antiboycott legislation? The benefits have been domestic and political and received by the government; the costs, less visible, have also been domestic, but are mainly economic and borne by particular exporters, their employees, and suppliers. Pain always seems slight to those who do not have to bear it, and benefits slight to those who do not receive them. That is probably why our government's position is that the negative effects of the antiboycott regulations have been slight, while our exporters' position is that they have been substantial. The myopic specialists lives on.

The Foreign Corrupt Practices Act

In 1977 Congress passed the Foreign Corrupt Practices Act after hearing testimony citing payoffs by U.S. firms or their representatives to foreign political officials. President Carter signed the bill with enthusiasm, noting that such practices had disturbed and often weakened political relationships between the United States and many of its key trading partners. The law forbids any domestic firm or anyone acting in its behalf from giving anything of value to any foreign government official, political party official, or anyone who might reasonably be expected to transfer the value to them; the same prohibition applies to recipients that are units of government or political parties. Penalties are stiff: up to $10,000 and/or five years in prison for the offenders and up to $1 million for the corporation involved. Companies are expected to keep very accurate records and employ stringent internal control measures to prevent such payments.[16]

To a very large extent, the law reflects American ignorance of the very significant differences between our culture and foreign cultures. In ancient times, kings exchanged gifts to cement political or military alliances; heads of state still do so today, as former President Nixon's gift of a helicopter to President Sadat of Egypt (and many other examples) can attest. In many countries, business is conducted in a highly ritualistic way that echoes the ancient patterns; business negotiators are expected to approach the nitty-gritty very slowly by first building close personal relationships, often by hosting one another and exchanging pleasantries and gifts. Times are changing, however. Today, an American executive can truthfully say, "the commissions we used to pay are still a social and business custom in some countries, but now they're crimes as far as we're concerned."[17]

In the United States, business or government negotiators are expected to maintain an "arms length" relationship with those with whom they are negotiating to avoid "conflicts of interest" that might permit them to profit at public expense, and properly so. In most other parts of the world, however, the economic, political, and social aspects of life are not as split apart as they are here; the arms length approach is simply not feasible. The local sales representative for a foreign company may also be an important political figure, and may feel incensed if he is asked to step aside so that the firm he heretofore represented can deal with someone else in the government. These nuances, however, are often not appreciated by U.S. lawmakers. And what is a legitimate "commission" in one country is seen as a "bribe" in another.

This is clearly another case of attempting to export morality. David Ball argues pursuasively that the law strengthens the market system by giving management more control and information and by reducing the chances that U.S. companies will be approached for bribes, but this argument assumes just one type of "market system" in the world and that is the American type. In fact, market systems are often almost inseparable from political systems. Although it is true that the economic side of life is becoming increasingly separated from the political as economic development occurs, in few places has it reached the stage it has in the United States. This is one reason (the dependence upon exports is another) why most other countries, including major industrial competitors of the United States, either do not consider payments to political officials a crime or do not enforce their laws with much vigor if they are on the books.

Again, the tool is fundamentally inappropriate to the task. Punishment of U.S. firms for doing what their competitors can do with impunity does not make the world more honest, nor does it extend American moral influence abroad. Bribery can be stopped only if all countries agree on what a bribe is and agree among themselves to put an end to it. Unilateral moves can only be self-defeating. Annual U.S. export losses attributable to U.S. antibribery legislation are roughly estimated by a White House task force on export disincentives at $1 billion.[18] Meanwhile, "an anti-commercial bribery treaty, proposed by the United States, is languishing in an inactive committee of the Economic and Social Council with little prospect for early agreement even in a working draft."[19]

The U.S. exporting community, predictably, is not completely happy with U.S. antibribery legislation but is reluctant to say so for fear the public will assume they are probribery. On the whole, businessmen have confined themselves to pointing out examples of lost exports without moral gains or to asking for more explicit guidelines from the Justice Department with respect to the 1977 law. The Justice Department, however, opposes identifying behavior that it will not prosecute, but will offer advice "on the type of conduct we think is most egregious."[20]

This leaves U.S. firms in a situation where they must turn down foreign business if they even suspect they could be charged with bribery. Thus, firms experience a "chill effect." They are then forced into marketing approaches that are "unnaturally conserva-tive" because the language of the law is "too sweeping" and "too ambiguous." As evidence, some have argued that a corporation can be held liable for violations of the act even when an employee disobeys expressed orders, or when an executive can be shown to "have reason to know" that sales agents abroad were making payoffs. Justice Department officials, however, apparently want to maintain the gray areas of uncer-tainty so that the chill effect can live on: "All they (businessmen) want to know is who they can bribe and who they can't. Well, we're not going to tell them -- we'll go down kicking and screaming on this one."[21] So much for cultural awareness in the Department of Justice.

Since the law does not achieve its intended purpose and cannot, and since the United States is not the monopoly supplier the law assumes, it should be repealed until an international antibribery code can be agreed upon. If this proves to be impossible for political reasons, it should be interpreted so broadly as to have the same effect as similar legislation in competitor countries. When the rest of the world finally recognizes that bribery merely reshuffles business instead of increasing it, when the market system in most countries evolves further from the socio-politico-economic milieu in which it is now bound, when the world comes closer to sharing the same values, the interpretation can narrow. For now, however, the law, far from being a beacon of morality guiding the saved from a corrupt world, is an instrument of self-flagellation that much of the world views with amusement.

Environmental, Health, and Safety Regulations

The United States has a wide array of environmental, health, and safety regulations (stemming from clean air and water legislation, occupational safety and health legislation, and legislation dealing with toxic substances, consumer product safety, and retirement security) that increase the cost of products and reduce export competitiveness indirectly. Until January 1979, many U.S. exporters were required to file environmental impact statements projecting what the effects of the sale would be upon the foreign environment. On 4 January 1979, President Carter issued an executive order that exempts more exporters from this requirement; nuclear reactors and certain toxic substances, however, still cannot be exported without such statements, which generally take thirty-one months to complete, even if the importing country has no such requirements.[22]

There is little question that environmental conditions affect the entire world. Air and water cross national boundaries, and we all share the world's oceans and seas. The world, however, is not yet of one

302

mind as to how safe the environment should be: rich countries who can afford to divert more of their resources to maintaining or cleaning up the environment have one set of standards, and poor countries with massive unemployment and low incomes have another. Ironically, the rich countries, with their large industrial sectors, are the biggest polluters. If the United States truly wishes to protect the world environment, nothing would be more effective than cutting our use of fossil fuels, chemicals, and other exotic substances to near zero. Since this is unthinkable for most people, we have chosen to make a trade-off. For example, we are steadily moving to eliminate the use of lead compounds in our gasoline, although we are not moving nearly as quickly to eliminate our usage of gasoline. (One estimate claims that reducing the lead content of our gasoline necessitates an additional $1.2 billion of crude oil imports into the United States each year, even though lead filters can be employed with catalytic converters on automobiles and even though it has not been firmly established that lead compounds are more hazardous to our health than the materials that replaced them.) Our trade-offs, in other words, are different from those of many other countries that still use lead in gasoline to reduce the need for imported fuel and are willing to suffer some deterioration in air quality to get it.

The loss of U.S. exports traceable to health, safety, and environmental considerations is large, indeed, if we include prohibitions on the export of nuclear equipment under this heading. U.S. suppliers of such equipment estimate that they have been prevented from bidding on $8.7 billion of nuclear power plants in Spain, Iran, South Africa, Switzerland, Brazil, Romania, and the Peoples Republic of China. In virtually all cases, the buyers were able to place orders with suppliers from other countries, particularly France and West Germany. In the words of Bodurtha and Hawkins, "administration policies may, in fact, kill the domestic nuclear industry."[23]

The problem is that requiring environmental impact statements before items can be exported, or prohibiting the export of nuclear equipment, does not really encourage environmental protection around the world. Importers simply turn to other suppliers. Large firms with large legal staffs and armies of technicians may be able to comply with remaining controls and still export, but many small firms cannot. The net effect is a decline in U.S. exports, greater concentration of those that remain in fewer hands, and, in general, little or no improvement in the environment.

The way to improve the world environment is to take a world approach. Multinational agreements to limit production of hazardous items are much more likely to be effective then unilateral attempts by single suppliers. It is true that agreements are difficult to negotiate and standards hard to set, but if the environment is really worth it -- and it is -- why not take steps that will work, however difficult, instead of steps that only create the illusion they are working?

Antitrust Legislation

The United States has the oldest and most vigorously enforced antitrust legislation in the world; indeed, only about thirty countries have such legislation. The benefits of the antitrust program have been substantial -- certainly the U.S. economy is much more competitive, efficient, and vigorous than it would be in its absence. What is more, antitrust laws have generally been applied with a keen appreciation of the real world. The thrust has generally been to promote "workable competition" rather than seek some theoretical degree of purity of competition. Thus we have found labor unions and farmers' organizations exempted from the antirust laws to better balance power in those particular marketplaces; cartel-like arrangements have been tolerated in coal mining and agriculture when it appeared that this would put these industries on better footing vis-à-vis less competitive sectors with whom they have to deal; mergers of competitive firms have been permitted when it could be shown that this strengthened competition in industries like automobiles and steel.

In the international arena, however, the norm of "workable competition" has yet to be applied in a consistent way, partly because of the many complexities encountered there. U.S. companies complain that no other government restricts their enterprises nearly so much in setting up joint ventures abroad, in engaging in consortium bidding, in licensing foreigners to produce patented or trademarked goods abroad, in dealing with centralized state trading countries, or in negotiating with commodity cartels like OPEC. No other government, they allege, offers so few firm guidelines for what is acceptable behavior abroad, or is so eager to apply its antitrust laws extraterritorily. No other government, they believe, takes such a strong adversary stance with respect to their own firms; most even encourage mergers and cartels among their firms in their overseas selling and investment activities.

Since 1918 the United States, under certain circumstances, has permitted its exporters to combine to promote their export trade. The Webb-Pomerene amendment to the Sherman and Clayton antitrust legislation allows firms to join together, share marketing costs, and bid jointly for international business to meet the competition of foreign cartels and consortia better, as long as this activity does not adversely affect competition in the U.S. market. Businesses complain, however, that there is too much uncertainty with shifting interpretations of what is legal and illegal, and they note that the number of Webb-Pomerene associations has declined, even as cartelization and state trading have grown abroad. Also, it has been mainly larger firms that have taken advantage of Webb-Pomerene; smaller firms lack either the legal expertise or the desire to become involved with their competitors for export purposes.

One peculiarity of the U.S. antitrust program is particularly burdensome to the small firm: wholly owned subsidiaries abroad tend to be more acceptable under the law than subsidiaries in which the U.S. firm has minority ownership in conjunction with some foreign competitor. Apparently, the thinking is that cooperation with a foreign competitor is more dangerous to competitive conditions than total ownership of a foreign operation. The net result, whatever the intent, is that large U.S. firms are more likely immune from antitrust prosecution for their overseas activities than small U.S. firms. How this serves to intensify world competition is something of a mystery. Also, since many Third World governments, in particular, tend to insist upon local participation in producing enterprises within their borders, U.S. firms find themselves at a competitive disadvantage vis-à-vis firms from other industrial countries who face no such restrictions. And when U.S. firms are barred from joint ventures in this fashion, the United States loses whatever "pull-through" exports (exports from the U.S. parent or its suppliers) that could be involved.

In truth, no one has been able to establish clearly what net effects the antitrust laws of the United States have upon its exports. According to one internal study by a major exporter of electrical equipment, the United States has lost almost $400 million in foreign sales in recent years because it was constrained by increasingly stringent interpretations of potential wrongdoing by the Justice Department; it had planned to form consortia with large U.S. and foreign firms (who were competitors in the U.S. market) to bid on various hydroelectric and metro-transit projects in Latin America and the Middle East. The Justice Department also barred another company from supplying commercial services to a joint venture it formed with two foreign government-owned companies in Europe in the 1960s. This company estimated that the lack of this input cost it $12 million of investment funds and up to $500,000 annually of lost export sales. Still another company, planning to form an export association under the Webb-Pomerene Act with two other firms to export to Japan, dropped the venture because its proposed partners did not feel the act offered enough protection from possible antitrust prosecution. This list could be extended at some length, but there is little point because of the nature of the evidence: it is a cataloging of exports that might have occurred if corporate decision makers had not been discouraged by antitrust prosecutions that might have been served.

On the opposite side of the coin, the Justice Department argues that U.S. antitrust legislation does not prohibit joint ventures or joint bidding abroad, as long as one company cannot singly undertake the project. It also notes that Webb-Pomerene associations have been prosecuted only when they made price agreements with their competitors abroad, attempted to share markets with them, prevented individual association members from competing with the association itself, and the like. In all, it argues that its actions have prevented restrictive behavior abroad that would have served to retard exports.

Overall, however, it is difficult to see how restrictions on U.S. firms that are not paralleled by restrictions on their foreign competitors can really improve competitive conditions around the world, or fail to hamper U.S. exports in general. The freezing out of U.S. firms hardly makes for greater competitiveness in world markets. The fact is that the structure of world competition has been changing rapidly in the last 20 years. Adam Smith's ideal of numerous small firms acting autonomously in competitive markets has faded into the reality of large multinational enterprises, state buying and selling organizations, and cartels. Galbraith's notion of countervailing power suggests that <u>de facto</u> competition in such a world is more likely to be created if similar-sized sellers on reasonably common ground compete for the buyer's money. This is not to argue that U.S. firms are infinitesimal while their foreign competitors are large; it is to argue that the day of unilateral restraint aimed at the reconstruction of war-torn economies and the development of viable producers in the Third World is coming to an end. The Marshall Plan era is over.

Competitive conditions in the United States and abroad are much more likely to result from a common code of unfair trade practices, uniformly enforced, than from a "good example" approach by the United States or any other country. Moreover, a common code is more likely to be developed if other countries feel the pressure of U.S. competition on the same basis on which they themselves operate than if the United States denies its producers equal access to foreign markets. If our antitrust stance abroad is one of "equal morality" rather than "superior morality," it is much more likely that there will be a common interest in a common code, or in making a common code more "moral." Common action requires a common interest.

In fact, the "superior morality" approach of the United States has provoked reactions from friendly countries. The British government recently introduced legislation that would block the enforcement of U.S. court decisions, multiple damage awards, and subpoenas on British soil when British firms are involved in U.S. antitrust actions. The British object to "the accumulation of attempts by the United States to impose its own economic and other domestic policies on individuals and companies outside its territorial jurisdiction."[24] Approval by the Parliament is considered by virtual certainty, and other countries are expected to follow suit with similar legislation. Interestingly enough, according to a British government official "We have tried to solve this situation quietly" through diplomatic channels, but "with little success. So we decided to show a little bit of muscle to defend our companies and our sovereignty."[25] The "equal morality" approach would clearly have a much better chance of success.

Tax Legislation

All countries levy taxes, but there the similarity ends. They may be laid on income, wealth, value added, sales, capital gains, exports, imports, or on a per-head basis. They may be based on window area, number of male children, size of herds, or anything else that is measurable. They vary in degree of enforcement, level of rates, and in incidence. They may be intended for revenue or for control purposes. Their overall impact on economic activity is still very much unknown. Guesses by experts are still guesses.

The United States taxes income from exports generally the same way it taxes other income. There are some exceptions, to be sure, but special treatment of some source of income or some category of expense is not nearly as common in the United States as it is abroad. Many other countries apply the "territoriality" principle, meaning that only income, property, or transactions within their national borders are subject to tax. Export incomes are thus exempt altogether from taxation, or are taxed at lower rates. Still other countries defer taxes for various periods on export incomes, thus giving exporters interest free use of funds for those periods. Nearly all countries permit drawbacks of customs duties on imported components that are later exported, many give special incentives to firms that invest in less developed countries, most subsidize certain exports indirectly or directly, and so forth. The list goes on and on.

Since 1971, the United States has used tax policy to encourage exports by permitting tax deferral through

Domestic International Sales Corporations (DISCs). Since foreign subsidiaries of U.S. firms are permitted to defer taxes on undistributed income until it is remitted home, it was considered likely that production abroad would be preferred over export activities unless exporters were offered the same benefits; hence, the institution of the DISCs. An exporter can set up a special sales corporation aimed at foreign markets where virtually all its income and assets have to be export-derived or export-related. Qualified corporations can effectively defer taxes on 50 percent of their income until it is remitted to the parent company. Moreover, tax-deferred income can be lent to the parent if it is a manufacturing company and if the funds are used to generate additional exports.

Opinion is divided regarding the effectiveness of DISCs in expanding exports at a reasonable cost in terms of foregone tax receipts. In general, the business community argues that DISCs have helped considerably, while the Treasury department contends that many DISC exports have merely replaced non-DISC exports while draining off excessive tax revenues. The balance of opinion in government seems to be that DISCs are not truly cost effective, but that removing them without offering some sort of alternative would be worse than leaving things as they are.

A report by the Senate Banking Committee suggests that DISCs could be made more effective by extending them to the small suppliers of exporters who are not exporting themselves (this is permissable at present, but seldom done) and by permitting DISC funds to be lent to firms other than the parent for export purposes.[26]

Recent tax legislation has also had its export-impeding effects. Congress has tightened many of the exemptions previously granted to Americans working abroad, with the result that many service-based firms, in particular, have brought much of their personnel home and substituted foreign nationals. After-sales service has deteriorated in some instances, resulting in lost business. Foreign nationals apparently do not represent U.S. interests as vigorously as do Americans. Tax changes of this type clearly should be reversed if this country hopes to expand its exports noticeably.

One proposal for U.S. tax reform that could have export impact is the value-added tax (VAT) currently used by most European countries. VAT works much like national sales taxes, levied on both domestically produced and imported goods, but rebated on exported goods. Many U.S. observers argue that this amounts to an export subsidy, even though it is perfectly legal under the General Agreement on Tariffs and Trade. Rebates of corporate income taxes on export income, however, are outlawed by the agreement. In consequence, many proexport groups are urging that the United States adopt value-added taxes to put the United States on more equal footing with its export competitors.

The proposal has merit, even if the impact of a U.S. value-added tax on exports is small at the beginning, because it is a step in the direction of worldwide tax harmonization. Congruity, in turn, provides a common base for world competition and keeps overly stringent tax arrangements in one coutry from impeding its exports vis-à-vis those of competing countries with more favorable arrangements. A switch to value-added taxes could also serve to raise the level of public awareness in the United States to the importance of export activity. Opponents to the VAT claim that it tends to be regressive, bearing more heavily on the relatively poor than upon the rich, but this drawback can be minimized by exempting basic necessities from the tax. Also, since it is a tax on consumption, it may serve to increase the rate of saving and an increased saving rate might dampen inflation and help to arrest the slide in U.S. productivity.

Overall, tax legislation is probably not as important as an impediment to exports as is commonly imagined. The advent of flexible exchange rates has eradicated some of the negatives associated with higher than normal tax levels (where they exist), and total exports are not likely to be significantly affected by taxes unless a country is making a concerted effort to shift the burden of those taxes onto foreign consumers of their exports. A tax structure can affect the structure of exports, however, if some sectors are burdened more heavily than others. This is an internal equity question that can only be settled by a nation's own citizenry.

Embargoes

The United States embargoes trade with a number of countries, including Cuba, Vietnam, Cambodia, North Korea, and recently Iran and the Soviet Union. Uganda under Idi Amin was also embargoed for a time, as was Zimbabwe-Rhodesia under the Smith and Muzorewa regimes. The object of these actions, at least initially, is to put pressure on unfriendly governments in the hope of modifying their behavior and perhaps eventually to bring them down. When the action is unilateral on the part of the United States, the impact of the action is mainly symbolic, however, since the offending nation merely turns to other suppliers. The resulting estrangement makes it virtually impossible for the United States to exert any kind of influence on the embargoed country, as the case of Cuba so amply demonstrates. Moreover, as Bingham and Johnson have pointed out, the use of embargoes for symbolic purposes "makes it difficult to lift them without seeming to send an unwanted signal. This alone suggests that trade embargoes are too insensitive to changes in another country's behavior to be a very appropriate tool for influencing that behavior."[27] So U.S. exporters lose business, U.S. political authorities lose leverage, and offending regimes typically remain in power, often more secure in their position than they were before because the United States can be represented as a common enemy.

Multilateral embargoes such as the U.N.-sanctioned embargo against Rhodesia are a different story. Although the blockade was far from total, the pressures were great enough to effect some change in behavior. Moreover, the costs of the embargo were spread among a number of countries, not just one. Again, embargoes can clearly only work when there is an element of monopoly or monopsony present.

Export Controls for Security Purposes

In 1917, the Trading With the Enemy Act gave the president the power to control export sales during wartime; in 1933 the act was amended to extend control to periods of national emergency. The Export Control Act of 1949 broadened the control to any items that

311

might contribute to either the military or economic potential of unfriendly countries. The Export Administration Act of 1969 extended the control to any kind of exports to any customer country if it were necessary to further the foreign policy of the United States, but trimmed controls on exports of nonmilitary items. The 1979 extension of this act further shortened the licensing list and provided for increased business participation in the control process.

The United States also participates with its NATO allies (Iceland excepted) and Japan in a joint effort to deny exports with potential military value to communist countries. An informal Coordinating Committee (COCOM) meets every three to four years to consult on which items should be denied and which permitted. Established in 1949, it worked reasonably well as long as its members needed reconstruction aid from the United States. As the supply capabilities of these countries began to build, however, it became apparent that some members were looser in their enforcement of the controls than others. U.S. exporters often found that they were denied export licenses for items that their foreign competitors could export. Morever, U.S. exporters often faced (and still face) lengthy delays in obtaining approval, apparently at times because some officials in the Commerce or Defense Department personally oppose trade with communist countries.[28] Internal squabbling and insufficient funding in the Commerce Department have further added to delays. Sometimes, too, export permits have been granted and reversed, contributing to the image of the United States as an "unreliable supplier."

Here is a classic case of a global approach to export denial that does not work well because the members do not agree completely on what should be denied. The United States has historically argued for a rather lengthy list of prohibited items, while our allies, being more export-dependent have argued for a shorter list. Evasion is common because, as Bingham and Johnson pointed out, "the United States attaches great symbolic importance to the continued existence of Western domination to maintain a common front vis-à-vis the East," and will not "blow the whistle for fear of risking COCOM's collapse."[29] So, thanks to uneven definition and enforcement, communist countries get almost everything they want, our allies increase their exports, and frustrated U.S. exporters are frozen out.

It is obvious what is needed: the list of denied products should be shortened to those upon which all participants can agree, and enforcement should be strengthened to make the controls uniformly effective. The licensing process, should be tightened by short-ening the list and streamlining procedures. The list should be subject to more frequent change, given the rate at which non-COCOM countries are generating technologies and goods that are equal, if not superior, to those coming from the members themselves. And if, as seems the case, the list shortens too fast for comfort, additional attention clearly needs to be devoted to the simulation of more research and development.

III. THE LEVEL OF AWARENESS

Recently there have been growing signs that the administration and Congress are becoming increasingly aware of the importance of export strength. On 26 September 1978, President Carter outlined several measures aimed at encouraging U.S. exports, including a directive that federal agencies take into account the export consequences of their regulatory actions before they carry them out. On 4 January 1979, the President issued an executive order exempting most exporters from the filing of environmental impact statements as a condition for receiving export licenses. The Department of Commerce has pledged to speed up its licensing procedures (but, as noted earlier, has yet to do so) and the Justice Department promises the same with its business review program. Fuzzy language is being clarified in various laws and regulations. Congressional committees are increasingly pointing to the need for a national export policy.

The difficulty is that there is still little unity in this emerging awareness. The Department of State is concerned about the foreign policy implications of export promotion, the Treasury Department worries about the monetary implications, Commerce Department counts the number of firms involved, the Labor Department the number of jobs involved, the Defense Department sweats the security implications, the Justice Department the legal situation, and so on. "Each expert and agency goes his own way and a battle results in which there is no logical statement of facts nor true logical resolution of differences."[30]

There is, of course, merit in the specialization process. Specialization permits handling of a greater workload, at least up to a point. Specialization, however, also requires integration of the specialized parts if there is to be consistent action towards a particular goal. This is where the United States falls short in the international trade arena.

The idea of a separate Department of International Trade with a cabinet level secretary should not be completely dismissed. This would serve both to increase public awareness of the importance of international trade and provide a common focus for the presently fragmented agencies and bureaus that often leave the impression that we have not one government, but many. It would give exporters some clout when they encounter regulatory barriers such as those discussed above. It could play a major role in negotiating common codes of commercial behavior, treatment of boycotts, and so forth.

The Carter Administration, by executive order, instituted a reorganization of the trade bureaucracy as of 1 January 1980. Its purpose is to provide better coordination, and a more unified approach to trade affairs. At this date, it is too early to judge its effectiveness in promoting trade and dealing with the declining U.S. export position. Whether specialists will continue to live in their restricted circles of awareness, knowing only the benefits of certain actions and blissfully unaware of their attendant costs, is yet unanswered. If the United States lacks the will and insight to organize its trade affairs properly, however, it may well expect to see its role in world affairs continue to decline, with all that this implies for long-term survival.

FOOTNOTES

[1] The Wall Street Journal, 2 August 1979, p. 1.

[2] U.S. Congress, Senate, Committee on Banking, Housing, and Urban Affairs, Hearings, Use of Export Controls and Export Credits for Foreign Policy Purposes, 10-11 October 1978 (Washington, D.C.: U.S. Government Printing Office, 1978), p. 400.

[3] Ibid., p. 396.

[4] Stephen Russell, "The Export Battle: Win or Lose?," Executive, June 1979, p. 23.

[5] Use of Export Controls, op. cit., p. 402.

[6] U.S. Congress, Senate, Committee on Banking, Housing, and Urban Affairs, Subcommittee on International Finance, Subcommittee Report, U.S. Export Policy, February 1979 (Washington, D.C.: U.S. Government Printing Office, 1979), p. 30.

[7] Penelope Hartland-Thunberg, "The Political and Strategic Importance of Exports," Significant Issues Series, vol. 1, no. 3, (Washington, D.C.: Georgetown University Center for Strategic and International Studies, 1979), pp. 4-10.

[8] Sandra Vogelgesang, "What Price Principle? U.S. Policy on Human Rights," Foreign Affairs, July 1978, p. 213.

[9] Rudiger Dornbusch, "Flexible Exchange Rates and Macro-economic Performance: The U.S. Since 1973," paper prepared for the Tripartite meeting in Tokyo, 14-16 November 1978, cited in U.S. Export Policy, op. cit., p. 4.

[10] Reported by Frederick M. Winship, Baton Rouge Sunday Advocate, 10 June 1979, p. 8-C.

[11] James M. Bodurtha, Jr., and Robert G. Hawkins, "The Trade Weapon," Executive, June 1979, p. 27.

[12] Congressional Record, 26 July 1978.

[13]Vogelgesang, op. cit., p. 210.

[14]London Times, 6 January 1977.

[15]U.S. Congress, Senate, Committee on Banking, Housing, and Urban Affairs, Hearings, U.S. Export Control Policy Extension of the Export Administration Act, Part 1, 5-6 March 1979 (Washington, D.C.: U.S. Government Printing Office, 1979).

[16]An excellent summary of the law is David S. Ball's "Official Piracy," Executive, June 1979, pp. 27-28.

[17]The Wall Street Journal, 2 August 1979, p. 10.

[18]Ibid., p. 10.

[19]Ibid., p. 2.

[20]Quoted by John F. Berry in The Washington Post, 10 October 1978.

[21]Ibid.

[22]Bodurtha and Hawkins, op. cit., p. 27.

[23]Ibid., p. 26.

[24]Leonard Downie, Jr., "British Act to Reduce U.S. Antitrust Power," Baton Rouge Morning Advocate, 1 November 1979.

[25]Ibid.

[26]U.S. Export Policy, op. cit., p. 26.

[27]Jonathan B. Bingham and Victor C. Johnson, "A Rational Approach to Export Controls," Foreign Affairs, Spring 1979, p. 908.

[28]Ibid. p. 902.

[29]Ibid., p. 906.

[30]Gary F. Cook and Robert F. Williamson, Jr., "Improving U.S. Policy-Making in International Trade," The Columbia Journal of World Business, Spring 1979, p. 16.

7

THE IMPACT OF THE TOKYO ROUND AGREEMENTS ON U.S. EXPORT COMPETITIVENESS

Thomas R. Graham

CONTENTS

320

I. INTRODUCTION

The Tokyo Round of multilateral trade negotiations was a comprehensive effort to adjust the accepted rules by which nations conduct international trade. This effort engaged 99 nations, off and on, for the five years between 1974 and 1979. Despite the name, the Tokyo Round negotiations were held primarily in Geneva under auspices of the General Agreement on Tariffs and Trade (GATT).[1] The name is derived from the fact that the ministerial declaration inaugurating the negotiations was issued from Tokyo.[2]

The Tokyo Round was the seventh major round of periodic trade negotiations to be held since 1947.[3] In most of the previous rounds, governments concentrated primarily upon bargaining down national tariff rates. Negotiations in the Tokyo Round, by contrast, produced not only agreements to reduce industrial and agricultural tariffs but also drafted some 700 pages of new rules on such diverse nontariff matters as:[4]

●   Government subsidies that distort trade competition and countervailing measures that other governments impose to offset the competitive advantages conferred by such subsidies;

●   Antidumping duties that governments impose upon imports that are sold at less than fair value;

●   Government purchasing practices that discriminate, overtly or covertly, against foreign products;

●   Product standards, test methods, and certification systems that are applied in ways that unduly burden international trade;

●   Customs methods for appraising the value of imports that are arbitrary or that artifically inflate the import duties payable;

●   Import licensing requirements that create unnecessary delay and red tape;

●   Consultations and exchanges of information regarding international trade in bovine meat and dairy products;

●   Trade barriers and special inducements to the international sale of civil aircraft;

●   Improved international procedures for settling international trade disputes; and

●   Basic reforms of the trade system to facilitate the granting of special preferences to the trade of developing countries.

The Tokyo Round agreements were accepted and implemented by the Congress in the Trade Agreements Act of 1979, which also made several important changes in U.S. trade laws.[5] As a political prerequisite for enacting the Trade Agreements Act, the Congress required President Carter to submit a plan for reorganizing the way that the executive branch formulates and administers U.S. trade policy and negotiates international trade agreements. The main thrusts of this plan, which went into effect on 2 January 1980, were threefold: first, to tighten the administration of U.S. laws to combat unfair import competition in the U.S. market; second, to vest in the United States Trade Representative (USTR) (formerly the Special Representative for Trade Negotiations) increased authority to coordinate diverse U.S. trade policies; and third, to organize the executive branch in a way that facilitates the promotion of U.S. exports.[6]

This essay is concerned primarily with the effects of the Tokyo Round, the Trade Agreements Act of 1979, and the recent executive branch reorganization on U.S. export potential. Those three events are, however, only some of the many factors that are currently affecting U.S. competitiveness. To avoid a distorted impression, the Tokyo Round and its aftermath must be set in the context of U.S. export activity and international trade relations in the 1970s.

In 1971, for the first time in this century, Americans bought more goods from abroad than they sold

322

to foreign purchasers.[7] The trade deficit for that year was $2.2 billion -- peanuts by current standards. But the shock of that first unfamiliar deficit helped to draw political attention to the declining competitive position of the United States in world market-places. This political attention, in turn, led to a series of official attempts to boost U.S. exports. By the end of 1971, the Congress had amended the Internal Revenue Code to permit U.S. exporters to form Domestic International Sales Corporations (DISCs) as devices for deferring payment of income taxes on a substantial portion of their export income.[8] The "Nixon shocks" of 15 August 1971, led, by 1973, to an international monetary system of floating exchange rates that could be expected to allow the value of the dollar to find a level at which prices for U.S. exports would become more attractive to buyers in other nations.[9] A White House Conference on Export Expansion in 1973 was followed by the creation of the President's Export Council, a group of top business executives, formed to advise the administration on how to increase U.S. exports. The Congress enacted the Trade Act of 1974 and sent U.S. negotiators off to Geneva with a mandate to secure "substantially equivalent competitive opportunities for the commerce of the United States."[10] In September 1978, a federal Task Force on Export Policy, chaired by then Assistant Secretary of Commerce Frank Weil, announced a new program for promoting U.S. exports.[11] For the last two years of the decade, the Carter administration and numerous members of Congress pressed the Japanese to buy more U.S. products.

Yet the U.S. trade deficit for 1978 was some 14 times greater than it had been in 1971.[12] The deficit has hovered at or above $25 billion for the past three years. Whole product lines -- such as black and white televisions, radios, 35 mm cameras, baseball gloves, and numerous household appliances -- are rarely produced in the United States anymore. Why have floating exchange rates, the DISC, and other U.S. export promotion efforts apparently not worked? What happened to U.S. export competitiveness in the 1970s? What, if anything, will the Tokyo Round and the measures taken to implement its results do for U.S. exports? What else can be done to assert U.S. interests in a rapidly changing international economy? It

is to these questions that we turn in the following
sections.

II. U.S. COMPETITIVENESS IN THE TURBULENT SEVENTIES

The cost of imported oil is the reason given most frequently for the unprecedented U.S. trade deficits of the last three years. In the late 1970s it was also said that exchange rate adjustments that foster economic growth in Europe and Japan would lead to an expansion of U.S. exports and thus would in time eliminate the trade deficit almost automatically. These arguments are both too simple and too reassuring. By ignoring more fundamental structural problems affecting U.S. trade, they risk diverting attention from needed policy changes.

The fact is that a sudden decline in the U.S. ability to compete both at home and abroad for sales of manufactured goods, more than the cost of imported oil, accounted for the dramatic increase in recent U.S. trade deficits between 1975 and 1978.[13] The U.S. trade balance for manufactured goods fell from a $20 billion surplus in 1975, to a $5.8 billion deficit in 1978. This shift in the trade balance for manufactures, a traditional area of U.S. export strength, was more than double the size of the increase in the U.S. oil trade deficit over the same period. In the years between 1970 and 1978, the U.S. share of total manufactured exports from industrialized countries fell from 21 percent to 17 percent. The Commerce Department has estimated that had the United States retained its 21 percent share of these manufactured exports, there would have been virtually no trade deficit in 1978, notwithstanding the $40 billion paid for oil imports.[14] A comparison of the U.S. trade balance for manufactured goods, for petroleum and petroleum products, and for other product sectors, for the years 1977 and 1978, is shown in Table I below.

Although the U.S. trade balance for manufactured goods bounced back to a surplus of about $4.35 billion in 1979, there were doubts about whether that positive trend would last.[15] The volume of U.S. exports of manufactured goods did not grow appreciably between 1975 and 1978, although manufactured exports of major U.S. competitors grew by an annual average of about four percent. This trend is illustrated in Table 2. Table 3 illustrates the decline of U.S. exports of manufacturer as a percentage of world

TABLE 1

U.S. SECTORAL TRADE BALANCES, 1977 - 1978
($ billion)

	1977	1978
Total Trade	-26.5	-28.5
Manufactured Goods	3.6	-5.8
*Chemicals (SITC 5)	5.4	6.2
Basic Manufactures (SITC 6)	-10.1	-14.7
Machinery & Transport (SITC 7)	15.5	11.7
Misc. Manufactures (SITC 8)	-7.5	-8.9
*Capital Goods (end-use)	25.7	26.7
*Food and Live Animals (SITC 0)	1.6	4.8
Beverages & Tobacco (SITC 1)	0.2	0.1
*Crude Materials, ex. Fuels (SITC 2)	4.5	6.2
*Mineral Fuels (SITC 3)	-40.4	-38.5
*Oils and Fats (SITC 4)	0.8	1.0
*Commodities N.E.C. (SITC 9)	1.0	1.0
*Petroleum and Petroleum Products, excluding Gas (end-use)	-40.1	-37.9

---

*Balance improved from 1977 to 1978.

Source: National Association of Manufacturers, 1978 Trade Update, citing U.S. Department of Commerce trade statistics, census basis.

TABLE 2

TRADE IN MANUFACTURES
UNITED STATES, FEDERAL REPUBLIC OF GERMANY, JAPAN
1970, 1975-77
($ billion)

		United States			Federal Republic			Japan		
		Imports	Exports	Balance	Imports (CIF)	Exports (FOB)	Balance	Imports (CIF)	Exports (FOB)	Balance
1970		25.9	29.7	3.8	17.4	30.7	13.3	5.6	18.1	12.5
1975		51.1	72.1	21.0	50.0	79.6	29.6	11.5	53.2	41.7
1976		64.8	78.5	13.8	48.6	90.7	42.1	13.4	64.6	51.2
1977		77.2	82.0	4.8	56.3*	99.5*	43.2*	14.4*	79.5*	65.1*
1977**	I.	69.8	80.3	10.6	55.0	98.9	43.9	13.8	68.5	54.7
	II.	78.4	85.5	7.1	55.6	101.5	45.9	15.2	75.9	60.7
	III.	79.0	79.3	0.3	56.3	99.5	43.2	14.4	79.5	65.1
	IV.	81.7	82.8	1.1	NA	NA	NA	NA	NA	NA
1978**	I.	94.8	82.2	-12.6	NA	NA	NA	NA	NA	NA

*1977, III at annual rates
**at annual rates
F.A.S. except where noted

Source: National Association of Manufacturers, U.S. Trade Performance Since 1970 With Special Reference to Manufactured Goods (1978), citing Commerce Department, International Economic Indicators, March, 1978.

327

TABLE 3

SHARES OF WORLD EXPORTS OF MANUFACTURES

	United States (excl. exports to U.S.)		Federal Republic	France	Japan	U.K.
1960	25.3	22.8	18.2	9.1	6.5	15.3
1969	22.5	19.3	18.7	7.8	10.7	10.7
1970	21.3	18.4	19.0	8.3	11.2	10.1
1971	20.1	17.2	19.3	8.3	12.7	10.5
1972	19.1	16.3	19.3	8.7	13.5	9.7
1973	19.5	16.7	20.3	8.7	13.3	9.0
1974	20.2	17.7	20.2	8.2	14.8	8.2
1975	21.2	18.9	18.6	9.0	14.2	9.0
1976	20.5	18.3	19.1	8.9	14.8	8.4
1977-I*	19.9	18.1	19.3	9.2	14.5	8.7
-II*	20.0	18.6	18.5	9.0	15.0	9.5

*Annual Rates

Source: National Association of Manufacturers, U.S. Trade Performance Since 1970 With Special Reference to Manufactured Goods (1978) citing Commerce Department, International Economic Indicators, March 1978.

manufactured exports, and compares the U.S. performance with that of other major competitors.

The reasons for this shift to weakness in a traditional area of U.S. trade strength are complex and are rooted in U.S. economic history since the end of World War II.[16] The United States emerged from the war as the only intact industrial power. The United States exported capital equipment as fast as other nations in the process of rebuilding could absorb it. Without really trying, the United States enjoyed, during the early postwar years, a strong trade position that masked underlying developments. Americans were spending much larger proportions of their incomes on consumer goods and were devoting much smaller segments of their incomes to savings and investment than were their Japanese and European counterparts. This pattern of high consumption pulled into the U.S. market imported articles such as textiles, apparel, shoes, consumer electronics, household appliances, and automobiles from nations that by the 1960s were back on their feet industrially and were turning out goods that -- in part, because of the lower wage rates and undervalued currencies of these nations in relation to the dollar -- were highly attractive in the U.S. market.

High U.S. consumption coupled with low savings and investment also meant that less capital was available in the United States for privately financed research and development and for modernization of U.S. plants and equipment. During the last decade, U.S. capital stock expanded at an average annual rate of only 2.8 percent. This was one-half the rate of U.S. capital formation during the 1960s. An average of 18 percent of U.S. gross national product went into investment during the 1970s; the Japanese invested an average of 33 percent of their GNP during the same period.[17]

Many other patterns that had been developing for decades came to a head in the 1970s. One involved direct and indirect export promotion by the European Economic Community (EC). Under the Common Agricultural Policy, the EC limited imports and subsidized exports of agricultural products, thus depriving U.S. farmers of export markets both in Europe and in other areas of the world. Over the years, European governments have

329

nationalized beleagured industries ranging from British steel to French automaking. These industries, backed by national treasuries, competed on world markets with U.S. companies that had to depend primarily upon private investment and financial markets. Short of nationalization, European governments intervened in private economies to support their industries through an array of subsidies: regional tax incentives to attract industry to depressed regions such as Brittany; soft credit terms for large, long-term export supply contracts such as the supplying of Rolls-Royce engines for new model aircraft; and a variety of research and development programs. These domestic subsidies aided European industries in international competition with U.S. companies that had not received similar benefits.[18]

The increasing internationalization of production raised a second set of issues that broke in the 1970s. Multinational companies accelerated the spread of their manufacturing and assembly operations to developing nations where labor costs were lower and government policies invited industrial development. Other firms that did not produce directly in less developed countries (LDCs) sold their technology to home-grown LDC entrepreneurs. In still other cases, manufacturers in developing countries acquired necessary know-how, quality control, and assured markets by building consumer goods to the specifications of huge U.S. retail chains. The immediate result of these shifts was a rapid transfer of industrial production, jobs, and export income from the developed West to a handful of nations in East Asia and Latin America. By 1977, Brazil, Hong Kong, Mexico, Singapore, South Korea, and Taiwan accounted for about one-fifth of U.S. imports of manufactured goods. The same industries that grew in these nations declined in the United States, Canada, West Europe, and, more slowly, in Japan. The first U.S. industries to be affected were labor-intensive ones such as shoes and textiles. Later, the shift of productive facilities affected more sophisticated manufactures such as color televisions, radios, and other consumer electronic products.

These developments placed U.S. trade policymakers in a political bind. For years, the United States had preached trade not aid to the Third World, but the success of some LDCs in international trade was now

330

generating formidable political pressures within the United States to limit import competition. To yield fully to these pressures would set an example that would damage U.S. attempts to persuade other nations, developed and developing alike, to open their markets to U.S. exports. Shutting out LDC exports would also impair the ability of those nations to earn the foreign exchange necessary to buy U.S. products. By the 1970s, the developing countries together purchased close to half of all U.S. exports -- more than any other single market.

Closely related to the sudden exporting successes of the newly industrialized nations was the rapid growth of Japanese manufactured exports ranging from automobiles to cameras to semiconductors. Effective cooperation with industry permitted the Japanese government to target for special assistance those industries that were most competitive internationally and to yield to Taiwan, South Korea, and other nations those industries in which Japanese competitiveness appeared to be declining. By the 1970s, competition from Japan was displacing U.S. sales at home and abroad.

At the same time, formal and informal Japanese trade barriers -- such as extremely restrictive import quotas on high quality beef and citrus fruits, as well as various customs regulations -- severely limited U.S. sales opportunities in the Japanese market. In 1977 and 1978, the U.S. bilateral trade deficits with Japan reached $8 billion and $12.2 billion, respectively. The trend of the U.S. merchandise trade balance with Japan over the 20 years between 1958 and 1978 is shown in Table 4.

These figures helped to produce enormous political pressures within the United States to limit Japanese imports or to open up the Japanese market to increase U.S. exports. In response, the U.S. Special Trade Representative, Ambassador Robert Strauss, brought pressures that were virtually unprecedented among allies in the postwar period to bear on the Japanese to accept more U.S. products and to expand the Japanese economy. These pressures were backed by threats that the Congress might act to limit Japanese imports.[19]

TABLE 4

U.S. MERCHANDISE TRADE WITH JAPAN[1]
(U.S. $ billions)

	Exports	Imports	Balance
1958	1.0	0.7	0.3
1959	1.1	1.0	.1
1960	1.5	1.1	.4
1961	1.8	1.1	.7
1962	1.6	1.4	.2
1963	1.8	1.5	.3
1964	2.0	1.8	.2
1965	2.1	2.4	-.3
1966	2.4	3.0	-.6
1967	2.7	3.0	-.3
1968	3.0	4.1	-1.1
1969	3.5	4.9	-1.4
1970	4.7	5.9	-1.2
1971	4.1	7.3	-3.2
1972	4.9	9.1	-4.2
1973	8.3	9.7	-1.4
1974	10.7	12.4	-1.7
1975	9.6	11.3	-1.7
1976	10.2	15.5	-5.3
1977	10.6	18.6	-8.0
1978[2]	12.2	24.4	-12.2

[1]Exports are f.a.s. and imports are customs values, generally the market value in the foreign country.

[2]Preliminary.

Source: U.S. Senate, Committee on Finance, Background Materials and Economic Data Relating to International Trade (1979) citing U.S. Department of Commerce data, p. 11.

The nations of the EC frequently managed the pressures of competition from Japan and the advanced LDCs by concluding voluntary restraining agreements (VRAs) that limited Japanese and LDC exports to European markets. Many of these arrangements were secret. Many consisted of little more than a handshake between, for example, the British and Japanese automobile industries (with the blessing of the British Ministry of Trade). Such confidential, industry-to-industry agreements were out of the question for U.S. manufacturers because they almost certainly would constitute gross violations of U.S. antitrust laws.

The proliferation of VRAs had two principal effects. First, these agreements often diverted to the more open U.S. market Japanese and LDC products that otherwise would have gone to Western Europe. The most publicized example of such alleged trade diversion involved a formal complaint of the American Iron and Steel Institute that a secret VRA between the EC and Japan diverted Japanese steel from Europe to the U.S. market.[20] The second effect of the VRAs was to increase pressure on U.S. policymakers to take similarly restrictive actions on behalf of U.S. industry, or to secure trade agreements exposing and reducing the number of such agreements by other nations.

In addition to the proliferation of VRAs in the 1970s there was perhaps increased use, and certainly a greater recognition of nontariff trade barriers that limited U.S. export opportunities. These devices ranged from the use of environmental regulations and other product standards to restrict imports by discriminatory customs formalities, and by preventing foreign suppliers from bidding for sales to government agencies. Increased attention to nontariff barriers in the 1970s raised political pressures for the executive branch either to protect U.S. producers by restricting import competition, or to seek greater discipline over actions that harmed U.S. trade interests and to promote U.S. exports. Viewed in this context, the Tokyo Round was the "free trade" alternative.

There were, however, many aspects of U.S. competitiveness that were beyond the reach of the Tokyo Round. One was the low rate of internal U.S. investment, described above. Another was the apparent imperviousness of many U.S. exports to price competition. Some who looked seriously into the question of why floating exchange rates had not automatically increased U.S. exports, by lowering the relative value of the dollar to a point at which the prices of U.S. products became attractive to other nations, came up with some interesting answers.[21] For many of these areas in which the United States is an effective exporter, it appears, prices are not the determining factor in sales. One of these areas is agricultural products, which accounts for a substantial portion of all U.S. exports. Agricultural trade is heavily regulated by governments; and agricultural export opportunities usually depend less upon price than upon foreign government policies, crop yields abroad, and the availability of favorable export credit terms.

A second major source of U.S. exports is military hardware, which is purchased by foreign governments on the basis of many factors other than price. As noted above, almost half of U.S. exports are bought by developing countries, where often government economic plans and credit terms play a larger role than does price. An increased proportion of U.S. exports consist of intra-company transfers between related operations of multinational companies. Price generally is not the determining factor in such transfers. Many of these intra-company sales are made between related companies in the United States and in Canada, which buys more U.S. exports than any other single nation. Many other sales to Canada are made as a result of lower transportation costs or special bilateral trade policies, such as the U.S.-Canada Automotive Agreement. The United States also is an effective competitor for many high-technology items such as sophisticated computers and telecommunications equipment. Frequently, overseas sales of such products are subject to direct government interference on such grounds as national security or the desire to develop similar technology locally.

After a generation as the unchallenged economic superpower the United States was poorly prepared for the shocks of the 1970s. The U.S. government had neither a coherent trade policy nor institutional machinery capable of establishing one. Instead, various aspects of trade policy were the bureaucratic domain of at least a half dozen federal agencies: the State Department for East-West trade, commodity agreements, commercial officers abroad, and the implications of trade issues for foreign relations; the Commerce Department for adjustment assistance to U.S. firms, liaison with U.S. industry, and such export promotion as existed; the Treasury Department for enforcement of antidumping and countervailing duty laws and for general national and international economic policy; the International Trade Commission for escape clause investigations and other questions regarding injury to U.S. industries resulting from import competition; the Labor Department for adjustment assistance to U.S. workers and the effects of trade policy on U.S. labor; and the United States Trade Representative for international trade negotiations under the loosely defined U.S. Trade Agreements Program. The USTR also had a vague mandate from the Congress and the president to coordinate some aspects of trade policy. Added to this group are the various specialized roles played by the Export-Import Bank of the United States, the Overseas Private Investment Corporation, the U.S. Agency for International Development, the antitrust functions of the Justice Department, the political interests of the president and his White House staff and the legislative prerogatives of the Congress. The inevitable picture is a governmental structure for trade policy that was almost wholly lacking in direction, and that contributed mightily to what is frequently called the absence of a U.S. export consciousness.

No one person or agency spoke clearly for the national interest in effectively promoting U.S. exports, eliminating from U.S. tax, antitrust, and regulatory provisions unwarranted competitive disincentives, consistently enforcing U.S. laws against unfair import competition, identifying and helping those U.S. industries that showed the greatest promise of being competitive internationally, and effectively easing the pain of scaling back those industries that did not appear to be competitive -- in short, for the national interest in an effective U.S. trade policy.

Until the end of the 1970s, in fact, there were strong indications that few Americans believed that there was a national interest in U.S. international economic competitiveness. Proposals to encourage

335

investment, modernization of plant and equipment, and exporting were regularly attacked as merely special interest benefits for the wealthy. No single powerful authority argued effectively for the workers whose jobs were saved or created by U.S. exports, or for more generalized economic benefits, such as the reduction of inflation, that could result from an open, competitive U.S. economy. In part because the national interest in a unified U.S. trade policy had no powerful institutional support in the U.S. government, export restrictions became the handiest means of expressing opposition to a host of international wrongs -- such as human rights violations, corporate bribery, the Arab boycott, and despoilation of the environment. No attempt is made here to defend such restrictions. The point instead, is that trade restrictions -- rather than some other vehicle -- almost unthinkingly became the means of expressing the U.S. position on these issues because no one in the government articulated or defended a coherent trade policy that might have included export expansion in the national interest.

The 1971 U.S. trade deficit was followed in rapid succession by the collapse of the Bretton Woods system of fixed exchange rates, the 1973 OPEC oil embargo with the recession and lingering stagflation that followed, and the existence of fragile political mandates for administrations in the United States, Canada, Japan, and most nations of Western Europe. These events raised real possibilities that the international trading system embodied in the GATT would, like Bretton Woods, be swept under by domestic political pressures increased in each nation by rapid changes and economic deterioration. If this happened, it was very likely that the United States and other nations would be unable to resist political pressures to limit imports severely as a shortsighted reaction to their trade imbalances and unemployment problems. Destructive trade wars that could only exacerbate international economic problems would almost certainly follow. The Tokyo Round was an attempt to prevent this from happening by revising substantially the accepted trading rules as well as liberalizing trade somewhat through a modest reduction of tariff barriers. In this sense, the Tokyo Round was a necessary, but scarcely sufficient step toward improvement of U.S. export competitiveness. In that limited role, the effort has, at least until now, been highly successful.

III. IMPACT OF THE TOKYO ROUND

As the preceding section indicates, there were many more causes for declining U.S. export performance during the 1970s than merely foreign barriers to trade. Thus, there are limits to what can be expected from the Tokyo Round as a cure for U.S. trade problems. In at least six areas, however, the Tokyo Round can have some positive effect upon the ability of U.S. exporters to penetrate overseas markets. These areas are: (1) direct trade liberalization through the reduction of tariffs; (2) potential trade liberalization through the negotiation of agreements that attempt to limit the use of several nontariff barriers to trade, but that have yet to be tested in practice; (3) stabilization of the international trading system and rejection of wholesale protectionism at least for a time; (4) tools provided in the U.S. legislation that implemented the Tokyo Round for U.S. exporters to seek removal of foreign trade restrictions; (5) a strengthened government-private sector-congressional working relationship on trade that grew out of the Tokyo Round experience; and (6) the reorganization of trade policymaking within the executive branch, which is perhaps a start toward consolidating a U.S. trade policy. The first two of these points are discussed in this section.

Industrial Tariffs[22]

Tariffs are the traditional subject of GATT negotiations. The results of tariff negotiations, moreover, are quantifiable and thus provide a comfortable if somewhat misleading sense of certainty. A U.S. industry can readily see how much of its protective tariff U.S. negotiators gave away, and what they got for it in duty reductions for the same product by other nations. Largely for these reasons, the Tokyo Round tariff negotiations assumed a political importance that was somewhat out of proportion to their real importance in relation to the other subjects under negotiations. The average incidence of industrial tariffs already is relatively low in most industrialized countries. The new tariff reductions are to be phased in through small annual increments over the next seven years. Exchange rate fluctuations, moreover, can have more significant impacts upon competitiveness than tariff rates.

The most effective way to negotiate tariff rate reductions for thousands of products from many countries is for the participants to adopt a general hypothesis, or formula, specifying the percentage by which all tariffs are to be reduced, and then to bargain about particular products that are to be exempted from the general reduction or subjected to higher or lower duty reductions than those called for by the formula. In November 1977, the principal participants in the Tokyo Round agreed to adopt a compromise formula that had been proposed by the government of Switzerland, that called for duty reductions of about 40 percent and that attempted to reduce higher tariffs by a greater amount than lower ones to promote greater uniformity among the duty rates of different nations.

At about the same time, negotiators for the United States and the EC agreed that the politically sensitive subject of agricultural tariff reductions would not be negotiated by applying the general formula. Instead, each interested country would advance specific requests for duty reductions, and the countries to which the requests were directed would respond by making offers. In addition, the United States, later joined by other Tokyo Round participants, agreed that the tariff reductions to be negotiated would be phased in over seven years and that a review after five years would determine whether external economic conditions warranted continuance of the reductions.

The industrial tariff reductions agreed upon by the United States, Canada, Japan, and the EC will, when fully implemented, average approximately 33 percent. (See Table 5.) The average U.S. industrial tariff rate will fall from 6.2 to 4.4 percent.

The EC will reduce its average industrial duty rate from 6.6 to 4.8 percent, a total reduction of 27 percent. For products imported from the United States, the EC will reduce its duties by an average of 34 percent. This will reduce somewhat the competitive disadvantage that U.S. exporters face in competition with companies that trade free of duty behind the common EC tariff wall, or with companies that enjoy special access to EC markets under arrangements between the EC and nations of Western Europe, the Mediterranean basin, Africa, the Caribbean, and the Pacific. EC tariff concessions of particular interest to U.S. exporters include certain chemicals, paper, printing, machinery, photographic equipment, machine tools, and scientific instruments.

Japan's average applied industrial tariffs will decline over the next eight years from 5.2 to 2.6 percent. For exports from the United States alone, the average applied Japanese duty rate will be only about 2.2 percent, compared with an average U.S. tariff rate on Japanese goods of approximately 4.5 percent. Several industries in which the United States has important export interests, including film products, computers, semiconductors, machinery, paper, and lumber, received particularly significant duty reductions by the Japanese.

Canada will reduce its applied industrial tariff rates by more than 38 percent, to an average of about 8 percent. Canadian tariffs on all U.S. imports -- both dutiable and duty-free -- will average about 6.4 percent. This will reduce somewhat the disparity that currently exists between several Canadian duty rates of 15 percent or more, and the much lower U.S. rates for the same products. The United States obtained particularly significant Canadian tariff reductions for such key U.S. export sectors as machinery, paper, photographic equipment, wood products, and computers.[23]

During the Tokyo Round, the United States also negotiated a score of bilateral tariff agreements with developing countries. These agreements carried out the U.S. policy of insisting that developing countries make some reciprocal concessions to the United States -- albeit in most cases fewer concessions than they received -- in return for U.S. tariff reductions of benefit to LDCs.

The United States made no tariff commitments at all with respect to nonrubber footwear, color television receivers, specialty steel, and other products that were subject to escape clause import relief actions. In addition, U.S. negotiators exempted some particularly sensitive categories of textiles and apparel from any tariff reductions. Where reductions

339

TABLE 5

TARIFF AVERAGES[a] ON INDUSTRIAL PRODUCTS (EXCLUDING PETROLEUM[b])
FOR TEN DEVELOPED MARKETS BEFORE AND AFTER THE IMPLEMENTATION
OF THE TOKYO ROUND AGREEMENTS

Market	MFN Imports 1976 ($'000 m)	Simple Average			Weighted Average[c]		
		Pre-Tokyo Round	Post-Tokyo Round	Percent reduced	Pre-Tokyo Round	Post-Tokyo Round	Percent reduced
United States	64.4	12.1	7.0	42	6.2	4.4	30
European Community	55.4	8.1	5.6	31	6.6	4.8	27
Japan	29.3	10.2	6.0	41	5.2	2.6	49
Canada	27.7	12.4	7.2	42	12.7	7.9	38
Sweden	3.3	5.9	4.8	19	5.2	4.3	23
Norway	2.3	8.5	6.5	23	4.2	3.2	23
Switzerland	2.2	3.8	2.8	26	3.2	2.5	23
New Zealand	1.8	26.2	20.0	24	22.4	17.6	21
Austria	1.5	11.6	8.1	30	9.0	7.8	13
Finland	0.9	13.0	11.2[e]	14	6.0	4.8	20
TOTAL	188.8	10.6[e]	6.5	38	7.2[e]	4.9[e]	33

Source: Hugh Corbet, "Importance of Being Earnest About Further GATT Negotiations," The World Economy, vol. 2, no. 3, September 1978, p. 328, citing Trade Policy Research Centre, London (preliminary calculations).

[a]The comparability of tariff levels, and of their practical incidence, is affected by differences in methods of valuation for customs purposes. The tariff averages set out in the table cover duty-free items. It should be noted that averages disguise the variation in tariffs, some countries having wider variations in their tariff schedules than others, with more tariffs at high levels and usually, it follows (if their tariff averages are closely related), more tariffs at low levels.

[b]Items CCN 2709 and 2710 are excluded.

[c]Here the simple average on each tariff line is weighted by each market's MFN imports on that line. In due course the GATT Secretariat will no doubt calculate weighted averages on the basis of total world trade in each tariff item.

[d]After implementing the Kennedy Round agreement Japan reduced her tariffs unilaterally by 20 percent across-the-board.

[e]Weighted by the trade of each country.

for textile or apparel articles were made, they were smaller than those called for by the general tariff formula. Overall, average U.S. textile and apparel duties will be reduced by only about 21 percent. These reductions, moreover, will not begin until 1982 and will be phased in at the slow rate of about one-half of one percentage point per year. In addition, the U.S. implementing legislation contains a "snapback" clause, which provides that U.S. tariffs on textiles and apparel will return to their pre-Tokyo Round levels if the existing international program for restraining textile imports -- commonly known as the Multifiber Arrangement -- or some suitable substitute does not continue in force. Finally, as the Tokyo Round was concluding, the U.S. administration initiated a comprehensive domestic program to aid the U.S. textile industry, including the tightening of current textile import restraint levels and government assistance in promoting exports of U.S. textiles and apparel.

Textile tariff concessions by the United States were made in response to various concessions by other nations. Among those concessions were undertakings by the EC to reduce its tariff rates on U.S. weaving mill products of man-made fiber by 28 percent, and by Japan to reduce its duty rates by 17 percent on yarn and thread mill products. These concessions should help U.S. exporters of mill products, a product category for which the United States has enjoyed for several years a positive trade balance.

Nontariff Measures

Subsidies and Countervailing Measures.[24]   For several years, the United States has sought to limit the use of foreign subsidies that confer competitive advantages upon the products of the subsidizing country. These subsidies can come in many forms, and their effects on U.S. competitiveness can be felt in several ways. The GATT rules, reflecting accepted national views, generally prohibit direct export subsidies for manufactured products -- such as the forgiveness of income taxes on all or part of export income, or the allowance of special tax deductions directly related to exports or export performance. The main reason for this prohibition is that such subsidies can readily be used as predatory devices to drive non-subsidized competition from a market.

But the GATT never was very effective in policing export subsidies. The rules were too weak and vague. They provided only that export subsidies for manufactured products were prohibited _if_ they resulted in export sales at a lower price than sales in the home market; and that export subsidies for agricultural and primary products were merely to be discouraged if they resulted in the subsidizing nation's having more than an equitable share of world trade in the agricultural or primary product. The "bi-level pricing" criterion for subsidies to manufacturers has been almost impossible to prove, and the rule with respect to agricultural export subsidies has provided virtually no discipline at all over such practices.

The GATT did not expressly address a second category of government subsidies that also affected U.S. trade in some instances. These were the "domestic" subsidies -- such as grants for research and development, tax holidays designed to attract industries to depressed regions of a nation, or infusions of public funds for the operation of a nationalized industry -- that usually were employed for domestic political or economic reasons but that almost incidentally conferred advantages upon the recipient industries that were not enjoyed by its U.S. competitors. These practices posed a difficult problem: how to balance the freedom to make these sovereign national policy choices against the rights of those whose international competitive position was thereby adversely affected.

Both export subsidies and domestic subsidies from abroad could affect U.S. competition in at least two ways. First, subsidized imports could hurt U.S. producers in the U.S. market; and second, the subsidized foreign competition could drive U.S. exporters out of markets in third countries where both the subsidized foreign producers and the U.S. producers competed for export sales. Domestic subsidies could, moreover, cause U.S. exporters to lose markets in the subsidizing country by encouraging import substitution.

Against this background, the main negotiating positions on subsidies and countervailing measures can be summarized as follows: The United States sought a more effective prohibition of export subsidies for manufactures; a better rule against agricultural subsidies; international recognition that domestic subsidies could harm the trade of other nations; and a more effective means of settling international disputes over subsidy practices. Behind these U.S. goals lay concern about the increasing involvement of European governments in industries that competed with U.S. producers and a desire to limit the effects of subsidized European agricultural exports in traditional U.S. export markets.

The EC, backed by most other industrialized nations, was less concerned with subsidies than with the fact that U.S. law permitted the Treasury Department to impose countervailing duties to offset the effects of subsidized imports without regard to whether such imports caused or threatened material injury to a U.S. industry. The U.S. countervailing duty law conflicted in this respect with Article VI of the GATT, but the U.S. law was technically "grandfathered" because it predated the GATT.[25] Thus the United States did not come to the subsidy-countervailing duty negotiations with entirely clean hands.[26]

U.S. and EC negotiations managed to put together an agreement that, on paper at least, appears to achieve major goals of each side. The agreement on subsidies and countervailing measures provides greater discipline over export subsidies by including nonagricultural primary products (such as minerals) within the flat prohibition on such subsidies, by eliminating the present requirement that a prohibited export subsidy be shown to result in a lower price than that charged domestically, and by updating an "illustrative list" of prohibited export subsidies that had been maintained by the GATT for some years. Somewhat greater discipline over export subsidies on agricultural, fishery, and forestry products is provided by prohibiting the use of agricultural export subsidies in a manner that displaces the exports of other nations or that results in material price undercutting in a particular market.

In addition, the agreement promises greater regulation of domestic subsidies by prohibiting signatories from using them in a way that would seriously harm the trade interests of other signatory countries, and by listing as "indicative guidelines" types of domestic subsidies that may have adverse effects upon international competition. At the same time, the agreement acknowledges that these politically sensitive domestic subsidies "[a]re intended to promote important objectives of national policy."

The agreement provides two methods for importing countries to offset the effects of subsidized competition. The first is the traditional unilateral application of countervailing duties to subsidized imports that cause or threaten material injury to a domestic industry. The second is to appeal to an international committee of signatories which was created to settle disputes under the agreements. The committee can authorize countermeasures to be taken to offset the subsidy practices of another country when such practices nullify or impair benefits accruing under the GATT to the complaining party, or result in serious prejudice to its domestic industry. Any such international complaints are supposed to be heard and settled within 150 days under detailed procedures for settling disputes. Countermeasures may take the form of ordinary countervailing duties or other trade retaliation. The concept of serious prejudice, moreover, includes not only adverse effects upon industries in the importing country as a result of subsidized imports, but also covers the loss of export markets if the subsidized products of one country displace nonsubsidized goods of another within the subsidizing country (import substitution subsidies) or in third countries where the subsidized and nonsubsidized exports compete (third country market displacement).

To gain these benefits, the United States agreed to write into its countervailing duty law a requirement that countervailing duties not be imposed unless subsidized imports should be shown to cause or threaten material injury to an established industry, or to materially retard the establishment of a new U.S. industry. Such a provision was incorporated into the Trade Agreements Act of 1979, which also shortens substantially the time limits for conducting U.S. countervailing duty investigations and amends countervailing duty procedures in other important ways.

How effective the agreement on subsidies and countervailing duties will be in promoting U.S. exports depends very largely upon how effectively the provisions of the agreement with respect to import substitution subsidies and third country market displacement subsidies are enforced. Since the harm caused by subsidies of this type is felt outside the U.S. market, the remedy must be found in an international complaint under the new subsidies code rather than in countervailing duties imposed upon subsidized imports. Thus, the effectiveness of the agreement on subsidies and countervailing measures in aiding U.S. exports depends ultimately upon the effectiveness of the new dispute-settlement procedures. Questions with respect to international enforcement of new international obligations recur throughout the consideration of nontariff agreements, and will be discussed later.

One final aspect of the agreement on subsidies and countervailing measures should be mentioned to put to rest fears that have been expressed by some in the U.S. private sector. U.S. adherence to the new agreements should not inhibit new initiatives to promote U.S. exports. As is discussed below, effective U.S. export promotion will require broad domestic measures to encourage research and development, promote plant modernization, secure better export financing for small businesses, and other similar measures. Such measures are not prohibited by the subsidies code. It is, of course, conceivable that in the future another government may find that U.S. research and development grants, or tax breaks for plant modernization, are "subsidies" that cause U.S. exports to materially injure an industry of that country. In such an event, the other government could, consistent with the subsidies code, impose countervailing duties on imports from the United States that received the U.S. benefits and that injured the foreign industry. Even if this occurred, however, the United States would not be under any obligation whatsoever to change its practice. As noted in the code, the signatories to the subsidies code have expressly recognized that domestic subsidies "are intended to promote important objectives of national policy."

Government Procurement.[27] Governments buy for their own use billions of dollars worth of goods such as pencils, paper, cars, trucks, and telecommunications equipment. Most governments traditionally have reserved this vast market for their own domestic producers. Some, such as the U.S. government, openly apply specified margins of preference in favor of

domestic bidders. Under the federal Buy America Act
and its implementing regulations, for example, government agencies are required to purchase from U.S.
suppliers unless the bids of all U.S. suppliers exceed
those of a foreign bidder by more than six percent or,
in certain cases, 12 percent.[28] Some other governments
achieve the same purposes less openly, by simply
excluding foreign bids, failing to give notice of
intended purchases, or declining to announce the basis
for awarding purchase contracts.

One goal of the United States in the Tokyo Round
was to open up to U.S. exporters the enormous government purchasing markets of Europe, Canada, and Japan.
U.S. negotiators sought to accomplish this goal through
an agreement to eliminate from government purchasing
all forms of discrimination against foreign suppliers.
They achieved a qualified success.

The government procurement code does require
elimination of virtually all forms of discrimination
against foreign suppliers. In addition to prohibiting formal preferences such as those set forth
by the Buy America Act, the code specifies rules that
are designed to ensure fairness and open procedures in
the drafting of specifications for goods to be purchased, the advertising of prospective purchases, the
time allocated for submission of bids, the qualification of suppliers, the opening and evaluation of bids,
the award of contracts, and the hearing and reviewing
of protests.

The government procurement code, if faithfully
observed by major U.S. trading partners, has greater
potential significance for U.S. exporters than any of
the other Tokyo Round agreements. The Carter administration has estimated that the code will open up for
U.S. suppliers, new foreign market opportunities
totaling some $20 billion annually.[29] Even allowing
for possible exaggeration on that claim, the opportunities for U.S. exporters resulting from access to
foreign government purchases will be very substantial
if the code works as intended.

Several qualifications are in order, however.
First, the government procurement code will not go into
effect until 1 January 1981. Second, the code is to
apply only to selected lists of agencies that the

signatories -- through intense bargaining intended to ensure reciprocal purchasing opportunities -- have agreed to subject to open, nondiscriminatory purchasing. Among the U.S. agencies that will not be covered by the code (and thus will still apply Buy America preferences) are the Departments of Transportation and Energy, the Tennessee Valley Authority, the Department of Defense Corps of Engineers, the Bureau of Reclamation of the Interior Department, three parts of the General Services Administration, as well as the Postal Service, the Communications Satellite Corporation, AMTRAK, and CONRAIL. A third qualification with respect to the operation of the government procurement code is that the code is to apply only to government purchases (by the designated agencies) on contracts that exceed 150,000 Special Drawing Rights, which equals approximately $190,000. The code does not apply to government services, such as transportation except those that are incidental to the purchase of goods (e.g., the delivery of an airplane). Fourth, the code will not apply to purchases by state and local governments, to purchases of strategic materials, or to purchases by ministries of agriculture for farm support programs or for human nutritional programs such as U.S. school lunch programs. Within the United States, the government procurement code will not affect programs that reserve certain government purchases exclusively for U.S. small businesses and minority-owned businesses, nor will it change the requirements that Defense Department purchases of food, clothing, and other products be purchased only from U.S. domestic sources. Finally, the United States and Japan still have not fully settled a dispute with respect to whether purchases of sophisticated electronic equipment by the Nippon Telephone and Telegraph Company will be opened on a nondiscriminatory basis. This dispute threatens to delay application of the agreement between the United States and Japan.

Thus the government procurement code faces many imponderables. Will other governments genuinely evaluate U.S. bids on the same basis as bids from local suppliers? Will the U.S. government vigorously press complaints? Will the dispute settlement procedures contained in the code function effectively? These procedures call for internationl reviews and findings in cases of alleged code violations. The government procurement code is to be reviewed after three years of operation to determine whether its coverage can be expanded. If this review fails to enlarge the coverage of the code, the entire principle of nondiscriminatory government purchasing could be in jeopardy.

Product Standards. Standards that regulate the quality, safety, or environmental effects of imported goods have proliferated in the past two decades. Frequently such standards, as well as test methods for ascertaining whether products conform to standards and certification practices for attesting conformity, have been used to keep U.S. goods out of foreign markets. The EC has, for example, refused to certify that U.S. electrical goods met European safety standards. Without such certification, the products could not be sold within the EC market. Until recently, the Japanese have been accused of requiring every automobile exported to Japan to be tested individually -- rather than testing on the basis of an entire product line -- to determine conformity with rigorous Japanese pollution standards. Australia reportedly required that imported live cattle be quarantined for an extended period, although there are no quarantine facilities at most Australian ports. These are examples of technical barriers to trade that the standards code is intended to eliminate.

The standards code attempts to promote nondiscrimination between domestic and imported products, as well as open and fair procedures in the development and use of product standards, test methods, and certification systems. The requirements of the code are entirely procedural; they do not require adoption of any particular standards or related practices. The code would not, moreover, prevent any government from adopting measures deemed necessary for the protection of human, animal, or plant life or health, the environment, national security, or the prevention of deceptive practices, as long as these measures were not merely disguised means of discriminating against imports.

The key requirement of the standards code is that product standards and related testing and certification are not to be used to create unnecessary obstacles to international trade. In addition, the code requires public notice and opportunities for comment with respect to standards under development; that

348

international standards be used as the basis for new domestic standards where appropriate; and that foreign testing and certification of conformity with product standards be permitted where feasible.

The standards code applies to product standards and related testing and certification of federal, state, regional, local, and private entities. Central governments undertake to use "such reasonable measures as may be available to them" to secure compliance by nonfederal bodies, and they accept international responsibility for such compliance. Special provisions call for technical assistance in the standards area to be made available to developing countries. Finally, the standards code creates an international Committee on Technical Barriers to Trade that will function under the GATT to review operation of the code and to deal with related disputes. Like most of the other nontariff agreements, the effect of the standards code upon U.S. exports will depend very largely upon how widely its provisions are observed, and how effectively its dispute-settlement procedures operate.

Other nontariff agreements. The remaining nontariff agreements can benefit U.S. exporters primarily by promoting stability in the customs rules of other nations and by requiring other nations to observe more open and expeditious procedures in the application of their customs laws. Thus the agreement on customs valuation promises to provide greater simplicity and certainty which will allow exporters to predict more accurately the duty to be assessed against their products. Similarly, the agreement on import licensing attempts to reduce red tape faced by persons who must acquire import licenses to export their goods to foreign markets. The new antidumping agreement requires more open procedures in the application of rules against dumping, or sales in a foreign market below the "home market value" or below cost. All of these agreements, if they work well, can reduce uncertainty and burdens faced by U.S. exporters.

Sectoral Agreements

Agriculture. The value of U.S. agricultural exports exceeded $30 billion in the fiscal year that ended on 30 September 1979. Overall, exports represented about one-fourth of all cash receipts from U.S.

farm sales. For particular commodities, exports comprised a much higher proportion of total sales: in the last fiscal year, 54 percent of all U.S. soybeans, 55 percent of U.S. wheat, and 73 percent of U.S. rice were shipped abroad. Some 40 percent of U.S. cotton and almonds were exported, along with 35 percent of all tobacco and about 30 percent of U.S. corn.[30] Obviously, a sustained high level of exports is essential not only to U.S. agriculture but also to the U.S. economy as a whole.

There has never been much effective discipline, however, over the barriers that nations erect to keep out agricultural imports in order to protect their own farmers. Past negotiating rounds have done little to reduce these barriers. The Kennedy Round, which ended in 1967, resulted only in a few relatively small agricultural tariff reductions, and was generally regarded as a disappointment by U.S. agriculture.[31] Among the perceived shortcomings of the Kennedy Round was the refusal of the EC to limit its movement, under the fledgling Common Agricultural Policy (CAP), toward virtual insulation of the EC market from most agricultural import competition. Another shortcoming of the Kennedy Round was its failure to deal effectively with nontariff distortions of agricultural trade, including export subsidies provided under the CAP that enabled EC farm products to move into traditional U.S. export markets.

Thus U.S. negotiators entered the Tokyo Round with determination -- and a mandate from the Congress -- to negotiate agricultural and industrial tariffs together, to apply any general formula for tariff reductions both to agricultural products and to industrial articles, and to secure greater discipline over the use by other governments of such nontariff measures as import quotas and export subsidies. The United States was only partially successful in these efforts. The EC would not apply the general tariff-cutting formula to both agricultural and industrial products. Such an approach, EC negotiators contended, would have undermined one of the cornerstones of the CAP: the system of "variable levies" imposed upon imports to equalize the costs of foreign and domestic agricultural products in European markets. The CAP, in turn, was widely regarded as one of the political foundations of EC unity.

350

In the summer of 1977, Robert Strauss, the chief U.S. negotiator, agreed with his EC counterpart that agricultural products would not be subject to the general tariff formula. Instead, in the agricultural tariff negotiations, nations would make specific requests for duty reductions, and the nations to which these requests were made would respond with specific offers. It was assumed that agricultural trade would be covered by the evolving nontariff negotiations.

The United States focused its tariff requests upon agricultural products with high potential for growth. These included such products as high-quality beef, pork, poultry, variety meats, tallow, tobacco, fresh and canned fruits and juices, vegetable oils, and vegetable protein products. Important concessions also were sought with respect to soybeans, rice, and cotton. These U.S. requests covered some $4.7 billion in annual U.S. exports.[32] The requests reflected the views of many agricultural experts from the private sector who served on committees to advise the U.S. negotiators.

Foreign offers in response to U.S. requests covered 480 products that accounted for about $4 billion in annual U.S. agricultural exports. These offers covered approximately 16 percent by value of all U.S. farm exports. Most of the foreign tariff offers were made for products in which the United States already is a major exporter. Japan accounts for one-third of the trade coverage of offers to the United States; the EC accounts for 28 percent; Canada for 13 percent; and Taiwan, 16 percent. Mexico, the Philippines, Korea, and India account for most of the rest.

U.S. agricultural tariff concessions cover products worth some $2.7 billion in annual imports. About one-fourth of these concessions cover trade in fresh or frozen beef, lamb meat and wool, live cattle, and various grain products in which concessions were offered to developing countries. Most of the remainder of the U.S. concessions cover vegetable oils, inedible molasses, fruits and vegetables, and preserved beef. The average U.S. duty reduction for these articles will, when fully implemented, be somewhat above 50 percent. The United States also agreed to expand existing import quotas on several foreign cheeses by some 15 percent. These quotas, however, will now include a number of cheese imports that previously were not subject to the U.S. quota system. Thus about 85 percent of total cheese imports will be covered by U.S. quotas, compared with some 50 percent of such imports that were covered previously.

The nontariff agreements offer a modest opportunity for the U.S. government to seek redress of nontariff practices that exclude U.S. agricultural exports. For U.S. agriculture, the most significant of the nontariff agreements appears to be the code on subsidies and countervailing duties, which may provide some discipline with respect to EC subsidies to third country markets in which the United States is also a competitor, the agreement on product standards is also of importance.

Forecasting future trade effects of complex agreements is always a risky business, but preliminary studies appear to indicate that the net effect of the Tokyo Round agreements on U.S. agricultural exporters will be small but positive. In one of the studies that was conducted for the Senate Finance Committee, Professor James Houck of the University of Minnesota concludes:

> The net change in overall agricultural trade due to the MTN agreements is an increase of $356 million. This corresponds to the annual value of sales of about 6,500 average-sized farms in the United States. A net increase of about 26 thousand jobs will occur as a direct result of these agreements. From the standpoint of income and employment, U.S. agriculture will receive distinct and measurable benefits from the agreements reached in the Tokyo/Geneva Round.[33]

Table 6 summarizes Houck's estimated effects of the Tokyo Round agreements with Japan, the EC, Canada, and others, upon U.S. agricultural exports, imports, and jobs.

Civil Aircraft. Toward the end of the Tokyo Round, negotiators for the United States, the EC, Canada, Japan, and Sweden embodied in a single agreement the elimination of tariffs and the creation of other nontariff rules affecting trade in civil aircraft. The agreement is open to other contracting

TABLE 6

ESTIMATED VALUE OF MTN AGREEMENTS
FOR AGRICULTURAL TRADE

Item	Net Change in exports (+) or imports	Net Change Employment
	(million dollars)	(thousand jobs)
Export Agreements		
Japan	+ $215	
EC-9	+ 168	
Canada	+ 56	
Other countries	+ 23	
Subtotal	+ 462	+ 34
Import Concessions		
Dairy products	- $ 66	
Other commodities	- 40	
Subtotal	- 106	- 8
Net change, overall	+ 356	+ 26

Source: James Houck, The Tokyo/Geneva Round: Its Relation to U.S. Agriculture, U.S. Senate, Committee on Finance (1979), p. 64.

parties to the GATT. This agreement resulted in the elimination on 1 January 1980 of all customs duties and similar charges of any kind levied on the import of civil aircraft and engines, as well as those levied on ground flight simulators for civil aircraft. Certain parts, components, or subassemblies of civil aircraft are also to be duty-free if they are to be used in civil aircraft. Duties on foreign repairs of civil aircraft also have been eliminated.

In addition to the elimination of import duties on civil aircraft, the agreement provides that governments are to avoid offering political or economic inducements (such as landing rights) or the threat of sanctions to secure export sales of their aircraft. From a U.S. point of view, this new discipline is intended to help U.S. aircraft exporters in their competition with EC producers for aircraft sales outside the U.S. and European markets. The agreement further provides that civil aircraft imports are not to be subject to quotas or to restrictive licensing agreements; that governments are not to require their national airlines to purchase only domestically produced aircraft to the detriment of trade interests of other signatories; and that the Tokyo Round agreements on standards and subsidies are expressly to apply to trade in civil aircraft and aircraft parts.

Developing countries and dispute settlement. Under pressure from developing countries, the United States and other developed countries added to the GATT a general "enabling clause," that authorizes future grants of certain types of preferential treatment to LDC trade. This clause constitutes a permanent international legal basis for the following types of actions: (1) the Generalized System of Preferences, by which most industrialized nations grant tariff preferences for selected products of developing countries;[34] (2) special treatment of LDC trade that is provided for in some of the Tokyo Round's nontariff agreements, and that may be provided in similar agreements in the future; (3) regional or global trade arrangements among developing countries; and (4) special treatment for the least developed countries.

The agreement regarding the settlement of international trade disputes provides slightly improved guidance for the GATT problem-solving machinery. This agreement affirms the traditional right of a government that is a GATT contracting party to have its trade complaints against other contracting parties reviewed be an impartial panel of three to five experts. The agreement also suggests target time limits for completion of various stages of such reviews. These provisions supplement the general rules for the settlement of international trade disputes that are set forth in Article XXIII of the GATT. Most of the new nontariff codes contain dispute-settlement procedures of their own that are generally modeled upon the procedures in Article XXIII of the GATT, as supplemented by the general understanding described above. The exact relationship between reviews of disputes under the nontariff codes and possible reviews of the same disputes under the general GATT dispute-settlement provisions has yet to be worked out in practice. As the following section discusses, however, the successful handling of disputes under the new trade agreements will be critical to the success of the entire Tokyo Round system.

IV.   AFTER THE TOKYO ROUND: IMPLEMENTATION AND EXECUTIVE BRANCH REORGANIZATION

Negotiation of the main Tokyo Round agreements was completed in April 1979. By mid-summer, the Congress had enacted legislation approving and implementing the nontariff agreements in the United States. Later in the year, President Carter proclaimed that the seven year phase-in of U.S. tariff reductions would begin on 1 January 1980. Most U.S. trading partners also completed during 1979 their domestic procedures for implementation of the Tokyo Round agreements. Except for the agreements on government procurement and customs valuation, which go into effect at the beginning of 1981, all of the new Tokyo Round agreements went into effect for those nations that had signed them on 1 January 1980.

For U.S. exporters, this inauguration of the new agreements merely opened a new phase in the struggle to gain and hold foreign markets. None of the Tokyo Round agreements -- with the possible exception of the tariff agreements -- will automatically create new opportunities for U.S. exports. Everything depends upon whether the new international principles are voluntarily observed, and upon how well the new agreements will be enforced when they are not observed voluntarily. Only the U.S. executive branch can assert U.S. complaints under the new agreements, either bilaterally with offending governments or in the multilateral forums of the GATT: yet in most cases only private U.S. exporters will in the first instance discover foreign trade barriers that abridge new U.S. rights. What will be needed, then, is a high degree of cooperation between the U.S. executive branch and the private sector in identifying foreign infringements of the new agreements and in pressing U.S. complaints. Beyond that, the procedures under the new agreements and the GATT for settling such trade disputes will have to function expeditiously, and the results of those procedures will have to be respected by sovereign governments if the whole 700 pages of Tokyo Round agreements are to amount to much more than lofty but ineffectual statements of principle. What signs are there that such cooperation between the government and private sector, leading to the vigorous assertion of new U.S. rights, will be forthcoming?

The first positive sign is to be found in the close working relationship that developed between trade policymakers in the administration, the congressional trade oversight committees (Ways and Means and Finance), and interested private sector representatives of industry, agriculture, and labor, that grew out of the five-year Tokyo Round negotiations. The culmination of this relationship was the congressional enactment of the Trade Agreements Act of 1979, by votes of 395-7 in the House and 90-4 in the Senate. This was done without amendment by the Congress, and in less than six weeks after the agreement and implementing legislation were submitted to the Congress by the president. All this was accomplished notwithstanding the fact that the legislation made extensive and controversial changes in existing U.S. trade laws.

This rather breathtaking legislative accomplishment was no accident. The Trade Act of 1974, which authorized and guided U.S. participation in the Tokyo Round, had set up a system of extensive participation by the Congress and the private sector in negotiations that were carried out by executive branch negotiators from the U.S. Trade Representative's Office. Under this system, several members of the House Ways and Means and Senate Finance Committees were designated as official members of the U.S. negotiating team; staff members from these committees were in almost constant communication with U.S. negotiators who were acutely aware that any nontariff agreements that they concluded would one day be submitted to the Congress for legislative action. In addition, the 1974 Trade Act mandated the creation of an elaborate network of more than 1,000 private advisors from industry, agriculture, labor, academia, and consumer groups. These advisors were kept informed of the progress of the negotiations and provided detailed suggestions to U.S. negotiators. Finally, the Trade Act of 1974 provided that the Tokyo Round agreements and implementing legislation -- having been prepared under these unprecedented procedures for national participation -- could not be amended by the Congress and would have to be acted upon within 90 working days after their submission by the president.

The overwhelming, expeditious congressional acceptance and implementation of the Tokyo Round results indicate how well, procedurally at least, this

357

experiment in national unity on trade policy succeeded. It also holds out hope that the executive branch, the Congress, and the private sector can work together to define and achieve national U.S. trade goals in the future. This hope is supported by the retention, in the Trade Agreements Act of 1979, of both the private sector advisory structure and the expedited procedures for gaining approval and implementation of nontariff agreements. The legislation expressly provides that interested private sector advisors are to be consulted with respect to disputes under the GATT or under the new agreements when the United States is a party to such disputes.

A second cause for optimism that the new U.S. rights may be more than empty promises is the revised statutory procedures under which affected U.S. persons can complain to the executive branch and secure expeditious reviews of alleged unfair foreign trade practices, including violations of the GATT or the new agreements. Under these procedures, the U.S. Trade Representative must announce within specified periods whether the private complaint is to be investigated, and if so, whether an international complaint under the GATT or a Tokyo Round agreement is to be filed. If such a complaint is filed, then the executive branch must, at the conclusion of the time allowed in the relevant international agreement for settlement of disputes, announce what action will be taken with respect to the matter. Such actions could include retaliation against the trade of offending nations.

Finally, there is reason to believe that U.S. export interests will receive greater attention from the executive branch as a result of the recent reorganization of the way trade policy is conducted. The executive branch reorganization, which was a political condition for congressional acceptance and implementation of the Tokyo Round results, was put into effect by an executive order of 2 January 1980, pursuant to a Reorganization Plan that President Carter had sent up to the Congress in September 1979.[35] The principal effects of the reorganization are to strengthen the ability of the USTR to coordinate overall U.S. trade policy; to move the administration of U.S. laws on antidumping and countervailing duties from the Treasury Department to the Commerce Department; and to strengthen the export promotion functions of the

Commerce Department by creating a position for an Assistant Secretary charged with promoting exports, and by providing for better coordination between the activities of the Commerce Department and those of other federal agencies, such as the Export-Import Bank.

All of these developments are hopeful signs that the U.S. government is moving toward a more comprehensive approach to U.S. trade and export promotion policies. The results of these efforts, however, will depend not only upon what is done in the United States but also upon what is done by other nations in the international trade policy forums.

V.   BEYOND THE TOKYO ROUND: UNFINISHED BUSINESS

Even if the U.S. government vigorously asserts new U.S. trade rights, what will be the response of other nations? What will be the response of the United States when another government complains about a U.S. trade practice that allegedly violates provisions of a new agreement? Will other governments, and the United States, respect formal findings of international dispute-settlement bodies convened under the new agreements -- particularly when such findings require changes in domestic laws of the offending country?

In short, now that the dust is beginning to settle from the main Tokyo Round negotiations, the next order of business will be to make the new rules work. This will depend, first, upon voluntary adherence by participating governments, and second, upon the effectiveness of the dispute settlement procedures in the new agreements and in the basic GATT rules. Both voluntary self-restraint -- to resist, for example, instituting new export subsidies -- and compliance with decisions of dispute-settlement panels may in some instances require governments to subordinate short-term political pressures to their longer-term stake in the new trading system.

Several things could go wrong in the first year or two. The dispute-settlement procedures could become glutted with cases as governments, under pressure from their exporters, race to test the new rules and procedures. The GATT secretariat, which is accustomed to handling two-or three major disputes a year, may become overwhelmed. Alternatively, the formal procedures for settling disputes may be underutilized if the United States, the EC, and Japan choose to settle their differences through direct negotiation. Depending upon the nature of the settlements, such a bypassing of the agreed means of handling trade disputes could discredit the new machinery as effectively as could an unmanageable flood of cases. There is a further danger that governments will dispute cases that are not politically manageable within the GATT-Tokyo Round framework, such as U.S. beef quotas, EC import restrictions and export subsidies under the CAP, or the speed with which Japan dismantles import quotas on citrus or beef. As the recent DISC case indicates, using the international trade machinery to complain of practices that are strongly entrenched politically is likely to result in damage to the machinery rather than in change of the practice. One or two failures by major participants to conform their practices to findings of dispute panels could seriously impair the operation of any of the new agreements.

In addition to making existing agreements work, several new subjects cry out for attention of the negotiators. The most pressing of these involves safeguards: the supposedly temporary import restrictions that governments impose to give a faltering domestic industry a chance to recover. This subject was under negotiation throughout the Tokyo Round, but in the end no agreement was reached for two reasons. First, the EC could not agree with Japan and the advanced LDCs about the conditions under which import-restrictive safeguard actions would be allowed to be taken selectively, that is, against a product from some rather than all nations; and second, few nations were willing to accept the requirement that informal voluntary restraint agreements (VRAs) be made public and subject to international scrutiny. Failure to achieve any discipline over the spread of VRAs is particularly serious to U.S. trade objectives. As other nations continue to use the VRA as a primary device for addressing their problems with import competition, exports that are shut out of European and Japanese markets by VRAs will (seemingly mysteriously) turn up in the United States and in third markets where U.S. exports compete.

A second subject that is ripe for negotiation is that of export restrictions and access to vital supplies. The United States tried unsuccessfully to negotiate international principles with respect to these matters during the Tokyo Round, and other nations agreed to continue the effort. A third area that remains untouched by the GATT Tokyo Round system is that of international trade in services such as shipping, banking, and insurance. Trade in services generally has been subject to far more government intervention than has trade in goods. Trade between developed and developing nations, and trade with nations having socialist economic systems will command attention in the 1980s. In all of these areas, U.S. exporters have important stakes.

VI.   WHAT MORE CAN BE DONE?

The obvious first step is to use the new agreements to attack foreign barriers to U.S. trade. As was indicated in the early part of this study, however, foreign barriers to U.S. exports are only one aspect of the difficulties that U.S. exporters have experienced in the last half of the 1970s. Breaking down foreign trade barriers is, to repeat, a necessary step but not a sufficient one. Above all, the U.S. government and U.S. business must stop looking at export performance in isolation from the economy as a whole, and the American public must be led to realize that U.S. export competitiveness deserves a high priority among national goals.

There are some encouraging signs. Last fall, 54 U.S. Senators, led by William Roth (R.-Del.) and Adlai Stevenson (D.-Ill.), formed the Senate Export Caucus to reflect "the Senate's deep concern over America's decreasing competitiveness" and to attempt to shape a more effective U.S. export policy. The Senate Export Caucus now numbers 67 members. For more than a year, a 21 member House Export Policy Task Force has provided a focus in the House of Representatives for discussions of export policy issues. In November 1979, President Carter announced a broad, nine part program to stimulate industrial innovation in the United States and to increase cooperation between the U.S. government and industry. Key parts of this program will increase government assistance for research and development, impose some order on a chaotic system of handling patents for inventions that result from government sponsorship, encourage agencies to reduce unnecessary regulation of business, and better explain the ways that U.S. firms can, under the Webb-Pomerene exemption from U.S. antitrust laws, combine to carry out export ventures. This program was criticized immediately, however, for its failure to include any tax incentives for innovation and exporting.[36]

In September 1978, President Carter announced an export promotion program that had been developed by an interagency task force, under the direction of then Assistant Secretary of Commerce Frank Weil. Although this program included increased loan authorizations for the Export-Import Bank, increased loan guarantees for small business exporters, and larger funding for export development programs by the State and Commerce Departments, it was generally regarded as insufficient to affect substantially U.S. export performance. Finally, another hopeful sign may be found in the fact that the recent reorganization of executive trade policymaking includes the designation of an Assistant Secretary of Commerce to be responsible for export development.

These are all good signs, but they are not enough. What, then, needs to be done? Most fundamentally, the American public must somehow be made to realize that U.S. competitiveness is a matter of vital national interest.[37] Acceptance of this simple point could pave the way for other, more specific changes by reducing political resistance that springs from the belief that measures to stimulate business are only special interest programs for the wealthy.

More specifically, the Commerce Department has produced an excellent and comprehensive inventory of recent proposals for the stimulation of U.S. export competitiveness.[38] Some of the most promising of these proposals appear to be the following:

1. Increase the exposure of the Export-Import Bank to small exporters, perhaps by greater joint projects in which the Eximbank and local banks together finance export transactions;

2. Create an effective "one-stop" office in the executive branch so that inexperienced exporters can obtain in one place all the information, forms, and assistance that they need;

3. Revise antitrust laws to increase the opportunities for U.S. companies to engage in joint ventures for research and development;

4. Broaden the Webb-Pomerene exemption from U.S. antitrust laws, which enables U.S. companies to form joint export associations, to include U.S. service industries;

5. Find ways to encourage savings and investment as compared with consumption. (One possibility is to eliminate the income tax deduction for interest paid on consumer loans);

6. Improve the administration of several of the regulations that currently serve as competitive disincentives. This could include repeal of the antiboycott provisions embodied in the 1976 Tax Reform Act, because similar provisions have now been promulgated under the Export Administration Act and the existence of two sets of antiboycott regulations merely increases confusion. The application of the Foreign Corrupt Practices Act, which in some cases imposes criminal sanctions upon U.S. persons engaging in business bribery, is highly uncertain and should be clarified. There is also uncertainty about the application of the National Environmental Protection Act to export transactions.

Finally, the consolidation of trade policymaking by the executive branch begun last year, should be completed by the creation of a new Department of Trade and Industry. This department should bring under one roof -- and thus under the control of one strong cabinet officer -- the following functions:

1. The trade negotiations functions currently carried out by the USTR;

2. The trade policy coordination currently done by the USTR;

3. The enforcement of U.S. antidumping and countervailing duty laws, currently performed by the Department of Commerce;

4. The adjustment assistance and Economic Development Administration functions currently carried out by the Department of Commerce;

364

5. The Export-Import Bank, together with other export promotion activities cur-rently done by the Commerce Department;

6. Research, creation of an information base, and the ability to anticipate competitive problems --tasks cur-rently performed, if at all, by a variety of agencies;

7. Investment policy, supposedly carried out at present by the USTR, and the insurance of certain U.S. investments abroad by the Overseas Private Investment Corporation.

All extraneous functions, such as fisheries regulation and the National Bureau of Standards, that are currently within the Commerce Department should be kept out of the new Department of Trade and Industry. The new department should be as small and lean as possible, and should be staffed only with the best possible personnel.

Such an approach would bring together several governmental functions that bear upon the same reality -- U.S. competitiveness. Placing one person in charge of each of these functions would help to eliminate the current piecemeal approach to U.S. competitive problems. It would more nearly enable the executive branch to use its resources efficiently to solve (and maybe even anticipate) competitive problems, rather than merely react in isolated ways to whichever crisis cries out the loudest for temporary attention.

[1]Opened for signature, 30 October 1947, 61 Statute A-11, Treaty and Other International Acts Series No. 1700, 55 United Nations Treaty Series 194. The Agreement has been modified in several respects since 1947. The current version is contained in General Agreement of Tariffs and Trade, vol. 4, Basic Instruments and Selected Documents (1969). The GATT rules were to have been one component of a more comprehensive International Trade Organization, which in turn was to have joined with the World Bank and the International Monetary Fund to form the pillars of the international economic system after World War II. When the International Trade Organization collapsed in 1949, principally because Congress failed to ratify the treaty establishing it, the GATT rules became the nucleus of a small international organization. For more complete background information about the GATT, see J. Jackson, World Trade and the Law of GATT, 1969, pp. 35-37, and R. Hudec, The GATT Legal System and World Trade Diplomacy, 1975.

[2]Declaration of Ministers Approved at Tokyo on 14 September 1973, reprinted in Basic Instruments and Selected Documents, 20th supplement, no. 19, Geneva, 1974.

[3]The first round after the formation of the GATT took place in 1949 in Annecy, France. The second round was held in 1951 at Torquay, England. The third, fourth, and fifth rounds took place in 1955, 1960-1961, and 1962-1967 in Geneva.

[4]The list presented here is adapted from one that the author presents in Thomas Graham, "Results of the Tokyo Round," Georgia Journal of International and Comparative Law, vol. 9, 1979, p. 153.

[5]Public Law No. 96-39, 93 Statute 144, 1979, (codified in scattered sections of 19 U.S. Code Annotated, West Supplemental, 1980.)

[6]Executive Order No. 12,188, 45 Federal Register 989, 1980. This order implemented a proposal that President Carter had submitted to the

Congress on 25 September 1979. See Reorganization Plan No. 3 of 1979, 44 Federal Register 69,273, 1979 and the President's Message to the Congress Transmitting Reorganization Plan No. 3 of 1979, Weekly Compilation of Presidential Documents, 25 September 1979, p. 1729.

[7]"The U.S. Trade Balance Less Oil: Is It Meaningful?" Staff Economic Report, Department of Commerce, Bureau of International Economic Policy and Research, August 1977, p. 6.

[8]The DISC legislation, in essence, permits U.S. companies to defer payments of income taxes on one-fourth of profits derived from export sales.

[9]Policies announced by President Nixon on 15 August 1971 included a temporary surcharge of 10 percent on U.S. imports and a suspension of the convertability of the dollar. See A. Lowenfeld, The International Monetary System, 1977.

[10]Public Law No. 93-618, 88 Statute 1978, (1975), section 2(2).

[11]This program is described in "U.S. Export Policy: New Directions," Washington International Business Report, 1978, p. 20.

[12]As this was written, trade statistics for 1979 began to become available. These statistics indicated unofficially that the U.S. merchandise trade deficit for 1979 would be about $24.5 billion. U.S. Department of Commerce, Bureau of the Census, Summary of U.S. Export and Import Merchandise Trade, 1979.

[13]This conclusion was demonstrated convincingly in Lawrence Fox and William Averyt, "The U.S. Trade Deficit: A Hard Look at Bad News," Business Economics, March 1979.

[14]A Survey of Export Expansion Proposals, U.S. Department of Commerce, September 1979, p. 1.

[15]The Wall Street Journal, 30 January 1980.

[16]In this part of the analysis, the author has drawn upon the excellent survey of historical origins

of current U.S. trade problems found in Fox and Averyt, op. cit.

[17]Op cit., "U.S. Export Policy: New Directions."

[18]It should be noted here, and borne in mind throughout the remainder of this essay, that the United States also maintains a number of trade practices that our trading partners regard as restrictive or unfair. These practices are not covered in this discussion because the focus here is upon phenomena that affect U.S. exports. This may cause the discussion to appear somewhat biased, particularly to non-U.S. readers. That is not intended, but is almost inevitable. A balanced discussion of possibly "unfair" trade practices that are maintained by the United States and other nations would take us far beyond the scope of this more limited analysis.

[19]For an account of this period of U.S.-Japanese trade relations, see I.M. Destler, "U.S.-Japanese Relations and the American Trade Initiative of 1977: Was This 'Trip' Necessary?" William J. Barnds, ed. Japan and the United States: Challenges and Opportunities (New York Press: Council on Foreign Relations, 1979), pp. 190-230.

[20]The petition of the American Iron and Steel Institute to the Office of the Special Representative for Trade Negotiations was published in vol. 41, Federal Register, 15 October 1976, p. 45628.

[21]Lawrence Fox and Samuel Katz, "Dollar Devaluation, Floating Exchange Rates and U.S. Exports," Business Economics, January 1978. See also U.S. Trade Performance Since 1970 With Special Reference to Manufactured Goods, National Association of Manufacturers, 1978.

[22]For factual descriptions of some aspects of the Tokyo Round agreements, the author has occasionally drawn upon two of his previous works, "Reforming the International Trading System: The Tokyo Round Trade Negotiations in the Final Stage," Cornell International Law Journal, vol. 12, 1979, p. 1., and "Results of the Tokyo Round," Georgia Journal of International and Comparative Law, vol. 9, 1979, p. 153. See also GATT document 1234, 12 April 1979, a press release by

release by the GATT Secretariat setting forth a description of the Tokyo Round agreements.

[23]Results of the Industrial Tariff Negotiations, Office of the Special Representative for Trade Negotiations, 1979.

[24]For an authoritative account of the negotiations on subsidies and countervailing duties, see John Greenwald and Richard Rivers, "The Negotiation of a Code on Subsidies and Countervailing Measures: Bridging Fundamental Policy Differences," Law and Policy in International Business, vol. 11, no. 4, 1979, p. 1447.

[25]The Protocol of Provisional Application of the General Agreement on Tariffs and Trade, which specifies the terms upon which the United States agreed as of 1 January 1978, to apply the GATT rules, states that the portion of those rules that includes the provisions pertaining to subsidies and countervailing duties is to be applied "to the fullest extent not inconsistent with existing legislation."

[26]In addition to problems with the U.S. counter-vailing duty law, the provisions of the U.S. Internal Revenue Code dealing with Domestic International Sales Corporations (DISCs) -- which permits U.S. companies to defer paying taxes on a portion of export income -- was found to be an export subsidy in violation of the GATT rules by a GATT dispute-settlement panel in 1976. The virtual failure of France, Belgium, and the Netherlands to tax repatriated earnings of sales subsidiaries located in tax haven countries was also found by the GATT panel to result in prohibited export subsidies. Neither the United States nor any of the three European nations took any action in response to this GATT decision. The Tokyo Round agreement on subsidies and countervailing measures expressly preserves this stalemate, by stating that "nothing in this text prejudges the disposition by the Contracting Parties of the specific issues raised in (the DISC case)." See GATT Document MTN/NTM/W/236, Note 2.

[27]For an authoritative account of government procurement, see Morton Pomeranz, "Toward a New International Order in Government Procurement,"

Law and Policy in International Business, vol. 11, no. 4, 1979, p. 1263.

[28]U.S. Code, vol. 41, 1976, p. 10a-10c, Code of Federal Regulations, vol. 41, 1-18.603-1, (1977).

[29]Government Procurement, Office of the Special Trade Representative for Trade Negotiations, Executive Office of the President, 1979.

[30]The Tokyo Round Agreements of 1979: U.S. Agriculture's Stake, Office of the Special Representative for Trade Negotiations, Executive Office of the President, 1979.

[31]MTN Studies, No. 1: Results for U.S. Agriculture, United States Senate, Committee on Finance, Subcommittee on International Trade, 1979, p. 8.

[32]Op. cit., The Tokyo Round Agreements of 1979: U.S. Agriculture's Stake.

[33]James Houck, "The Tokyo/Geneva Round: Its Relation to U.S. Agriculture," United States Senate Hearings, Committee on Finance, 1979, p. 64.

[34]For a discussion of the Generalized System of Preferences, see Thomas Graham, "The U.S. Generalized System of Preferences for Developing Countries: International Innovation and the Art of the Possible," American Journal of International Law, vol. 72, 1978, p. 513.

[35]Supra, footnote 6.

[36]The Wall Street Journal, 1 November 1979.

[37]At this writing, see for example, "The Reindustrialization of America," Business Week, special issue, 30 June 1980; James Fallows, "U.S. Industry, What Ails It, How to Save It," Atlanta Monthly, September 1980, pp. 35-50; "The Productivity Crisis, Can America Renew its Economic Promise?" Newsweek, special report, 8 September 1980, pp. 50-69.

[38]*A Survey of Export Expansion Proposals*, U.S. Department of Commerce, Industry and Trade Administration, September 1979.

SELECTED BIBLIOGRAPHY

Dam, Kenneth. The GATT: Law and International Economic Organization. Chicago: University of Chicago Press, 1970.

Destler, I. M. Making Foreign Economic Policy. Washington, D.C.: The Brookings Institution, 1980.

Evans, John. The Kennedy Round in American Trade Policy. Cambridge: Harvard University Press, 1971.

Executive Office of the President, Office of the U.S. Trade Representative, various papers summarizing the results of the Tokyo Round negotiations, including Results of the Industrial Tariff Negotiations, Government Procurement, Subsidies and Countervailing Measures, and The Tokyo Round Agreements of 1979: U.S. Agriculture's Stake. 1979.

Fox, Lawrence and Averyt, William. "The U.S. Trade Deficit: A Hard Look at Bad News," Business Economics. March 1979.

Fox, Lawrence and Katz, Stanley. "Dollar Devaluation, Floating Exchange Rates and U.S. Exports," Business Economics. January 1978.

Graham, Thomas R. "Revolution in Trade Politics," Foreign Policy. Fall 1979.

Givens, William and Rapp, William. "What it Takes to Meet the Japanese Challenge," Fortune. 18 June 1977.

Herzstein, Robert E. "The Role of Law and Lawyers Under the Multilateral Trade Agreements," Georgia Journal of International and Comparative Law. vol. 9, 1979, p. 177.

Hudec, Robert. The GATT Legal System and World Trade Diplomacy. New York: Praeger Publishers, 1975.

372

Houck, James P.   The Tokyo/Geneva Round: Its Relation
    to Agriculture, United States Senate.   Committee
    on Finance.   Subcommittee on International Trade.
    MTN Studies No. 2, 1979.

Jackson, John.   World Trade and the Law of GATT.
    Indianapolis: The Bobbs-Merrill Company, 1969.

Marquand, David.   "Learning   from   the   Germans,"
    Listener. 5 April 1979.

National Association of Manufacturers.   U.S. and
    World Trade Developments, 1978.   30 March 1979.

National Association of Manufacturers.   U.S. Trade
    Performance Since 1970 With Special Reference to
    Manufactured Goods.   1978.

Preeg, Ernest.   Traders and Diplomats.   Washington,
    D.C.: The Brookings Institution, 1970.

Rowland, Ted and Nemmers, Barry H.   "After the MTN:
    What is in Store for Importers?" Georgia Journal
    of International and Comparative Law.   vol. 9,
    1979.   p. 207.

Schnittker Associates.   Results for U.S. Agriculture.
    United States Senate.   Committee on Finance.
    Subcommittee on International Trade.   MTN Studies
    No. 1.   1979.

United States Congress. 1st Session.   House Document
    No. 96-153.   Part I.   Agreements Reached In The
    Tokyo   Round   of   the   Multilateral   Trade
    Negotiations.   1979.

Washington International Business Report.   U.S. Export
    Policy: New Directions.   1978.

Weil, Frank.   "The U.S. Needs an Industrial Policy,"
    Fortune.   24 March 1980.

8

POLITICS AND THE EXPORT MESS

Richard J. Whalen

On 3 September 1980, the Senate voted by an overwhelming 77-to-0 margin to approve a bill that would permit U.S. corporations and banks to join forces and establish Japanese-style trading companies to improve the flow of information on foreign business opportunities, strengthen overseas marketing, facilitate trade financing, and generally boost U.S. exports. Although the bill is scarcely a cure-all for complex U.S. trade problems and faces some opposition in the House, it nevertheless represents a legislative breakthrough for the new "export lobby." The emergence since the mid -- 1970s of a congressional caucus seeking to promote the interests of export-oriented corporations, financial institutions, industries, and labor unions is belated, but encouraging, evidence of growing realism among those responsible for legislating the rules under which the U.S. political economy operates at home and competes abroad. The congressional caucus includes the Senate Export Caucus, a group now numbering 66 senators, and the House Export Task Force, consisting of 21 House members.

Throughout U.S. history, until recent years, lawmakers in Washington felt little need for creating an "export policy" or establishing competitive vehicles such as trading companies. Like so much else in the private enterprise system, exports were assumed to take care of themselves without the need for encouragement from public policy and government incentives. A secure and prosperous United States, safe behind its ocean moats, dealt with the outside world mostly on its own terms. Congress was absorbed in parochial concerns and disinterested in the intricacies of the world economy and the U.S. competitive position in it. In this, of course, Congress faithfully represented the attitude of the nation as a whole, including most of the business and financial community. Americans were preoccupied

The author gratefully acknowledges the invaluable research and editorial assistance of Dr. Robert Kilmarx and Ms. Jennifer White of CSIS.

with exploiting the opportunities of the vast domestic marketplace.

All this has now changed, at least at the level of political perceptions of what is important enough to demand the time and energies of elected officials, who must be responsive to shifting public moods and priorities. Restoring America's position of respected leadership in the world -- being number one beyond doubt or argument -- is now a broadly popular goal, according to opinion polls. U.S. leadership is defined by public opinion not only in familiar political and military terms but also in terms of economic revitalization ("reindustrialization") enabling the United States to reassert its competitive vigor in domestic and foreign markets.

This generalized public desire for the recovery of national strength and pride, which has been growing since the ignominious end of the Vietnam War, provides a political climate in which basic economic policy change becomes possible but does not offer anything remotely resembling a specific legislative blueprint. That can be fashioned only by the interplay of forces and interests in the political process, defining policy in a succession of ad hoc legislative actions shaped by circumstances and pragmatic compromises.

Thus, the political/legislative process in the U.S. system tends to work from the bottom up rather than from the top down, as in the parliamentary regimes in Japan and Western Europe. Public opinion leads legislative opinion, which, in most cases, sets firm limits on presidential aspirations. The White House may announce a program, but it cannot impose one.

Policy, while it may be proclaimed by the president as a goal, does not exist in any real sense unless and until Congress sets its own direction and follows it through legislation. In determining whether it will recognize the goal of a coherent export policy and consider legislating export incentives, Congress is guided, not by expert opinion or presidential prescription, but by the balance of interests actually or potentially involved in, and affected by, legislative changes. In the eyes of Congress, the most compelling interests are, simply, those best organized to press their case. Often, their advocacy becomes more persuasive as it becomes narrower in scope, for this will tend to reduce the impact of upsetting the status quo.

Although export promotion has the appeal of being a goal to which all sides aspire, it also has the disadvantage of having been, until quite recently, something of an orphan. Exports have not been, and are not, deliberately neglected; they are simply not considered. Or, if they are, rising exports are assumed to be the automatic result of a healthy domestic U.S. economy, which is assumed to be, self-evidently, the sole focus of U.S. policy and politics. To draw an extreme but perhaps provocative parallel, a typical member of the Congress probably spends as much time thinking about promoting exports as his counter-part in the Japanese Diet spends thinking about, say, liberalizing foreign imports. In both nations, the established political and economic systems are geared to reward the unquestioning pursuit of traditional goals: in the United States, ceaseless domestic economic expansion; in Japan, relentless export expansion.

There is one crucial difference, however. Japan has created institutional mechanisms for rapid polit-ical adjustment to changing economic conditions. For example, Japan's Industrial Structure Council, composed of representatives of government, business, and academia, basically determines which are "sunset" industries, destined to lose out in the international competitive arena and therefore not worthy of further aid, and which are "sunrise" industries, to be empha-sized and favored with financial and other assistance. The United States has only begun to think about adopting a similar approach. At present, the United States now bails out its industrial losers on an ad hoc basis and ignores its winners.

The U.S. tradition of taking exports for granted rests on the dubious assumption that the market-centered, "free enterprise" economy is reliably self-correcting at home and abroad -- able to compensate internally and to adjust without sustained government intervention to changing external forces and conditions. In short, the United States long believed it was -- and could remain -- economically autonomous and self-sufficient. This myth is dying hard.

In the first post-World War II generation, Washington defined U.S. national interests almost exclusively in strategic, geopolitical, and military terms. In the 1950s and early 1960s, the enormous U.S. economic, technical, and financial advantages over war-torn former adversaries and new allies, especially Japan and West Germany, bred a dangerous complacency in the attitudes of political and business leaders toward such mundane considerations as maintaining U.S. competitive position in the radically altered world economy. Indeed, when our diplomats thought of foreign economic policy at all, it was usually to make unilateral concessions to trading competitors.

By the late 1960s and early 1970s, however, former U.S. advantages were fast fading before the competitive assaults of the newly rebuilt, more efficient, and politically coordinated industrial economies of Europe and the Far East, especially the surprising economic superpower, Japan. Japan's success proved that politically directed and fully mobilized human resources could more than compensate for a dearth of natural resources.

In the winter of 1973-74, the crushing arrival on the world economic scene of the Organization of Petroleum Exporting Countries (OPEC) shattered U.S. complacency and destroyed old assumptions of economic invulnerability. Since then, the United States has been attempting to come to terms with a harsh new international environment of fragile interdependence and insecure access to resources threatened by political and economic blackmail. Massive trade and balance of payments deficits since the mid-1970s underscore not only U.S. dependence on oil imports but also the steep decline in the competitiveness of U.S.-manufactured products.

Especially symbolic is the plight of the domestic automobile industry in the face of a tidal wave of fuel-efficient Japanese imports. The automobile is the American dream machine, the means of individual mobility and independence that preserves at least a psychological open frontier in urban America. Now the combined onslaught of OPEC and Japanese autos have flattened the nation's self-image.

Philip Caldwell, president of the embattled Ford Motor Company, noted in a thoughtful speech that the United States helped set the ground rules by which Japan has played a globally winning game. Caldwell declared: "For the Kennedy Round of the GATT [General Agreement on Tariffs and Trade] negotiations beginning in 1962, Japan was treated as a developing country. Only 15 years later, she was producing 8.5 million cars and trucks annually compared with 12.5 million in the United States; 113 million tons of raw steel to 125 million; 10 million color television sets to 7 million. Japan used the protection of severe import quotas, high tariffs, and prohibitions against foreign investment to develop industries of world scale."

In short, Japan used a combined political and economic strategy to stage its "miracle," and so have every other successful U.S. competitor. Until recently, however, Americans were still pretending that economics and politics were entirely separate and that the twain should never meet.

In his speech, Mr. Caldwell observed that "the United States has become essentially a service economy, with too little emphasis on expanding manufacturing capacity to serve developing hard-goods markets abroad.... Manufacturing now accounts for less than 25 percent of all U.S. jobs." He concluded on a somber note: "In effect, we have become an economic colony for much of the industrialized world, exporting agricultural products and raw materials, and importing manufactured goods. If we continue in that direction, we will not have the sinews for a vigorous, well-balanced economy."

Because this is the case, enthusiastic talk of America's "reindustrialization" in the 1980s will ring hollow until we embark on a radical modernization of the political framework for managing our economic system. We must accept the discipline of global interdependence and change outmoded laws, institutions, and practices in light of the way the new world economy actually works. We have no real choice.

The congressional search for direction, for a politically acceptable path leading to a coherent and effective export policy, should be understood as part of this much larger undertaking. As noted above, it is politically safe to advocate export promotion, but it may well be politically difficult and dangerous to support specific remedial measures that will adversely affect powerful vested domestic interests. The underlying causes of the decline of U.S. trade competitiveness extend far beyond the realm of trade policy alone; indeed, they go much deeper than politics and economics into the cultural mores of the country. We have built, more or less unintentionally, a post-industrial society dominated by a consumption-leisure ethic and a universal sense of federally guaranteed "entitlements" adding up to a secure, comfortable life whether or not we choose to work. We have built a noncompetitive, nonproductive, and increasingly inefficient society, and we should not be surprised by the results.

Seen in this perspective, enormous U.S. trade and payments deficits are external signs of internal economic imbalances: excessive government stimulus to consumer demand and neglect of expanded productive capacity; obstacles to business innovation and risk taking; declining investment return on capital since the mid-1960s; increasing disincentives to work, production, and capital formation; stagnant productivity per worker; and -- the all-encompassing negative factor -- the relentless growth of public sector spending for two generations at the expense of the tax-burdened private sector, generating a chronic inflation and inflationary psychology.

Our best hope lies in the fact that most of the advanced industrial nations are experiencing basically the same social trends and grappling with similar economic consequences. The international competitive struggle is actually a little understood contest among governing elites, testing their relative ingenuity and skill in devising new political and economic arrangements (subsidies, incentives, and so forth) to offset mounting social and cultural obstacles to productivity. In this contest thus far, which pits ideas instead of factories against each other, the United States is running well behind. This country probably will remain an also-ran as long as Congress is reluctant to upset the status quo in the domestic political economy and legislate economic rewards and penalties with much closer attention to the criteria dictated by international competition.

The status quo is formidably entrenched in the Congress because it represents a balance of power among opposing interests agreed solely on avoiding disruptive change and joined in mutual defense beneath a banner bearing the stark legend: no! Who is willing to say yes to the far-ranging implications of a truly effective export policy? The answer, alas, is too few even in the business community, where guardians of the status quo are numerous and vigilant.

So it may be said flatly that the United States lacks a coherent and comprehensive national export policy because it lacks a sharply defined and committed exporting constituency. Whereas the United States is a leading exporting nation, its commerce is completely dominated by the domestic market. Only a small percentage of U.S. manufacturing firms -- mostly larger ones -- are major exporters. Many of these firms are also more concerned about domestic economic programs than international trade issues. Thus the export caucuses in the Senate and the House are not supported by broadly based political and economic constituencies that agree on particular measures needed to improve U.S. trade competitiveness.

Another big obstacle to the adoption of a national export policy is the diversity of views of congressional politicians on free trade. In principle, the removal of artificial barriers to U.S. trade competitiveness and, to a lesser extent, the adoption of more effective trade promotion policies similar to those of our competitors would seem consistent with a commitment to free trade. Indeed, the objective of free traders should be to provide the government with bargaining leverage to enable it to negotiate downward the tariff and nontariff barriers of other nations. So far, proposed export-related legislation has been limited mainly to reducing self-imposed barriers to U.S. competitiveness and does not include measures that would give discriminatory advantages to U.S. companies over foreign competitors.

Discussions with leading members of Congress who have spoken out on trade issues suggest that many of them are not committed to free trade principles or even to the more politicized, interventionist concept of fair trade, which sanctions government intervention in export markets to counteract unfair practices by competitors. Many congressmen are utterly pragmatic about trade issues.

They can sanction threats of protectionism when basic U.S. industries -- especially those located in their districts -- face economic hardships and at the same time vigorously support GATT and other international measures to reduce obstacles to the expansion of world trade. Many congressmen lack the background (or interest) to make consistently sound judgments of trade policy issues. As on domestic issues, they ask: What does this mean to my constituents?

During a recession, the temptations and pressures mount in Congress to seek the solution to U.S. trade problems by favoring domestic industry regardless of the effects on the trading interests of other countries. Controlling imports attracts more attention than promoting exports. Appeals for specific import restraints gain political support more readily than pleas for changes in basic laws impeding U.S. exports in general. So far, to be sure, Congress has resisted the protectionist serpent. Specific bills to aid particular distressed industries since the signing of the GATT agreements have not gained much support. This situation, however, could change if the recession proves to be deeper and more prolonged than now expected.

Congressional trade-related initiatives are also hampered by the law between American perceptions and the actual development of the international economy. While the United States still expects market forces to topple tariff barriers and move the world toward freer trade, governments have in practice become the main actors on the world's economic stage. This development is understood on Capitol Hill but the appropriate response within the constraints of the U.S. system is unclear. We cannot have a market-oriented economy at home and a government-centered trade policy abroad -- or is there an alternative yet to be devised?

A further political problem is that several specific policy obstacles to U.S. export competitiveness, such as the Foreign Corrupt Practices Act and antiboycott and environmental protection legislation, are each supported by a dedicated single-interest constituency that knows how to mobilize opposition to needed changes. Their individual causes have been endowed with moral or ethical sanctions, regardless of the economic consequences. Their legislative gains made in an earlier time will not be easily surrendered, even though the sweeping powers given government over corporations in the Foreign Corrupt Practices Act and other "moral" legislation far exceed the bounds of prudent and necessary regulation. And what brave lawmakers will face single-issue antagonists on behalf of the broad national interest, which lacks a sure majority?

To understand the sentiment of Congress on trade issues, a census was conducted of the voting records of all 100 senators and 435 congressmen, focusing on proposed protectionist legislation. The census was based on House and Senate votes from 1977 through mid-1980 that can reasonably be characterized as addressing free trade versus protectionist issues. Eleven votes were used for members of the Senate and sixteen for members of the House. Issues covered were as diverse as "Buy American" amendments, legislation to exclude textiles from the multilateral trade negotiations, and prohibitions on U.S. development assistance for export-oriented projects abroad. Members of Congress were then classified according to six categories: free trade, leaning toward free trade, mixed record, leaning toward protectionism, protectionist, or unknown.

The findings reveal that the 96th Congress is evenly split between free traders and protectionists, with a substantial portion of the members in the "mixed record" or "unknown" categories. It does not appear that party affiliation is a significant factor in determining the trade views of most members, although liberals apparently incline more to be free traders while conservatives, more often than not, lean toward protectionism. The South is the most protectionist region of the country, while the Northeast is the most oriented toward free trade. As expected, the Senate is more sympathetic to free trade than the House. The reason, of course, is that senators are more immune to constituents' political pressure than representatives. This is the breakdown of senators in the 96th Congress on the basic free trade vs. protectionism split: free trade, 13 members; leaning toward free trade, 23; protectionist, 0; leaning toward protectionism, 4; mixed record, 44; unknown, 16.

The makeup of the House of Representatives in the 96th Congress on this issue is as follows: free trade, 67 members (15.4 percent of the entire House); leaning toward free trade, 38 (8.7 percent); protectionist, 63 (14.5 percent); leaning toward protectionism, 47 (10.8 percent); mixed record, 140 (32.2 percent); unknown, 86 (18.4 percent).

An important fact about the congressional power structure: the key trade-related committees -- the House Ways and Means Committee and the Senate Finance

Committee -- are more sympathetic to free trade than Congress as a whole. On the Ways and Means Committee, 38.9 percent of the members have voting records showing a pattern of support for free trade while 22.2 percent are considered protectionists. On the Senate Finance Committee, 50 percent of the members have voting records supporting free trade, and none are in the protectionist camp. Both committees, however, have relatively large proportions of their memberships with mixed records or no previous voting record -- 38.9 percent on the Ways and Means Committee and 50 percent on the Finance Committee.

For a more comprehensive evaluation of a member of Congress's voting tendencies, it is also useful to consider the voting record of Congress on labor issues. Organized labor is the most influential force behind protectionist legislation. To measure that influence, we examined the record of each member of Congress according to the Committee on Political Education of the AFL-CIO (American Federation of Labor -- Congress of Industrial Organizations) plus other voting records produced by the Americans for Constitutional Action, Americans for Democratic Action, and the Chamber of Commerce of the United States. We found that many congressmen who may be characterized as free traders or leaning toward free trade are also consistent pro-labor voters. Until recent years the AFL-CIO supported liberal trading policies. The pro-labor senators and congressmen, however, soon may be forced to choose between their patrons and their principles in view of the protectionist policy positions taken by the AFL-CIO, the United Auto Workers (UAW), and other unions. The AFL-CIO also takes views ranging from equivocal to critical on issues favoring exports, because of their special concern about the alleged danger of exporting jobs. As yet, pro-labor sentiment in Congress has not significantly overcome the members' free trade dispositions.

Congressional interest in changing laws (such as antiboycott acts) that impede U.S. exports is lukewarm at best, but the typically inconsistent commitment of President Carter and his White House aides makes the task virtually impossible. With much fanfare, the president declared the expansion of U.S. exports as an important national policy goal in the fall of 1978. An interagency task force was created to implement this goal, headed by the able Assistant Secretary of Commerce Frank Weil. The results, however, were trivial. As Business Week complained: "The new export policy works like the old -- badly."

Politically difficult reforms were avoided by the White House and, of course, by the Congress. The president's prestigious Export Council, headed by Chairman Reginald Jones of General Electric, languished in neglect and was denied influence, access, and -- the worst indignity -- its own budget. Again, the president's attention had shifted elsewhere.

On 22 July 1980, President Carter's special trade representative, former Governor Reubin Askew of Florida, testified before the House Ways and Means Committee and candidly admitted what was wrong. Askew told the committee that President Carter had assured him that export policy was high on the administration priority list. Askew added, however, that the White House's dedication to exports "will have to be more than what it has been to save its hide." He identified a particularly glaring area of gross neglect: lack of adequate funding for the Export-Import Bank, which had run out of money to lend. Without a fully funded Eximbank there is no way to match the export subsidies other governments provide to their corporations, said Askew. Without adequate funds for the bank, the United States is denied the leverage needed to negotiate export subsidies out of existence, he said.

Askew also endorsed the bill to permit export trading companies -- a bill that had been moving at a snail's pace with only tepid support from the administration. Thereafter, the White House finally made a concerted effort, and, in early September, the bill passed the Senate unanimously. Concerns about the role of banks and competing committee jurisdictions, however, make passage in the House a question.

The most hopeful sign is an omnibus bill, the National Export Policy Act of 1980. Although there is no expectation that it will pass into law during this Congress, it has begun to focus attention on the importance of exports. The retirement of one of its outstanding sponsors, Senator Adlai Stevenson of Illinois, will mean that new leadership will have to be found.

Looked at more broadly, no single piece of legislation, however inspired, will begin to fill the trade policy vacuum, which is merely part of a greater policy deficiency. The United States will continue to lack an effective export policy until it acquires a realistic policy for guiding the domestic economy. In a world economy we no longer dominate or even understand very well, clarity begins at home.

ABOUT THE AUTHORS

DR. JACK N. BEHRMAN is the Luther Hodges Distinguished Professor at the University of North Carolina Graduate School of Business Administration and an advisor to the U.S. Department of State, the United Nation's Center for Transnational Corporations, and the Fund for Multinational Management Education. He served as assistant secretary for commerce for domestic and international business under the Kennedy and Johnson administrations.

DR. JACK CARLSON is the executive vice president, chief economist, and corporate secretary of the National Association of Realtors. Prior to joining the National Association, he served as vice president and chief economist for the Chamber of Commerce of the United States.

DR. MARK G. FARAH is visiting professor in the College of Business Administration at the University of Oregon. He worked as a research economist at the National Economic Research Associates, Inc. and the Oregon Research Institute.

DR. ROBERT A. FLAMMANG is professor of economics at Louisiana State University and serves as a consultant for the Port of New Orleans and the Gulf South Research Institute. He has been a consultant with the Agency for International Development in the Philippines, Indonesia, and Thailand.

DR. LAWRENCE G. FRANKO is coholder of the U.S. Professorship of the Corporation and Society and director of research at the Centre d'Etudes Industrielles in Geneva, Switzerland. He also is a consultant to the Conference Board (Europe), the OECD, the World Bank, and the International Labor Office. He served as deputy assistant director for international affairs at the U.S. Congressional Budget Office, was a fellow at the Carnegie Endowment for International Peace, and taught at the Georgetown University School of Foreign Service.

MR. HUGH GRAHAM is director of the Forecasting Center at the National Association of Realtors. He was formerly the deputy director of the Forecast Center of the Chamber of Commerce of the United States.

MR. THOMAS R. GRAHAM is adjunct professor of law at American and Georgetown Universities, a resident associate of the Carnegie Endowment for International Peace, and a senior associate of the Southern Center for International Studies in Atlanta. He served as deputy general counsel to Special Trade Representative Robert Strauss under the Carter administration, participating actively in the Tokyo Round negotiations.

DR. ELEANOR M. HADLEY is group director and senior economist in the International Division of the U.S. General Accounting Office, adjunct professor of economics at the George Washington University, and an associate member of the George Washington University's Sino-Soviet Institute. She served with the U.S. Office of Strategic Services, the Department of State, and the U.S. Tariff Commission.

DR. PENELOPE HARTLAND-THUNBERG is director of economic research at the Georgetown Center for Strategic and International Studies and adjunct professor of economics at Georgetown University. Before joining CSIS, she served on the Board of National Estimates of the Central Intelligence Agency, the Council of Economic Advisors, and the U.S. Tariff Commission.

DR. HARALD B. MALMGREN is president of Malmgren, Inc., Washington, chairman of Malmgren, Golt, Kingston, and Company, Ltd, London. He is also adjunct professor at Georgetown University and a director of the Atlantic Council of the United States, the Overseas Development Council, the Council on Science and Technology for Development, and the Trade Policy Research Centre in London. He served as deputy special representative for trade negotiations under the Nixon and Ford administrations.

DR. RAYMOND F. MIKESELL is the W.E. Miner Professor of Economics at the University of Oregon and a consultant to the Department of State, the Office of Technology Assessment, and the Office of Science and Technology. He has served on the Advisory Council of Overseas Private Investment Corporation and on the Council of Economic Advisors.

DR. SIMON SERFATY is director of the Washington Center of Foreign Policy Research and a faculty member of the Johns Hopkins School of Advanced International Studies.

MR. ROGER E. SHIELDS is vice president and head of the International Economic Research Unit of the Chemical Bank. He served as deputy assistant secretary for international economic policy at the U.S. Treasury Department and as deputy assistant secretary for international economic affairs at the U.S. Defense Department. He has also served on the faculty of the University of Texas and the University of Virginia.

MR. R. CRAIG SONKSEN is an international economist at the Chemical Bank, joining the Economic Research Department in 1978 after receiving his M.P.A. from Brigham Young University. His specializations include Eastern European economies, East-West relations, and Asian affairs.

MS. SHERRY STEPHENSON is a research associate with the Centre d'Etudes Industrielles in Geneva, Switzerland and is completing her Ph.D. from the Graduate Institute of International Studies. Before joining CEI, she served as an associate economic affairs officer with the United Nations Conference on Trade and Development.

DR. WILLIAM G. TYLER is senior economist at the Research Institute of the Brazilian Planning Secretariat and a member of the economics faculty at the University of Florida. He has also served as a consultant to the World Bank, USAID, and the Brazilian Institute of Economics.

MR. RICHARD J. WHALEN is chairman and editorial director of Worldwide Information Resources, Ltd., adjunct senior fellow at the Georgetown Center for Strategic and International Studies, and international business editor of the Center's Washington Quarterly. He served as senior editor to Fortune, and was given the American Book Award for his bestseller, Founding Fathers, a biography of Joseph P. Kennedy.